English Ways

Conversations with English Choral Conductors

Contributors

Ralph Allwood
Sue Barber
Matthew Best
Michael Brewer
Peter Broadbent
Ken Burton
Andrew Carwood
Harry Christophers
Stephen Cleobury
Pamela Cook
Sir John Eliot Gardiner
Simon Halsey
Stephen Layton
Richard Marlow
Paul McCreesh
James O'Donnell
Andrew Parrott
Peter Phillips
Vivien Pike
Paul Spicer
David Temple
Geoffrey Webber
Edward Wickham

English Ways

Conversations with English Choral Conductors

Jeffrey Sandborg, Editor and Interviewer

ISBN 0-937276-26-X
Cambridge: Trinity Great Court & King's College Chapel
Cover Photograph by Tim Rawle ©

For Marianne.

Contents

Acknowledgements ix
Foreword by John Rutter xi
Introduction xv
Ralph Allwood 2
Sue Barber 10
Matthew Best 16
Michael Brewer 26
Peter Broadbent 42
Ken Burton 54
Andrew Carwood 62
Harry Christophers 74
Stephen Cleobury 82
Pamela Cook 92
Sir John Eliot Gardiner 98
Simon Halsey 102
Stephen Layton 112
Richard Marlow 120
Paul McCreesh 134
James O'Donnell 146
Andrew Parrott 158
Peter Phillips 166
Vivien Pike 180
Paul Spicer 192
David Temple 204
GeoffreyWebber 218
Edward Wickham 228
Appendix 239
About the Author 253
Index 254

Acknowledgments

The completion of this collection has involved many people at every level of its preparation, and the project simply could have not come together without their generous and cheerful contributions.

First are the conductors, all of whom have enormous professional obligations and all of whom gave freely of their time, energy and spirit. Each contributed in unique ways beyond the interview itself. Without their cooperation, proofreading, suggestions, and continued assistance throughout the duration of the project, the final product would have been greatly diminished. I am deeply indebted to all.

Working on the behalf of several of the conductors were assistants or management companies. These folks provided timely information, pictures, biographical materials, or contact with the artists. Among them are Victoria Newbert and Malcolm Bruno for Andrew Parrott, Anne-Marie Norman and Sophie Emery at Hazard-Chase, Ltd., representing Simon Halsey, Stephen Layton, and Stephen Cleobury. Gijs Elsen assisted with information for Harry Christophers, Debbie Rigg for Sir John Eliot Gardiner, and Mark Anyan for Michael Brewer. J. Audrey Ellison helped with Ken Burton's materials, as did Chris Bagnall for Stephen Cleobury. All were always thoroughly professional through countless requests which, at times, must have become irritating.

Vanessa Reed and Matthew Greenall from the British Music Information Center gave valuable advice early in the project and also helped with contact information, as did Louis and Eve Halsey from beginning to end. Jane Capon of Choir Schools Today furnished important background information.

My institutions of employment, Roanoke College and Second Presbyterian Church, Roanoke, were especially instrumental in providing grant support for travel, as well as release time. The Mednick Foundation also furnished a grant to facilitate travel to England.

My colleague, Dr. Gordon Marsh, and Chairman, Dr. Bruce Partin, offered encouragement, advice, and professional perspectives. The Vice President for Academic Affairs and Dean of Roanoke College, Dr. Kenneth Garren, was supportive in all phases of the project. Others at Roanoke College who helped expedite the process of the book's completion were Chris Henson, Director of College Publicatons, Mark Poore of Information Services, and Joann Barfield of the Fine Arts Department, who kept the fax machine running through frequent, heavy use.

Cathy Skinner of Ambassador Travel set up travel aspects of the trip, both for England and Holland. Christopher Wade of Barnes and Noble, Roanoke, and Seth Williamson of WVTF-FM helped obtain recordings of the various artists.

Robert Walter, Professor Emeritus at Roanoke College, served as proof-reader for the manuscript, and I was helped by able student assistants, Barry Hubbard and Sara Feagan, especially in the transcriptions of the conversations. My wife, Marianne, helped in innumerable ways all along the way.

Finally, in addition to providing the Foreword to this collection, John Rutter offered counsel, important dialogue, and gave valuable advice from start to finish, and graciously corrected numerous errors.

Foreword

For anyone interested in European choral singing, this is a fascinating and valuable book, not least because nothing like it has previously been published. The editor has conducted a series of wide-ranging interviews with British choral conductors, in which their differing philosophies, techniques, backgrounds, ideals, likes and dislikes are candidly revealed. From their answers, a complex and contradictory picture emerges of choral music in Britain at the start of the twenty-first century. On the one hand, our expert cathedral, collegiate and professional choirs appear to thrive; on the other hand, state schools struggle with minimal music budgets and the decline of a general culture of singing, while (with notable exceptions) amateur choral societies face the problems of aging membership and shrinking audiences. Like sport, choral music appears to be turning into a professionalized pursuit, where we pay a small elite to do it for us rather than do it ourselves.

To the American reader, some of the issues raised in this book will be familiar, others perhaps less so. To understand why choral music in Britain is the way it is and how this differs from the USA, some context needs to be established, especially as it affects the institutions of church and school. Those readers already well versed in what follows (which is no more than my own personal perspective) should feel free to skip to the first interview.

To take church first, the most singular difference between the USA and the UK is the vastly greater proportion of the US population attending church: over 40%, as opposed to under 5% in Britain and other European countries. In the USA, several Christian denominations thrive musically; in the UK, the Anglican church is musically predominant, mainly because only our fifty or so Anglican cathedrals maintain resident boys-and-men choirs singing frequent choral services (among Britain's Roman Catholic cathedrals, Westminster and Liverpool alone do this). Below the level of the cathedrals, church choirs in Britain are on the way to extinction because of dwindling church membership, lack of funds to pay organists, difficulties of recruitment and the growth of charismatic pop-style worship where a traditional choir is unwanted. The recent emergence of choral music in the mainly black urban Adventist churches is a happy exception. Increasingly, our cathedral choirs stand at the apex of a pyramid whose base is rapidly eroding, and as such they are more vulnerable than they perhaps realize, since they depend on the continued patronage of a church uncertain of whether it wants them. Any US choir directors inclined to romanticize the Anglican choral tradition should be aware that it thrives, for the most part, only in the cathedrals and in Oxbridge college chapels – and not even there for much longer if present trends in society and in the church continue.

To turn to education, an equally worrying picture emerges. Approximately 92% of British children are educated in state schools. Most of these do not have choirs: some never did, others abandoned them when music educators in the 1960s began to promote instrumental and free creative work instead. School choirs are found mainly in the private sector; many private schools are religious foundations or at least have a school chapel and so are more likely to support a choir and a trained choir director. I would be happy to be proved wrong, but I suspect that the great majority of school choral activity is concentrated in the 8% of the population attending private schools. County youth choirs (roughly equivalent to US All-State choirs) have been disappearing as a result of budget cuts and the dismantling of local education authorities. At the level of higher education, university choirs certainly exist in Britain, though not in the extraordinary profusion of their US counterparts.

The two ancient universities of Oxford and Cambridge (familiarly shortened to 'Oxbridge') are the principal patrons of choral music in the education world, and their rather unique set-up perhaps deserves describing here because it is such a common source of understandable confusion. To go back to the medieval origins of Oxbridge, the students needed lodging during their studies at the university, and colleges were founded by private benefactors (sometimes kings or queens) to provide this lodging; as the number of students increased, more colleges were founded and existing ones expanded. Some colleges were given valuable endowments of land and money, and became centers of teaching and research in their own right; being modeled on monastic abbeys, they all had chapels, some quite small, a few almost as grand as that of King's College, Cambridge, endowed with a resident choir. Today, Cambridge University has around 30 colleges, Oxford 45 colleges. Every student at Oxbridge belongs to a college (they range in size from about 150 to about 800 students); the college is more than just a hall of residence or dormitory, and yet less than a self-contained place of learning because, like all universities, Oxford and Cambridge have a faculty structure. Students may receive some tuition within their own college, but most of it will come from their faculty. They live, dine, make friends, and (if so inclined) worship more within their own college. Oxbridge chapel choirs range from modest once-a-week student volunteer groups directed by the organ scholar (an undergraduate who has been selected by audition for this post prior to entry) to such world-famous choirs as those of King's College, singing almost daily and conducted by a experienced professional Director of Music specially appointed by the college for this task. In Cambridge, the choirs of King's and St John's Colleges have, by tradition, boy sopranos who are educated at choir schools supported by the college. Jesus College has boy sopranos recruited from local schools. All other Cambridge chapel choirs are mixed undergraduate groups made up of auditioned members who are either receiving financially nominal scholarships or singing as volunteers. Of these mixed chapel choirs, Christ's, Clare, Gonville & Caius, Selwyn and Trinity College choirs are conducted by a professional Director of Music, the others are undergraduate-led. In addition to this network of college chapel choirs, Oxbridge has university choruses and chamber choirs, but generally it is the leading college choirs which are more widely renowned and which make recordings. To add to the confusion, there are numerous choirs and vocal groups – the King's Singers, the Oxford Camerata, my own choir the Cambridge Singers, the Cambridge Taverner Choir, Cambridge Voices and so on – which have institutional-sounding names but which are in fact independent enterprises. Until 1972, all Oxbridge colleges were single-sex; men's colleges without boy sopranos therefore had ATB choirs. After 1972 colleges one after another became mixed, and mixed chapel choirs became possible. One exciting result of this change has been the creation of a pool of young female ex-Oxbridge singers versed in the style and literature of church music and early music; they, along with their male counterparts, have formed the nucleus of such professional mixed choirs as the Monteverdi Choir and The Sixteen.

A question often asked is, "where can you study choral conducting in Britain?" and the answer until recently has been "nowhere," at least in the sense of taking a dedicated course at a university or music college. Conducting courses exist at our music colleges, but their focus has been orchestral (there is an issue here of whether choral conducting ought to be regarded as a separate, specialist study, but that's another story). In one way, therefore, all our choral conductors who have not studied abroad are self-taught. On the other hand, those who have worked in cathedrals or Oxbridge chapels have learned their craft by a rigorous apprenticeship system whereby they first observe, then assist, and ultimately replace their mentors. And Oxbridge students can, even as undergraduates, gain surprisingly wide conducting experience by organizing their own concerts or even founding their own choirs (as Sir John Eliot Gardiner and Sir Roger Norrington did); no one stops you. The results of this anarchic system are that Oxbridge has produced a plethora of conductors characterized by idiosyncratic stick technique but, at their best, inspiring and historically-informed approaches to the music they conduct.

Those reading this book in search of 'methods' may be disappointed. There is quite a degree of consensus among the interviewees about the dos and don'ts of choir training, but pragmatism generally prevails. If this seems over-casual and pedagogically unsound to the American reader, it should be seen as a symptom of the different histories of education in Europe and the USA. In Europe, learning in the Middle Ages and Renaissance was seen as primarily abstract and speculative; the highest form of music to the medieval mind was 'musica mundana' (the inaudible music of the spheres), the lowest 'musica instrumentalis' (music you could actually play and hear). Practical skills did not gain academic respectability until astonishingly late: Cambridge University instituted a music honors degree only in 1948, and included practical performance as part of it only in the 1970s. The European educational system was traditionally geared to a small elite strong on independent thought but weak on specific skills. America, by contrast, set up its educational system from a more practical standpoint: there was a vast country to be tamed. Essential skills in engineering, agriculture, medicine and so on had to be efficiently imparted to a large and scattered population much of which did not have English as its mother tongue. Such a monumental achievement was only possible with a severely methodical approach (a cast of thinking particularly suited to the German immigrants who played such a major role in the dissemination of music in America). Gradually, of course, the 'useful learning' of the American system and the 'useless learning' of the European system began to converge; but even now, I believe it to be at least residually true that faith in method and system is stronger in American education than in British. Interestingly, those interviewees in this book who work in the less privileged environments tend to come across as more technically methodical (and more internationally-minded), perhaps because they have to be.

Choral music is international yet in some ways strongly national, and thank goodness for that: if choirs the world over begin to sound as uniform as orchestras the world over, they will be the duller for it. I expect an English choir to sound in some sense English, just as I expect a Russian choir to sound Russian. Yet, in the case of one or two of the distinguished interviewees, I am a little disappointed not to read more evidence that they are inspired by, for example, the stunningly fine choirs and vocal groups of Finland, Estonia or Cuba from which we can all learn so much. Can it be that insularity lives on in the British Isles, even in this age of cheap air travel and readily available CDs?

What of the personalities of the interviewees themselves? I can promise you a good read as you compare, say, the diplomacy of Stephen Cleobury with the outspokenness of Peter Broadbent. Outspokenness, of course, tends to make for more exciting reading, though I suspect that as some of the interviewees peruse each other's contributions, names may be indignantly crossed off Christmas card lists (if they were ever on them). Granted, it is sometimes easier to define what we are in favor of if we can identify what we are against, yet I am saddened by the needlessly ungenerous attitude revealed in some of the interviews towards the achievements of fine colleagues (though, come to think of it, Beecham and Toscanini didn't have much time for each other). You don't have to hate the sound of a flute to appreciate the sound of an oboe; choirs past and present in all their wondrous variety are a many-sided miracle for us to enjoy, and, at a time when in Britain the whole edifice of choral music is tottering – or, to use another analogy, the flowers are blooming brightly while the roots are decaying – it would be heartening to see more signs of collegiality and a sense of all being on the same side.

John Rutter
Cambridge, England

Introduction

English Ways
Introduction

This is a collection of interviews with twenty-three of the most important English choral conductors working today. Most of the conversations took place in England in January, 1999, though two were conducted at the World Symposium on Choral Music in Rotterdam, the Netherlands, in July, 1999. Three conductors provided recorded responses.

Background and Purpose

Choral musicians on every continent are familiar with the sounds of English choirs – from the ethereal, treble-dominated cathedral choirs (which remains the stereotype for much of the world) to the hard-edged perfection of the professional ensembles. For many in the choral profession recordings of English choirs have been a deep wellspring of great literature, and English conductors have been at the vanguard of performance practice developments for the past thirty years. My own experience with "English ways" of making choral music has been through hosting some touring English choirs, having the opportunity to talk with their directors, and through studying with Louis Halsey, an English choral conductor, at the University of Illinois. From observations and conversations, I began to notice that many directors seemed to have a substantially different approach from most Americans to choral music making. For example, I had been told that warm-ups were rarely done in rehearsals, and "methods" used by so many Americans were nearly non-existent.

One set of hazy assumptions I had, that seemed to be shared by many, suggested that people in England are steeped in a national tradition, that they absorb choral styles almost by osmosis, and that they can sight-read anything that is put before them. Indeed, choral music "over there" can appear to be just a matter of "add water and stir."

With a sabbatical leave before me, I wanted to explore some of the sources for this excellence, to confirm or correct my stereotypes, to ask, in short, "How do they do it?" By questioning some of the leading figures in English choral music, I hoped to expand the palette of approaches, philosophies, ideas and practices available to the rest of the choral world. As with most stereotypes, I immediately learned that mine were either inaccurate or outdated. Furthermore, I learned that the choral landscape in England is undergoing changes that have been underway for several years.

Precedents

In addition to my conversations with English and American choral musicians, a germinal idea for this book was drawn from an interview I had with Harry Christophers, Director of The Sixteen, while the ensemble was on tour in Roanoke,

Virginia, in December, 1993 (published, Choral Journal, November, 1994). A precedent had also been set for this genre of book with Carole Glenn's In Quest of Answers (1991) which asked a series of questions of noted American choral musicians. Another inspiration was Richard Dufallo's Trackings (1989), a collection of interviews with American composers.

Choices

While the importance of the choral cultures in Ireland, Scotland, and Wales is recognized, this collection focuses exclusively on English choral musicians. The decision to do so is based on several factors. First, was the practical consideration of integrating geography with the time available to me, and to the conductors. Second, at this writing, it is a fact that English choirs and conductors are the most famous abroad. This is due to England's relatively larger size, the choral institutions that trace their origins back centuries, and to the broad exposure English choirs have received in the USA through recordings, television, radio, and tours. An early decision was to focus on professionally active conductors who are presently associated with a choir. Conspicuous by their absence are Sir David Willcocks of King's College, Cambridge, and Dr. George Guest of St. John's College, Cambridge, both retired from those institutions. They each were profoundly influential figures in English choral music for decades, and their influence is still felt by those who worked with them or even heard their work. Though neither was interviewed for this collection, their presence through constant reference is a sort of idée fixe throughout this book.

An additional word needs to be said about how the conductors were chosen, for when a list of anything is made, a second list is implied: the list of those not included on the first. And so it is with the conductors who appear in these pages, and the many prominent ones who are missing. Again, the limitations imposed by time, distance, and the availability of the interviewees put practical limitations on the number of conductors who could be interviewed. Along with including choral conductors who are well known in England and abroad, a guiding purpose was to select those who represent a cross-section of English choral music at the highest levels. Therefore, this collection includes directors of professional choirs and consorts, university choirs, cathedral choirs, cathedral/university choirs, a prep-school choir, amateur groups, gospel choirs, girls' choirs, and a children's choir. The choral categories follow. It will be noted that some directors conduct more than one ensemble.

Professional Choirs and Consorts

The Sixteen	Harry Chistophers
The Monteverdi Choir	John Eliot Gardiner
Gabrieli Consort and Players	Paul McCreesh
Tavener Consort and Players	Andrew Parrott
The Tallis Scholars	Peter Phillips
BBC Singers	Stephen Cleobury
Finzi Singers	Paul Spicer
Polyphony	Stephen Layton
The Cardinall's Musick	Andrew Carwood
The Clerkes	Edward Wickham

University (College) Choirs

Trinity College, Cambridge	Richard Marlow
King's College, Cambridge	Stephen Cleobury
Gonville and Caius College, Cambridge	Geoffrey Webber

Cathedral Choirs (Catholic)

Westminster Cathedral (at time of interview)	James O'Donnell
Westminster Abbey (January, 2000)	

Independent Secondary School Choir

Eton	Ralph Allwood

Symphonic Choir

City of Birmingham Symphony Chorus	Simon Halsey

Amateur Choirs

Crouch End Festival Singers	David Temple
Corydon Festival Singers	Matthew Best
Joyful Company of Singers	Peter Broadbent
Holst Singers	Stephen Layton

Youth Choirs

National Youth Choir	Michael Brewer
Rodolfus Choir	Ralph Allwood

Girls' Choirs

Cantamus	Pamela Cook
City of Sheffield Girls' Choir	Vivien Pike

Children's Choirs (non-cathedral)

Stoke Brunswick Choir	Sue Barber

Gospel Choirs

London Adventist Choir	Ken Burton
Croydon Adventist Choir	Ken Burton

This list does not represent parish churches, boys' choirs, or barbershop groups. Neither has the somewhat controversial topic of "girls in cathedrals" been discussed with any of the directors who have been at the forefront of this controversy, most notably Richard Seal and David Hill at Salisbury and Winchester Cathedrals. Nonetheless, this issue is addressed by several of the interviewees. And the widely respected choral work at the various colleges in Oxford University is not represented here because of the aforementioned limitations. Though this collection of interviews is by no means comprehensive, the conductors interviewed in these pages are acknowledged in the choral world for the excellence of their choral music making.

Types of Choirs and Institutions
Professional Ensembles

The large number of professional choirs in England, principally in London, is sustained by an abundance of choral musicians who have come through the cathedral and university choirs, especially at Oxford and Cambridge. These singers provide the London area, and much of the British Isles, with a large supply of excellent singers who read fluently and sing with a sensitivity to style. The high skill level of the singers allows many conductors of professional ensembles to prepare concerts and recordings with astonishingly little rehearsal time by almost any measure. The BBC Singers are the only full-time choir in England at this writing; therefore, many singers in London sing in more than one group.

College (University) Choirs

There are two kinds of university choirs represented here. First, the choir with university-age students (men and women) is represented in this section by Gonville and Caius College and Trinity College, both of Cambridge University. The other college choir, of boys and university-age men, is represented by King's College, Cambridge, in this examination.

Choir Schools

In Great Britain there are approximately forty choir schools in which all of the children choristers receive their education. Schools may be attached to a college chapel like King's College, Cambridge, or New College Oxford; or they may be a part of a cathedral like Westminster in London. The Cathedral School Association is the umbrella organization that represents the forty described above. One criterion for membership in that organization is that the singers at the schools must sing as least four times per week.

While the choir schools give young boys (and in some cases, girls) musical training in addition to their general education, they are also significant in that they account largely for the boys who sing in most cathedral and collegiate SATB choirs. Thus in Cambridge, St. John's and King's, there are choir schools and thus boys in the choir, whereas Trinity, Gonville and Caius, and Clare do not have choir schools and therefore use college-age women, instead.

Girls and Boys and Choir Schools

The children enrolled in choir schools are typically eight to thirteen years of age. Some cathedral choirs now have girls, and this trend, as is seen in a number of the interviews, is somewhat controversial. The Cathedral School Association counts only four schools that offer choral-school education to girls: Salisbury Cathedral, Exeter, Wells and York Minster. The practice was started in 1990 by Richard Seal at Salisbury Cathedral. Numerous other schools have girls singing on a volunteer basis, but they are not educating them.

Cathedral Choirs

Many of England's cathedral choirs are well known the world over. Among the famous names are Winchester Cathedral, St. Paul's Cathedral, Westminster Abbey, and Westminster Cathedral. These are classified as either Anglican or Roman Catholic. Most use boys and men, but some, notably

Winchester and Salisbury, have begun to introduce separate girls' choirs. These institutions often have affiliated choir schools.

Amateur Choirs

The amateur choirs whose directors were chosen for this study may well be untypical of amateur choral singing in England. Indeed, they were first chosen for this collection without knowing that their groups were amateur. All are well known for the professional level of their choirs' performances and their outstanding recordings.

Gospel Choirs

The gospel choir movement is an urban phenomenon of the last several years. These ensembles, too, are classified as amateur, though some seem to be reaching professional levels in activity. It is worth noting that most of the singers in the gospel choirs see their singing as worship, not as performance.

Youth and Children

In England, "public" schools are equivalent to American "private" schools, while "state" schools correspond to American "public" schools. It was a surprise to learn that choral singing in schools is not pursued with the vigor that is seen in the choir schools, although there are excellent exceptions. Each of the directors chosen for this collection represents a different kind of educational circumstance. There are two girls' choirs represented and one choir of children. The girls' choirs meet independently of school, while the children's choir (Stoke Brunswick) is in a "public" school. The National Youth Choir is a summer gathering of England's best high school- and college-age singers.

The Questions

Questions were devised with both the general and specialized reader in mind, but they obviously reflect my own interests, curiosity, and biases. Given limited schedules, there never seemed to be enough time to cover everything of interest. When the project began, it seemed that there might be value in asking each conductor the same questions and that the comparison of responses would be useful. It became clear however that, given the broad sampling of choral specialties, this approach would be too inflexible to be interesting and, further, it tended to stunt the spontaneity and natural flow of conversation. Thus, while several fundamental questions are presented to most interviewees, many others grow out of the conversation, or are asked with the particular choir and conductor in mind.

Biographies

The most basic information is provided as an introduction to the conductors and the principal groups that they conduct. Again, because this information is constantly changing (as some of it has during the preparation of this book), readers will generally find the most recent data they seek from a simple on-line search. Information presented in this collection includes the conductor's year of birth; choirs with which each is most associated; last degree-granting institution attended; the date and location of the interview; a biographical/career sketch, and a brief description of principal choirs.

Several of the conductors have ongoing relationships with other choirs in England or abroad. I have listed only those choirs with which they are most closely associated, usually through recordings. It should be understood that given the stature and accomplishments of these musicians and choirs, no overview here is close to being complete or even as the conductor might have it. That said, the inquiring reader may easily pursue more complete information at leisure through the World Wide Web.

Discographies

A sampling of no more than six recordings is provided for the reader's review in Appendix I. A complete discography for each conductor became unwieldy, given the fact that several of them have many dozens of recordings stretching back decades. Also, any such list would be immediately out of date as soon as it was published.

Editing Practice

While editing these interviews, I was frequently reminded of the phrase, "two nations separated by a common language!" An attempt has been made to retain the flavor of the British language, as well as the spontaneity of conversation. However, spellings have been Americanized, for the most part; for example, "practice" instead of "practise." Also, while some usage has been changed to accommodate the American ear, occasionally words like "quaver" (eighth note) are retained.

These interviews reveal a rich mixture of ideas, aesthetics, and approaches. And while I began with assumptions, stereotypes, and misconceptions about English choral music making, I ended not only by having those assumptions corrected but also by having my own understanding of the choral craft broadened and fortified. I wish the same rewards for the reader.

Jeffrey Sandborg
Salem, Virginia

English Ways
Conversations with English Choral Conductors

Ralph Allwood

Born: 1950

Eton College Chapel Choir
Rodolfus Choir

Education: King's College, Cambridge

Interview: January 16, 1999, Eton College, Windsor

Ralph Allwood has directed the Eton College Chapel Choir since 1985. In that time he has broadened its international exposure through tours and recordings. Allwood is the founder and director of the week-long "Eton Choral Courses," which he established in 1980. Members of those courses, past and present, provide singers for his Rodolfus Choir. He is also a regular lecturer and clinician abroad, and is a judge for the Sainsbury's "Choir of the Year Competition."

An independent boys' school, Eton was founded in 1440 by King Henry VI. The Chapel Choir has been singing services almost continuously since then. Today's Choir has fifty-four singers, from the ages of thirteen to eighteen. The Chapel Choir's annual Easter tours have taken it to nearly every corner of the globe. Allwood's Rodolfus Choir ranges in age from seventeen to twenty-five years of age, expanding or contracting from twelve to sixty voices.

Website: **www.etoncollege.com**

Ralph Allwood

Photo: Clive Barda

Ralph Allwood
Eton College
Rodolfus Choir

JS: How do you go about selecting singers?

RA: It's very different for each of the various choirs I direct. There is Eton College Choir, there is Eton College Musical Society which is a big choral society, all-school, and then there is a town choral society which is Windsor and Eton Choral Society. We take part in the Windsor Festival and do three concerts a year with orchestra. Then I do four choral courses in the summer – each one has about sixty boys and girls. From those 260 boys and girls who come to us in the summer, I choose a small chamber choir of about forty called the Rodolfus Choir. They record frequently and tour occasionally.

For the big choirs and the choral courses, I don't audition at all, and I believe that that is right. There should be some unauditioned choirs. The Rodolfus Choir is selected by the singing teachers and the choral course staff. Here at Eton I have a simple audition, but singers are recommended by their singing teachers. Before they can join the choir here, they have to be having singing lessons, and then their singing teachers will make recommendations to me. I will then hear them, test their sight-reading, put them on the waiting list, and give them a place when it comes available.

JS: What materials do you use for auditions?

RA: When I'm interviewing boys for music scholarships here, I use a piece which I think works extremely well and that's "O Little Town of Bethlehem" to the Walford Davies tune. If I get them to sing, then it tells me whether they've got perfect pitch or not, if they miss the C-natural towards the end. I make up melodies for other auditions, which start very simply and gradually get more and more complicated till they're ridiculous at the end. Then you see where people founder. You can sort the sheep from the goats with a simple tenor or alto part from a hymn because even the best singers will make a little mistake in the audition. I reckon that the singing of runs and the like can be learnt. So it's basic musicianship and the sounds of the voice one wants to hear in an audition.

JS: How do you approach blend?

RA: Blend comes from vowel sounds as much as anything, making the vowel sound the same from everybody. I'm never too worried what the vowel is except to ensure that the singers are all singing the same one. Bad blend in a part, of course, comes from pitch and tone quality, but vowel sound is the big difference. I use a hand gesture to get them to go from one vowel sound to another and ask them to recognize what is going on inside the mouth during that change. That's the quickest method I know to getting the vowel sound right.

JS: What is your view on vibrato?

RA: Vibrato needs to be controlled. A certain kind of vibrato is fine, but a wobble is not fine. A pleasant vibrato is not a pitch vibrato but one of intensity. That is, it is loud and soft.

JS: How do you build intonation with your young singers?

RA: That's a very long story. They must listen to themselves and the others and learn to change the pitch slightly. I talk a lot about harmonies. Do you know about Mongolian chanting? (Demonstrates overtones by changing vowel formants while singing a drone. Intones "In dulci jubilo" with the formants.) Basses need plenty of bright sound because it pervades the whole texture. Others hear the harmonies and learn to match them. When one is talking about this kind of accuracy, one is talking about the best choirs only, particularly consorts. The best consort I know for doing it is the Hilliard Ensemble. Rogers Covey-Crump leads the tuning. He has first-class perfect pitch himself, but he also knows exactly how slightly flat to make a major third and how slightly sharp to make a minor third and how very, very slightly sharp to make a perfect fifth, for example. If you listen to the Hilliards' most recent records, their blend is absolutely stunning. Of course, they'll sing the same vowel sounds; of course they don't have vibrato; of course they have identical phrasing, and of course they're balanced, but the intonation is the exceptionally good thing that they do. It's far from equal temperament. Every note is adjusted in their scores, and they have arrows up and down on most of them to say just how slightly sharp or flat they should be. That's how they do it.

Now, you can get that with a really good choir. If people are aware of that kind of intonation and you ask it of them, they will sing with it. I do like sharp minor thirds and not-too-sharp major thirds. However, with inexperienced singers, they tend to sing a major third too flat, anyway.

4

JS: When you speak of the sharpness or flatness of an interval, are you talking about horizontal voice-leading or the vertical tuning of a chord?

RA: The chord. In a single part, it's not so crucial.

JS: Do you work this tuning out for every vertical sonority, or just cadences, or long note values?

RA: The latter, and particularly those points because that's where tuning is most audible.

JS: What is your approach to tone quality?

RA: I have various exercises to develop tone quality. We're lucky here because every boy in the choir has individual singing lessons. I'm very fussy about singing teachers, and I have a team of absolutely first-class teachers. One of the things I will do in rehearsal is say, "Remember a particular thing your singing teacher just said to you." That's all you need. Suddenly, you hear the tone improve.

JS: What personal musical characteristic makes your groups sound the way they do?

RA: If you listen to my choirs, I hope you will hear a clean, blended sound and hope it will always be scrupulously in tune. But, I like to think that one takes that as given. It's absolutely basic. On top of that, I think you will hear an attention to text and words and the phrasing that results from that, and those are the things that I'd like to be noted for. If I see a review of a record and they say that there was exquisite phrasing which came from the text, then I am very happy.

JS: Therefore, is that the principal focus of your rehearsal?

RA: Yes. And, I think also by the way I conduct and the way I talk and demonstrate; I am always asking for that.

JS: Do you do warm-ups?

RA: Yes, I do little warm-ups. They don't last long. I will do more in the morning than in the evening. The singers do find them valuable. They're a teaching exercise as much as for warming up.

JS: Is there an English choral style?

RA: Well, you see, the cathedral style is the cathedral style because the little boys have only just learned to sing. They haven't all learned to put real power into their voices and they are with lay-clerks or choral scholars who are blending with them. Nowadays, choirs have much better singing teaching, and so the little boys learn how to do it properly and at a much earlier age can make a much richer sound. Look at James O'Donnell, David Hill, John Scott, George Guest, for example. What they produce is usually helped very much by a singing teacher. Once they become adults, they become much more biddable. You can say, "Will you sing it like this?" or "Will you sing it like that?" Even with the Tallis Scholars or the Monteverdi Choir, there is no one sound they make because they change from year to year, and, indeed, the individual singers sing in many different choirs. I really don't think there is an English sound. In England, choral music is in the blood so much in certain families that you will get a lot of people singing who don't necessarily have fine voices. They just want to sing. In a lot of other countries, some people come to singing because they were singing in the shower one day, and Mummy said, "Oh, that's a good voice. You've got to get it trained." So off they go and get it trained. They don't know much about music, but they've got a fine voice. So in England and, I suppose, Sweden and Hungary, you will often get people with less-than-outstanding voices who, nonetheless, are singing well.

JS: What does that mean in choral sound? Do you mean that English choirs don't have as many good voices as a result?

RA: Well, if you have a line of three people, one of them has an outstanding voice and the other two have reasonable voices, the sound will become that of the best. On the other hand, if you have three singers and one of them is singing flat and the others are in tune, it will sound flat. That's just the way it happens. So, richness of singing is more influenced by a single person on a line. Bad intonation is influenced by a single singer on a line. So you need the whole lot to be in tune, and you need a good smattering of good voices, but you don't need them all to be good voices. Lots of people have said that, in the collegiate and cathedral chapel choirs, you have a pair singing bass, a pair singing tenor and so on, and one of them will say, "He gets the notes and I sing them." One of them is musical but hasn't got such a great voice.

JS: What do you identify as the sources of excellence in the English choral tradition?

RA: The choir school is the source. We haven't got a choir school here. We have lots of boys who come from choir schools. Our boys start at age thirteen and go to eighteen.

JS: So you might get some boys from, say, Westminster Cathedral School?

RA: Yes, and we've got a couple. And some from King's, John's, St. Paul's, The Abbey, Winchester.

JS: What do you see as the role of choral music in English culture?

RA: I go over to America and I can see England from your perspective. You see these incredible cathedrals and college chapels, schools that have this amazing music. Yet, when you are here, you realize that this music is coming only from certain places, and it's only five percent of the whole output. Ninety-five percent don't know the difference between a B-flat and a photocopier. In fact, music is dying out in the schools here, and so the big choral-society tradition is in decline because there isn't singing in schools as there used to be. There's much more instrumental music in schools now, and so we have incredibly fine youth orchestras in many places. The pendulum could swing back, though.

JS: Given the deep choral roots, how did this switch come about?

RA: I think it was economic. In the old days, instruments were quite expensive, but suddenly they became more affordable, so kids who were musical could play instead of sing. There's quite a culture of instrumentalists who sing, and in the last twenty years it has tended to divide state schools from the independents. The state school tradition, which feeds the National Youth Orchestra and youth orchestras, doesn't sing so much, and there are quite a lot of them that won't sing at all, whereas independent schools have a lot of singing going on as well. I think pressure from other subjects in the curriculum led to the demise of singing lessons in schools.

Also, the demise of the Christian religion and the church in England. People just don't sing hymns much anymore, and you find people who don't know the hymns we take for granted. It's worrying. I feel there is something in all cultures that sings, and when it's stifled, as we're stifling it at the moment, you don't hear workers singing on building sites nowadays, the way they used to.

The reason they don't is that they have a radio on, so they don't need to make the music; they just hear the music. I think this transition from active to passive is rather worrying. It means that one or two people get enormous amounts of money by making records, and the mass of people ought to be singing rather than listening. There's a terrific thing about the human heart which wants to sing, which wants to express; and if it doesn't, there is something stifled about it.

JS: Do you have lay clerks who are paid here at Eton?

RA: No! They are entirely boys. Similarly, the orchestra is made up entirely of boys in the school.

JS: What do you do to raise money for tours and other projects?

RA: The parents pay a lot for our tours. We get a little bit from the school; we get a little bit from our CD sales, and we get occasional sponsorship. Obviously, audiences and fees bring us a little bit, but they don't usually cover what we do. For the Rodolfus Choir, we have an anonymous sponsor for our *B Minor Mass* in January, 2000, and we're coming on tour to the States in April, 2002.

JS: Who have been important influences for you?

RA: John Walker, senior choral scholar at King's, Cambridge, under Boris Ord – an amazing, inspiring man. David Willcocks. The other two teachers at school – Bruce Pullan and David Nield.

JS: In all, what did you learn from them?

RA: Spirit. Musical spirit. Musical enthusiasm. I think I learn from everybody I see work. When I organize people to come and conduct our choral courses, I get them because I can learn from them, in addition to the fact they're good at what they do. With that in mind, I couldn't begin to list the people I've learned from. Barry Rose is extraordinary. When I do Bach, I learn a lot from the way John Eliot Gardiner does things. I've learned a lot from the early-music and period-orchestra movement.

Sue Barber

Born: 1949

Stoke Brunswick Choir

Education: Royal College of Music

Interview: December 1999 (taped responses)

Director of Music at Stoke Brunswick School (East Grinstead, Sussex) since 1982, Sue Barber is one of England's best known music educators. She is an award-winning student of the Kodály method from the British Kodály Academy. In addition to directing the Stoke Brunswick Choir, Barber directs the children's choir at the Saturday Stilgoe Concerts at Royal Festival Hall.

The Stoke Brunswick School Choir is comprised of thirty children, eight to thirteen years of age, and is recognized as one of the finest children's choirs in Great Britain. The choir has traveled extensively and has appeared frequently on television in Britain. In 1992, 1996, and 1998, the choir reached the semi-finals of the Sainsbury Choir of the Year Competition, and has also received a Silver Medal at the International Choir Festival in Greece. Among their many performances has been Benjamin Britten's *Owen Wingrave*, with the Glyndeborne Festival Opera.

Website: none

Sue Barber

Sue Barber
Stoke Brunswick Choir

JS: Please tell me about your choir.

SB: My group is called Stoke Brunswick Choir, and we are based in East Grinstead, which is in West Sussex. We have thirty-two children in the choir aged seven to thirteen years, roughly half boys and half girls. The children are all members of an independent preparatory school that spans the ages of three up to thirteen. There are 140 children in the school, but because there are only 100 children aged seven to thirteen, I choose my choir from that group.

JS: Do the singers receive voice lessons outside the choral setting?

SB: Yes, some receive voice training, but this is voluntary. Just as when parents want their child to learn the violin, they sign them up for lessons; and if they want singing lessons, they do likewise. Currently, approximately one-third of the choir is having extra singing lessons.

JS: What kind of music do you sing?

SB: Our repertoire is quite varied; for example we have performed a number of Doreen Rao's "Choral Music Experience" songs, published by Boosey and Hawkes. These are original songs by American and Canadian composers, as well as good arrangements of spirituals and folk songs. Some of the twentieth-century English composers we enjoy are, for example, Benjamin Britten's *Ceremony of Carols*; John Rutter, especially his Christmas music; also the Vaughan Williams *Dirge for Fidele*; William Mathias, *Lear Songs*; Edward Gregson, *Dona Nobis Pacem*; Bob Chilcott, *City Songs*; and songs by Ronald Corp and Andrew Carter.

We particularly enjoy singing in other languages, among them Israeli, Russian, French and Italian. We always perform from memory. We also have a school Chapel, and so, on occasions, we sing an Anthem for the Chapel service, and we are quite often asked to sing at weddings.

JS: How do you audition the children?

SB: Auditions are hardly necessary because the children have class lessons with me from the age of three upwards. By the time they are aged seven or eight, I know quite well how they sing and their general musicianship. But I do a token audition so that the children will feel they are being fairly treated. They sing a song of their choice, a few scales and are given some ear tests. Basically, they must be able to sing with good intonation and have a reasonable level of intelligence.

JS: How often do you rehearse?

SB: We rehearse four times a week for about thirty-five minutes.

JS: Do most of your children continue singing when they move on to other schools?

SB: This is quite a problem, especially for the girls. If they go on to an all-girls' school, the majority do not have a choir that is at a level anywhere near the one that our children have been used to. Some of them find they are singing simple unison songs with other children who have not been trained, and so are inexperienced singers, and often are rehearsing infrequently. Consequently, there is little motivation for them to continue singing. The co-ed schools are better because often there is a choral society. However, the choral society is not the same as singing in a close-knit choir such as we have at Stoke Brunswick.

JS: Do you teach sight-singing?

SB: Yes. I teach the Kodály method in my class-music lessons. This uses relative sol-fa. This is similar to the French solfege, but uses a moveable "doh." When the children are young, they learn first how to read my hand signs, and eventually we go onto the staff when they are age seven. By that stage they are reading quite competently.

JS: What is your typical rehearsal like?

SB: We always start with some physical warm-ups to relax the children. The Head Chorister begins these before I arrive at the rehearsal. I pride myself on the fact that even if I arrive a few minutes late, the children have already started in a well disciplined manner. We also make different vocal sounds, and the children take turns leading this part of the rehearsal. It is fun, and also of value, I believe. We follow this procedure before a concert or festival because it is good to make the children laugh and relax before performing. We also do scales and arpeggios to stretch the vocal range. I am a believer in singing high into the head voice, and the children have no problem with this. With scales, I tend to start at the top and vocalize down, using different vowel sounds. I also use sol-fa for intonation warm-ups. To improve intonation we sing patterns up and down in thirds in three parts, a third apart. For example:

Soprano 1 - d m r f m s f l s t l d t r' d'
　　　Soprano 2 - d m r f m s f l s t l d' t r' d'
　　　　　Alto - d m r f m s f l s t l d' t r' d'

Many of these simple exercises can be found in the education books of Kodály published by Boosey & Hawkes, and all of them are unaccompanied.

In addition, I am incorporating more movement into our rehearsal because I think the children need to feel the music in their whole bodies, not just in their voices. This takes the form of either swaying, clapping, clicking, stamping, stepping on the spot or from side to side, always with the pulse. All the children play and sing very rhythmically. When they are using their bodies, children relax into their bodies and sing all the better for it. When it comes to performing, very few songs actually incorporate movement, apart from the African traditional songs, e.g. *Syahamba* (*Zulu*, arranged by Doreen Rao), and *Kenyon Melody* (arranged by Stephen Hatfield), and some other songs from shows such as *West Side Story*.

I would say that the training I give them is very comprehensive and thorough. There are also many opportunities for individual singing. In all rehearsals, I will have a few children singing on their own at certain stages. It may be one tiny little phrase or a longer passage or just a couple of intervals. They are used to singing on their own and don't have worries about it.

JS: How do you approach choral blend?

SB: Blend and intonation are greatly helped by soft singing, humming and concentrated listening. Most of the rehearsal is spent away from the piano, and I take care to demonstrate often the particular sound I want. We aim for one uniform beautiful sound, and I think we do achieve a good blend, judging from comments received from adjudicators at choral festivals. On the whole our intonation is very good, but you have to remember that I am training young children and do not have a large number to choose from. Not all of the children are fantastic musicians, so occasionally intonation lets us down in a performance when under stress. It is usually sharpness rather than flatness.

JS: What is your position with vibrato in children's voices?

SB: As the children are young, this is not a problem as it might be with older girls. Some of my children develop a light natural vibrato which they probably pick up from me, but I think this just adds to the color of the overall sound.

JS: How do you approach the development of tone quality in the choir?

SB: I think that tone quality is very important, and we pride ourselves on aiming for and achieving a beautiful sound. We want good color, shade and light, and also dynamic contrast in particular. I do a lot of patterning all the time. That is, I sing a phrase, and the children copy. Also, they listen to themselves and to each other, never forcing the tone; and always aiming for a beautiful sound does seem to bring good results, as does unaccompanied singing.

JS: Does your choir have a sound that is distinct from its peers?

SB: I would say that my choir has a quite distinctive sound, and this sound has remained the same for a number of years. I started the choir eighteen years ago. Twelve years ago, I discovered the Kodály method, and since then I would say that the choir really started to improve. Without a doubt, it's the Kodály method that has made a huge difference. At the risk of sounding immodest, I would say that we are one of the best school choirs of our age group in the country. We are not perfect, but you can never get perfection with young children. It seems to me that we do have the ability to move an audience and to communicate the music, whether the mood is sad or joyful. I would say that our diction and the way we project our voices are both far better than the average choir.

JS: What have been your most important professional influences?

SB: Studying the Kodály method of musicianship training has had a profound effect on my choir training and general music teaching. It made me a better musician, and I see it doing the same for my pupils.

JS: Please describe your musical training?

SB: I studied the piano and the organ at the Royal College of Music in London. I did not study singing, and at that stage I had not had a particularly good music education at school. I had not been involved in a choir. Once I started teaching, I had to find out how to conduct and train choirs. I started going to summer schools, the first of which was at Canford in Dorset with Simon Halsey. Then I attended the British Kodály Academy and passed the advanced course with Distinction under Cecilia Vajda, pupil of Zoltan Kodály. I also spent three weeks in Hungary at the Kodály Institute in Keckemet.

JS: Do you have an educational philosophy that guides your work with children?

SB: I would say that I always aim for high standards. I think praise and encouragement are extremely important, and I have to keep reminding myself to give praise when it is needed. I am immensely proud of my choir. They work extremely hard and are very enthusiastic, so they well deserve praise and encouragement. I like to be uplifting in my approach, to be humorous, to be joyful, and to be enthusiastic all the time. I also try to be kind to the children and treat them as my equal. We talk about the music that we are singing. They tell me how they feel, and I do likewise. It is not a question of me and them. We work together as a team, and I find this very rewarding. I love the relationship between myself and the choir, and I think that they do too. That is probably why I am able to get such good results. At the same time, I am quite a strong disciplinarian, and in the early days I used to have to get cross quite often because I wanted a high standard and a good discipline. Nowadays I have no need to raise my voice because the children are so keen and responsive. The choir rehearsal is always a positive and energizing experience.

The other interesting thing, I think, is the effect the choir training has on the children's daily lives. It is noticeable that the members of my choir are well behaved in school, good at their work, and their concentration is good. The choir experience teaches them so many important values: getting along with each other, working as a team, social values as well as music values. I think the children realize the importance of these things too. I think they appreciate even more after they have left what a very positive experience it has been for their singing in this choir.

Matthew Best

Born: 1957

Corydon Singers and Orchestra

Education: King's College, Cambridge
National Opera Studio

Interview: January 19, 1999, Royal Festival Hall, London

Matthew Best navigates successful careers both as conductor and as singer. He founded Corydon Singers in 1973, at the age of sixteen, and the Corydon Orchestra in 1991. Among the roles he has sung as a bass-baritone are the Dutchman, Jochanaan (*Salome*) with the English National Opera, Kurwenal (*Tristan*), Scarpia (*Tosca*), Amfortas (*Parsifal*), and Wotan with the Scottish Opera. He is also heard frequently in concert appearances with many of the world's leading orchestras.

Corydon Singers have a core of about sixty amateur singers but fluctuate in number given the needs of the repertory. The group, almost entirely amateur, appears regularly at major festivals and is known for its many recordings made with Hyperion. Four times they have been runners up for the Gramophone Awards. Among their many other honors, Corydon Singers' recording of music by Vaughan Williams (including the *Five Mystical Songs*) received the "Record of the Year" in 1990 from both *The Guardian* and the *Sunday Times*.

Website: www.hyperion-records.co.uk/artists/mbest.html

Matthew Best

Photo: Jim Four

Matthew Best
Corydon Singers
Corydon Orchestra

JS: Where does the name Corydon come from – mythology or literature?

MB: It's a name we stumbled on by accident. I founded the choir just over twenty-five years ago, so it's been around a long time. I was still in school and had no plans for it to be anything other than a group that met for one concert. We needed a name, and were singing some English madrigals – hardly my thing but we happened to be doing some in that one concert. Anyway, someone coined this name because Corydon is a character who appears in English madrigals, rather like Phyllis and Amaryllis. It has absolutely no relevance to what we do; it never has, and frankly the name has been a pain in the neck. This is partly because there is a borough of South London by the name of Croydon. For many years (and even now) people assumed our name was misspelled and printed it as Croydon!

JS: Is your group made up of professional singers?

MB: It's almost entirely amateur though I reserve the right to bring in one or two professional singers if I need something very specific. Many in the choir are the sort of singers who either are on the verge of turning professional or could easily have been but who have decided for family or business reasons not to be. We also have quite a number of people who sing with us for a while and then move on to become professional singers. They're the sort of people whom we like occasionally to invite back as a one-off thing to help out with something. Generally speaking, the majority of what we do is entirely amateur though people often assume we are professional, especially abroad.

JS: Is the group fixed in size or does it fluctuate?

MB: It fluctuates dramatically. I rarely go below thirty-five or thirty-six; the most we've ever been is 140. The most regular size is between forty and fifty. We used to be quite a bit smaller years ago, but because the majority of our repertoire now is nineteenth and twentieth century and because we don't do much unaccompanied repertoire, I like a slightly larger sound. Also, because we use singers who are vocally very competent, forty can sound like a much bigger group. The one time we went with 140 was to record the Bruckner *Te Deum*. But for the Bruckner masses, for example, we recorded those with around sixty or seventy. For Mozart, I might use about forty. It all depends on the repertoire we are doing.

JS: How have you managed to remain bi-vocational at such high levels?

MB: I can't pretend it's been easy. There have been a number of occasions where I have been tempted to give up one or the other. But they're both important parts of what I do. There have been times when the pressure has become very considerable. I try to avoid as much administration as possible, but there is still an awful lot of planning and decision-making to be done. Inevitably I have to work longer hours, and I have to know when to shut one out. I think that's the secret. When I'm a singer, I try very hard to live as a singer, to be disciplined as a singer, and not to stay up into the small hours catching up with loose ends, or to spend hours on the phone or feeding things into the fax machine. I don't do little parts anymore. I sing big roles in big places. Sometimes, I will be asked to sing a concert, conduct a concert and sing another concert – do a package deal. The answer to that is nearly always "no." I'm either one or the other, and I try not to mix them. I used to look after all of my own affairs because no management seemed equally interested in both sides of what I was doing. So I found it easier to manage my own diary even though that obviously meant more administration. But now I have a very good manager at IMG here in London. We've sat down and worked out exactly where my priorities are. I sing maybe three or four operas a year, and my conducting centers around the work that I do now with the Corydon Singers, Corydon Orchestra and my guest conducting. It is very much a matter of saying, "Now I am a singer. Now I am a conductor. Now I am a singer." People accept me as doing both, and I'm doing very interesting work in both. As long as I stay upright, I hope to continue this way.

JS: Where did you develop your love of the choral medium?

MB: I developed it in school. From about the age of twelve, I knew I wanted to go to Cambridge and sing in the King's Choir. I had a very enthusiastic music teacher at school who fostered a budding interest in singing and choral repertoire.

JS: Were you a treble at King's?

MB: No, I went as a bass, as a choral scholar.

JS: Please describe your audition process for the Corydon Singers.

MB: Auditions are usually a very straightforward process. I don't have a very complicated audition. I ask each singer to come and sing one prepared piece which is of his or her choice. I like it to be whatever they feel the most comfortable in. I don't normally request any particular style. I like quality voices so, in addition to the ability to sing, the primary thing I'm looking for is the sheer quality of the voice. As a result, I turn away far more than I take. The other most important criterion is the ability to sight-read well.

JS: How do you evaluate sight-reading?

MB: I choose some quite difficult pieces! I usually start with a very awkward Bruckner fugue. I don't expect people to get it right the first time, but if they don't get it right, I expect them very quickly to work out where they went wrong and put it right by the second time. You can very quickly see if someone makes a quick slip and puts it right or if someone has major difficulty with it. Then, I might introduce a piece of Handel or Bach just to see how flexible the voice is. The sight-reading is very important because I just don't have time to teach people the notes.

JS: If someone is hearing the Corydon Singers and several other groups on recording, how would that person know that they were hearing your group? Is your aesthetic audible to the listener?

MB: People have often said that the Corydon Singers have a very distinctive sound, but I am probably not the best person to know why that's the case. Over the years we have had quite a fluctuating personnel because inevitably people come and go. And if we fluctuate between thirty-five and a hundred, we're dealing with a huge number of people who come through the choir at various stages. Yet there is a character to the sound, so there must be something to do with the way I ask them to sing. I think the fact that the choir is an amateur group that a lot of people think is professional, is an indication that there is a particular attention to vocal color and the sheer quality of sound. There is a real physical and vocal engagement. I often ask the choir to think of singing as soloists. This can give a richness and intensity to the sound. We're not as refined as some, but I think we sing with quite a lot of depth of color. I want the sound to be arresting.

JS: How much do you employ your special knowledge of singing in rehearsal?

MB: A lot and increasingly so, I find. Certain things have to be simplified. Much depends on how receptive choirs are to this sort of approach. I'm lucky with Corydon Singers in that they are, by and large, very interested. I'm probably more successful in some areas than in others, but we have had some interesting results. For instance, we were told that only the Russians can sing the Rachmaninoff *Vespers*. Though our recording is still considerably more English than any Russian choirs would be, I think it is considerably more Russian than most English choirs would be because together we were able to find colors and look at technical ways of getting them to free-up inhibitions and create a depth of sound. That is always my priority in rehearsal.

JS: Is choral blend an important objective for you?

MB: I always think it is the thing I try to get last. What I like to do is to find the individual character of people's voices. People are very shy at letting their voices go because the English style is very disciplined, but also very restrained. That probably has something to do with the English character. Because I spend half of my life in opera, working with professional singers of all types and vocal colors, what I'm looking to find in a choir is the character in the voice – the maximum color that a voice can create. Then, once I've got that, I might smooth the rough edges. Once I've got everyone vocally engaged, then I think about blend.

Another thing, which I think is terribly important, is the clarity of vowel color and knowing what vowel is right at any part of the vocal register. There are certain vowels that need to be open and ones that need to be narrow in different situations, in the same way a solo singer needs to know which vowels are open and which closed. It's not necessarily always the same. This ability helps to create the best tone quality one can; it helps to create a blend and, in a strange way, it also helps with intonation.

JS: What is your view of vibrato?

MB: I personally do not like vibrato-less singing. I think that vibrato is a natural part of any voice. Occasionally, one can sing without vibrato for a particular effect, but there has been an increasing trend, particularly in the last twenty or thirty years, for this so-called "pure," "white," vibrato-less sound. And I think it's been very specifically in this country.

JS: Do you think that has been influenced by the early-music movement?

MB: I do. I also think that many women are afraid of sounding like women. They are afraid of what I would regard as the natural vibrato that goes with a sound technique. It seems to me that the majority of people working with amateur choirs want this very pure sound. It may be very appropriate for Renaissance music, but applied to the whole range of choral music, I find it rather inappropriate. I'd be the last one to say that I want big, wobbly voices. I don't want that at all. I think this vibrato-less trend is a reaction against voices that are regarded as operatic. I always like a choir to sing with warmth, and warmth involves some vibrato.

JS: Some have traced much of this phenomenon to King's during the Willcocks years.

MB: I think this may be the case. The King's Choir under Willcocks was probably the foremost choir of its type at the time (certainly the one with the highest profile through the Christmas broadcasts and recordings), and it undoubtedly acted as a model for a whole generation of other choirs and choir directors. Over the years a great many members of the choir have gone on to direct other choirs all over the world, so it is hardly surprising that there has been a strong stylistic influence.

The passion for a cool, unemotional and "pure" sound has even spread to some of the big choral societies. I am all for precision and discipline. However, if you listen to some of the old choral society recordings made in the middle years of the twentieth century, for example, you will hear a warmth and a passion, and in some cases a sheer quality of sound which can be lacking today. The cool and slightly detached sound of the King's Choir under Willcocks had a special character that was ideally suited to the building at that particular time. I feel that sound is perhaps less appropriate when applied to other types of choirs, other venues, and other repertoire.

JS: What do you do in a typical rehearsal?

MB: We don't generally do warm-ups or exercises. We just go straight in to the music. I might invent an exercise for a specific purpose, but we always use the maximum amount of rehearsal for the music that is being prepared.

JS: Do you pass out the music in advance so that it is learned before the first rehearsal?

MB: No. Copies are picked up at the first rehearsal, and I expect the choir to sort the music out pretty quickly. These are busy people with busy lives, and they get bored easily. They want to put together a program with as little rehearsal as they are allowed to get away with and get the best out of it quickly. They expect to be drilled for three hours, get up to the highest standard they can achieve, do the concert, then go off and do something else.

JS: How do you form your conception of a piece?

MB: I like to prepare it over as long a period of time as I am able to. I never like to prepare anything in a hurry. Sometimes one's schedule demands that something has to be learned in a hurry, but I never feel comfortable doing that. I like to take a lot of time to think into an interpretation. I like to be influenced by other people as little as possible. By and large, I go a great deal on my own instinct. Obviously, I like to be historically informed as far as I can, but I'm a great believer that what is right speaks out at you from the page, if you let it. Having said which, one has to be aware of the performance convention of the time and aware of how one can be influenced by an over-Romantic approach to things. By and large, I like to try to see what the music is trying to say. It's very important to me to find out how it's put together.

JS: What kind of analysis gives you your structural understanding?

MB: I do an awful lot of scribbling into my scores; I divide everything up into phrase lengths; I often change my mind. I will often be looking for a particular way of doing something and then months later will suddenly find that I've been thinking it wrongly. The overall shape of a piece is something that I like to come to terms with over a period of time, and I think my most successful interpretations have been those that have had time to evolve.

JS: On what do you focus in the performance of a piece?

MB: What I'm always looking for in any music, whether it be choral or orchestral, apart from looking for the real truth behind the piece, is the drama in it. I think this reflects my operatic side. That's why I'm interested in structure. It might just be the way that a symphony is put together, the way one theme might be fighting against another theme, which is a drama in itself. Or it might be the fact that I'm trying to get the choir to sound like an opera chorus and make the sound more dramatic. I'm always looking for the internal drama in the music.

JS: How do you select Corydon's programming and repertoire for recording?

MB: I've had a long-standing relationship with Hyperion, which goes back a number of years. I've tended to fill a sort of nineteenth-century slot for them together with English repertoire from the first half of the twentieth century. The general repertoire area has been laid down by Hyperion, but within that framework the planning is very much a two-way thing. Sometimes Hyperion puts ideas forward, but more often it's a case of my suggesting things I'm keen to do. Hyperion either says "yes" or they don't. They won't record things they don't want to, and neither will I.

JS: How do you develop audiences for your concerts?

MB: Freelance organizations have real problems in making ends meet. Audiences are dwindling badly, particularly here in London. It's a really depressing situation. Even with excellent soloists and players, we have no guarantee of getting an audience. Concert halls in London are regularly half or even a quarter full. The Vienna Philharmonic has played to empty seats in London. Ten or twenty years ago this would have been unheard of.

JS: To what do you attribute this?

MB: The whole music business has become saturated. The compact disc boom of a few years ago meant that everybody was making records. Then, suddenly, the market became saturated, and now people are not buying records at the rate that they used to. So the record companies are having to cut back very dramatically. The effects on concert audiences are even worse. Concert tickets are not cheap, and however much you try to persuade people that a concert is a one-off experience which they can't get by listening to a record, it's easier and cheaper to put on a favorite record, open a bottle of wine and stay at home. There is so much on record now that is of very high standard. People who want tidbits have Classic FM and the like. Getting people to go to concerts now is a very big problem in the major cities. If you go farther afield where they have far fewer opportunities available, the chances are better.

JS: If ticket sales represent only a small percentage of total operating revenue, where do you find the rest?

MB: It comes from a number of sources or it doesn't. We have lean patches. If the choir and orchestra are invited to do a concert in a festival or as part of a series somewhere, then there is a fee payable to us. That can help keep the organization afloat. We only have one part-time employee, a general manager. Everybody else is employed on an event basis, so if there isn't any work, then there are no fees to pay.

JS: How many performances do you do?

MB: However many we can find or can afford to promote. A couple of years ago, for example, we had five concerts in the summer from five separate festivals. By and large, they invited us to come and paid the fees. Then we also have to look to sponsorship. There are certain charitable trusts to provide funding on a one-, two-, three-year basis. For us the financial aspect is never a certainty, and one simply does what one can afford. And one tries to get as many engagements as possible with someone else footing the bill. More and more promoters are finding joint promotion is viable. We say that we'll provide part of the funds, and the promoter will provide the rest to enable something to happen. Even with a full house, ticket sales actually make up a very small percentage of total concert costs.

JS: How then would you describe the role of choral music in English culture?

MB: The short answer is "strong, but declining in certain areas." There was a time when every major town had a big, thriving choral society, and it was a big part of community life. Nowadays there are still some very good regional choral societies, but I do think that the situation is declining. And, unfortunately, the average age is getting older, and the choirs are failing to attract younger singers. By contrast, with a lot of the smaller choirs of which the Corydon Singers might be regarded as an example, there is a great leaning towards youth. In the Corydon Singers I have a wide range of ages: I've had people who are not yet twenty and others who are over sixty. I like a mixture of age, though if somebody gets vocally past it, then I have to say "goodbye" to them. But if the older singers can still sing well, I like to have that maturity mixed into the sound.

JS: Finally, what have been your most important choral influences?

MB: In the early days, I was probably influenced in very different ways by both the King's College Choir and The Monteverdi Choir (having sung in both at various times). As I get older I find that I am influenced less and less by other choirs and other directors. As I have very wide range of activities, including a great deal of opera, I think that what I now bring to the choir is a kind of fusion of all these experiences.

Michael Brewer

Born: 1945

National Youth Choir

Education: University College of Wales

Interview: January 2000 (taped responses)

Michael Brewer is perhaps England's most prominent conductor of youth choirs, today serving as music director of the National Youth Choir and the chamber choir drawn from it: Laudibus. Choirs under his direction have twice won the international choral competition, "Let the Peoples Sing." He is author of the popular manual *Kick Start Your Choir*, and has collaborated on two sight-singing books. He is an active clinician and adjudicator worldwide. Before taking up residence in New Zealand for part of the year, Brewer was Director of Music at Chethams, Britain's largest school for musically gifted children.

The National Youth Choir of Great Britain convenes twice yearly for intense rehearsal and instruction, followed by concerts and tours. The choir of about 120 is selected from auditions held throughout Great Britain, and it embraces singers from the ages of sixteen to twenty-two. The Choir's tours have taken them to South Africa, Mexico, California, Australia, and throughout the Pacific.

Laudibus is a chamber choir of twenty-two singers auditioned from the NYC. Its growing reputation has been enhanced by winning the Tolosa (Spain) International Choir Competition and its best-selling recording, *20th Century English Choral Classics*.

Website: www.nycgb.org

Michael Brewer

Michael Brewer
National Youth Choir

JS: Please describe the National Youth Choir.

MB: National Youth Choir is really my main involvement these days, and I've been associated with it since it was formed in 1983. Before that, there was a choir called the British Youth Choir, which was run from the city of Sheffield by Carl Browning, the music advisor there. When Sheffield stopped supporting, he kept the choir going and changed its name to National Youth Choir so as to be the equivalent of our National Youth Orchestra and, in fact, we've performed with them a couple of times already. We will do so again on July 12, 2000, when we will sing *Belshazzar's Feast* by William Walton, which will be very exciting.

JS: How long do the choral courses last?

MB: Each summer course or camp lasts between eight and eleven days, depending on how many concerts there are. We tend to settle on a school in a particular region of Britain, rehearse there, and then perform within a bus journey of where we're camping. I think we've covered most of Britain over that time, but every third or fourth year we do an extended tour. In 1999, for example, there was a Pacific Tour, which also took in South Africa as a starting point and went across to Australia and across Australia, New Zealand and them some South Sea Islands to finish off with a kind of postscript in California.

JS: How many singers participate in these courses?

MB: The numbers in each course tend to be about 130. Such has been the demand for this choir that, for the last six years now, we've had a training choir of the same size, if you can believe it, but slightly younger so we've rationalized the ages. The concert choir is now aged sixteen to twenty-two with a younger cutoff than many youth choirs because we're trying to limit it to college-age and under. The training choir is essentially a secondary-school choir, in the British sense of the word, going from thirteen to eighteen. Because of the millenium, we have both choirs, one after the other, at Easter and again, one after the other, in July. Normally, we'll have just one at Christmas and one at Easter.

JS: Does the National Youth Choir receive any sponsorship?

MB: Now we don't have a sponsor as such. We have a small grant from our Arts Council, but such grants in Britain are now towards projects and because we are essentially providing a specific service and want help with administration, we're not very attractive to those forms of help. We have obtained money for specific projects in the last five years. A wonderful time we had performing African music with drummers; we did a concert in the Royal Albert Hall in '94. We try to perform a great deal of contemporary British music as well and to take it on tour.

One form of sponsorship, which really works, is to have local help for individual choristers. We find that also a wonderful way to advertise the choir because local papers, especially free papers, will write about a locally sponsored student who's just joined the choir. Everybody in the area reads it, so it's wonderful, free publicity. It's also good for actual sponsorship for members on courses because the local branch of Safeway is much more likely to sponsor one person than the national organization is to fund a national organization. It's just the way it works now.

JS: Please describe your approach to rehearsals.

MB: Our rehearsal day is pretty long. We aim at seven and one-half hours of singing, which is essentially a full morning, a fairly free afternoon when people can do recreation and sports, or sleep, or read books, or organize their own singing if they want to. Then we start again at four o'clock in the afternoon, have a session until around dinner and then another session after dinner, eating into the evening with recreation at the end of the evening. It's because of our licensing laws and because of the fact that we don't allow people over age to drink until the end of the rehearsals, that it works rather well. They just have a quick drink afterwards, at about nine at night. But we also arrange a huge number of social activities for everybody, and that really makes the family unit work well.

JS: Do you have additional staff to help with rehearsals?

MB: Yes. For one thing, all the members of the choir receive at least one and nearly always two individual singing lessons from a private teacher in the course.

Of course, there's a lot of small-group work and sectionals as well as the full rehearsal led by our staff. It's very important to us that the young members of staff are recruited from the choir itself. That's working very well. The section leaders have a wide- ranging role, especially in the senior choir: teaching music; looking after morale and discipline; helping with social activities; and helping with things like punctuality and pencils – you know, everything from the most profound to the most simple. This again strengthens the family unit and some of the section leaders then go on to be staff. This also works very well with the training choir, which is run entirely by present and former members of the senior choir. So it really is a pyramid system.

We also have a chamber choir called Laudibus, which now has about fifty-five on the books. It covers a ten-year age span – my oldest daughter, who sings with us, just turned thirty.

JS: How many times a week do you rehearse with Laudibus?

MB: It meets for just two days at a time. We have to do all of our concerts at weekends because people work. In one sense it's a good-old English telephone choir, but all the people on the end of the line are former members of the National Youth Choir. Chamber choir has become increasingly successful, and we do a number of festival appearances each year.

We've made a number of recordings over the last four years, including one in Germany for a project for new choral music. We've done some very way-out and difficult things for them. And we've also recorded English composers, most recently Humphrey Clucas, who writes a wonderful conservative style of English church music. It's beautifully accomplished. And we've recorded some old favorites for American Jewish Archive, for which we also have a project of recording American Jewish music over the coming year. The choir essentially aims to do absolutely anything, and try to do it as well as anybody else could. I've mentioned Indian and African, we've done music from the South Pacific, including a special commission on the Cook Islands, and Maori and New Zealand music.

I should say that I live in New Zealand for a third of the year now and enjoy very much a more peaceful lifestyle while trying to write books and music.

JS: What is your musical background?

MB: I came to music through jazz, having given up the piano at the age of eleven, as boys tend to do. I formed a group of school friends, persuaded them to learn instruments, did arrangements for them, toured around the Midlands of Britain and made pocket money. I wasn't a brilliant treble, but my voice broke quite well, took up singing lessons, and went to Birmingham School of Music for a year as a part-timer, while still at school. I did two degrees, the second one in composition and at the same time kept up the singing. I did a bit of oratorio singing in my twenties and then gave up out of fear and more importantly because I was become increasingly fanatical about choral training, and applying vocal techniques to helping other people. So I was a schoolteacher, including twenty years as director of a specialist music school for talented children. As a teacher, I was able to devote quite a lot of time to connecting choirs, learning more about it and began doing workshops for other people, which I've been doing for twenty-five years. In 1985, I did a European tour on my sabbatical, and I listened to every choir and conductor and singing teacher I could find. I amassed so much information that I was using, that it reached a point where I was able to put things together into a book called *Kick Start Your Choir*. That book came out three years ago. I'm now writing a second book, which includes everything from warm-ups to ways to sing in foreign languages without too much effort, ways particularly to find an authentic choral sound quickly. I don't have any other choirs of my own apart from the three national ones, but I spend the rest of my time wandering around the globe giving workshops. I have a pretty extensive English season, from Easter to summer and another one in October and November. Also, I get a fair bit of guest conducting as well and visiting conferences.

JS: How do you audition singers for the National Youth Choir?

MB: These are great fun because we try to make the audition into a little bit of a vocal challenge, rather than just going through their party pieces. And because the musical background of applicants is so varied, you can't rely on good sight-reading, or even their having been in a school choir, because so many schools in Britain don't have an active choir anymore. Maybe they've been performing musicals or learning things by rote. Especially in the training choir, we have to take things from scratch, and look very much at potential. I've drawn on my experience for that in auditioning for Specialist Music School over all those years and we've designed a form which tries to label different forms of vocal technique which might need attention or may be OK. We look at musicianship and of course the performing skills too. This means that when they meet their singing teacher in a course, they can be given practical help along those lines. If they don't gain a place in the choir, then they can have a letter, giving a fair amount of detail, as to what we advise that they can work on for future consideration.

In selecting for the choir, we're looking for clear voices, good pitch and quick response as first priorities. And then after that we're looking for potential and response. So if someone has a naturally quite good voice, but doesn't quite sing in tune and is slow to respond, then we know that they're going to find the choir very difficult. Sometimes we disappoint singing teachers about their star pupils. On the other hand, we're not looking for safe, inverted choir voices. We really want people with personality, and the ability to blend and vary sound, and the ability to sing in tune. Sight-reading can be taught and improved rapidly; and because ninety-five percent of successful applicants go into the training choir first, that's how we can do it, if they're not getting that help somewhere else. Needless to say, the people from independent schools are liable to be much better equipped, and they're also liable to be the ones who go to Ralph Allwood's marvelous courses at Eton, which prepare them for choral scholarships as well as giving them a great experience of church music. My main concern now, on one hand, is for that vast majority of young people in the state system in Britain who won't get the chance to sing some of the great music and, on the other hand, to develop their potential as choral singers. This is crucial as we enter the new millennium, of course. It's true to say, and obvious to say, that an organization like the youth choir can only scratch the surface. However, that's one of the reasons I'm spending so much of my time doing workshops with school choirs of all levels – to encourage them to have fun, to do world music repertoire, and to learn basic vocal skills quickly.

JS: What do you mean by response and potential, and so on?

MB: I'm really talking about the ability to change something instantly. So if someone comes to an audition singing an obviously very well prepared piece, it's wonderful to ask them why they did it that way, and what other ways they could have found to interpret a particular phrase or mood. I'll ask them to do that on the spot. Then there are more basic musical games to play: to alter the rhythm, to do in the minor, to improvise on a short phrase and so on. There isn't time to do much of that in an audition, but it's very helpful to see how much someone can handle that natural approach. And it's amazing how many can, and how many have simply learned their music as taught without having to think about these things. It's a very exciting area of creativity and music, I think, and contributes enormously to the eventual quality of a group like the National Youth Choir, and to the fact that they need to be ready for anything.

31

JS: In what ways do you develop blend?

MB: In fact, I'm just now in the middle of the chapter on blend for my second book and it's something which I find a very exciting topic to worry about and try to and improve. It's hard to put in just a few words, but basically I'm looking to teach vowels through sensation, through awareness of what people call breath management and resonance. I use lots of games to reinforce that and also try to develop some understanding of harmonics. This is coupled with relating those vowel sounds to specific languages. The second stage, for me, is to look at individual voices, and in rehearsals I regularly go down a line of singers and make adjustments or by inviting individuals to change their jaw, lips, tongue, posture, position and to identify with the sounds of the person next to them. This is very stimulating, and once they get over their initial fears, the students love it. Then, as a third stage, I get them to sing to each other in pairs so that the sound waves face each other; the students face each other and the sound waves blend. And then they sing in different pairs. A fourth stage is to move the people around so that the clearest blended voices are towards the middle, but the darker, richer voices are mixed in with them. Depending how many problem voices there are in a section, they are cunningly placed either at the edges, or between two very clear voices. It's very important to me that singers change position in the choir every couple of rehearsals so that, on the one hand, they get used to singing and blending with a neighbor, and, on the other hand, they adapt quickly to blending with a new person. I also think it's very important that singers listen to another section while rehearsing. I invite them to comment on blend from another section in a very open way when they're singing a particular part. It's amazing how the group identity develops through that open opportunity to be positive. Of course, we keep the negative comments classified as "out of order." And I find it very stimulating to do that. The great thing about it is that, if you have at least a reasonable resonance in the room, the whole choir can hear the difference and the sound blends. The harmonics start to ping, and the room gives its own bloom to the sound. As soon as that's been done once or twice, the singers are right with it and understand that they are not being victimized for singing something wrongly, but are being invited to contribute to an exciting sound.

I had one crazy experience on a workshop where a singer refused to play this game because he said he had the right to his own sound. My answer to that was yes, of course he did, and we all did but that we had a contract in a choir to enjoy blending with other sounds in this kind of music. So that was a tricky one.

JS: How do you develop tone quality in your groups?

MB: To me, tone quality comes from blend, but blend applied to the sound that we want to create for a particular style. So we look for high resonance for Italian, richer, rounder covered sounds for German, very bright sounds for Bulgarian and some islander music and so on. We can achieve this in a short time by having specific signals for kinds of sound, partly in the conducting, but also coming from the warm-ups. These things are reinforced in the singing lessons so that when I ask them for an open Italian "oh" or "ah," they will do that fairly quickly. It needs constant reinforcement to eradicate, as far as possible, the English diphthongs and the unsupported backward tongue and clipped speech of some kinds of English, which is why we spend a lot of time singing in an Italian sort of way, and applying that back to other styles.

JS: Do you have specific ways that you achieve ensemble?

MB: This flows naturally from blend and tone. And it has the additional central kind of pivot of breathing and pulse and rhythm of words. We spend a lot of time on supported sound, of breathing in, of feeling whole phrases, on lip and tongue articulation, sitting on top of long phrases and so on. And as well as watching a conductor, we are trying to get the young people to feel each phrase together, and we keep stressing that, even with one hundred voices. We need to think like a chamber choir.

JS: Is intonation something that you work towards deliberately?

MB: In my *Kick Start* book, I give a kind of troubleshooting page on pitch problems. A quick summary would be, first of all breathing and support, and maintaining consistency of vowels through the vocal tract. Secondly, we must understand vowel modification. I ask for high resonant vowels in the bass part of a chord, whoever happens to be singing it, and then gradually modifying to a more rounded sound in the top part. Then I would add to that the need for approaching the *schwa* vowel in sopranos from roughly F sharp above the staff onwards. All these things help with listening, and that in itself helps with pitch. That brings me to the third point, which is listening – listening to one's self and listening to the sound. Another aspect of this is pitch memory. The biggest fault I think singers have is forgetting a note they sang a few seconds ago. I *don't* use a rehearsal keyboard – repeat, I *don't* use a rehearsal keyboard except for emulating the radio, and playing one or two very high arpeggios to reinforce the upper partials and when there are difficult passages needing pitch security. I think it's especially important not to give a note for a phrase that you

are singing several times. Let the choir remember it. If, over a few minutes, the pitch slips, then I would go over to the piano, play something irrelevant and start again. Other aspects of pitch that are important to me are, first of all, not to get neurotic when the choir starts to go flat because it normally has a psychological cause: it might be doing too difficult music too early in the rehearsal or too early in the morning; it might mean not enough oxygen in the room; it might mean bad sitting position and you need to stand up; it might mean low morale and you need to tell a joke; it might mean something totally external like somebody's had a family problem or something. So my solution to all that, if technical means and fun and games and jokes don't work, is to sing another piece of music, or have a coffee break. Sometimes in a long rehearsal period, like in the middle of a music course, if we're having a bad rehearsal, we just let it finish and let the people learn the music that they're learning, come back after coffee all fresh, and the problem is
nearly always solved.

In reestablishing morale, for example, after singing difficult music which then flags, I would engage the choir in sirens, calls, a simple song they know well, a bit of African music, vowel sounds, chords, or humming. I should mention specifically that we love to improvise chords, and learn about chord progressions. This is a skill that's declined a lot over the last fifteen years, and I'm keener than ever to keep it going. To teach them that when you call out, say, G-major, somebody finds a G, they can then sing any note in the chord, and if you then call out D, or E minor, they're allowed to slide until they find a note in the new chord. That's a lot of fun, and once they realize they have the freedom to move where they want within the chord, you can achieve tremendous things over a course of five or six tries, maybe three or four minutes each time. We will sing diminished sevenths, Neapolitan chords and, of course, going completely chromatic or atonal, then coming back to a tonal chord again. The possibilities are endless.

JS: How do you go about putting together programs for the NYC?

MB: In program selection, I've mentioned that we have specific projects – be it African, Indian, Russian, whatever, and we sang some Mongolian music last year. It's more important to us to offer a wide experience. So our programs always include at least one multi-choir Renaissance piece, one contemporary piece, (often commissioned), several major works from the past, and then a world music component. Our concerts seem like a bit of a mish-mash, but they are always intended to demonstrate the variety of sounds which young people can make.

JS: What guides your choral aesthetic?

MB: This is the most difficult question of all. The point at which I seem to differ with colleagues in Britain is what I call the lapidary approach. Many conductors talk about the music and the aesthetic of it from the beginning. I like to build the music stone by stone, starting with the notes, analyzing the harmony, analyzing the rhythm and the words separately, because of course, they come from a different part of the brain. I seek to gain an experience of how it fits together and, after that, to look at the reason the music was written. We like to deconstruct and then synthesize the piece into a whole. I find that it's very easy for busy singers to skate over the surface of music, and to gain quite a good feeling for its message. But with a choir like the Youth Choir, we have the opportunity to explore much more deeply and to enjoy the detail of the sonorities as we learn. I believe, in the youth choir, that it takes five rehearsals of a piece to begin to reach the automatic understanding which a performance needs. And unless we've reached that five-rehearsal stage, it's dangerous to perform it. Parallel with that comes the memorizing of the music. The obvious result of that is that singers and conductor are as one, and the performance can be created with an immediacy which I derive directly from my experience of jazz as a teenager.

To put it another way, I don't think I would have a perfect performance of anything in my mind because I would still be asking questions, even on tour after twenty performances. I would want to be still exploring and surprising the choir with new angles so that, in a sense, every audience hears the piece fresh. I hope this doesn't come over as a kind of arrogance that I would know more than the composer; in fact, it's exactly the opposite. I think we are exploring to find what was in the composer's heart or spirit. To set something down in stone as to how a piece must be sung goes against that kind of exploration. Of course, some things in a composition are blindingly obvious, and it would be stupid to mess about with speeds, for example. I'm looking more at the subtlety of phrasing, and the shaping of sounds to create moods. In short, I think that an audience gains from a two-fold emotional condition in listening to a choral performance. On one hand, they sense that the choir is relaxed and confident, and communicating well; on the other, there is a kind of excitement of creativity going on. I don't think that performances should be comfortable. On the other hand, I do think that they should be assured.

JS: Who have been your greatest influences?

MB: In brief, I learned from watching John Eliot Gardiner at Chethams (my school) twenty years ago, the excitement of bright vowels and incisive, dancing Baroque rhythms, and all that alongside his great analytical, historical, scholarly approach to music. From Andrew Parrott, I learned also scholarship but, as well, a kind of crazy enthusiasm, infectious humor, and physical involvement by amateur performers. I also was inspired by his effortless teaching through keeping people excited and laughing and on their toes while learning. I spent a week watching Eric Ericson. I admired his calm, demanding approach with which he seemed, with very little verbal communication, to create a remarkable response in the students he was working with. Of course, they were Swedish people imbued with all that that country has in musical tradition: a natural feeling for singing, for harmony, and for making a beautiful sound. Watching him was a life-changing experience, and I have to say it's been very hard to emulate his approach in my own work. Where it comes home to me is at exasperating moments when all seems to be slipping away, that it is possible to sit down and do something very quietly and intensively. That really does work, and it's something I feel everyone can learn from.

Apart from those specific influences, I have learned so much from dozens or hundreds of conductors, partly on my 1987 tour, but also in every encounter since. To me, the most important thing is the magical relationship between the conductor and the singers; every conductor achieves it in a slightly different way, of course, but that's what is so exciting about it.

JS: Do you have what would be called a "typical rehearsal?"

MB: I don't think there is such a thing in the way I work with the youth choir, but there is a range of rehearsal types. There's the sectional, where people are largely working with section leaders, carefully learning notes. Sometimes this is done in groups of only six. They report back when they've learned a particular passage in, say, twenty minutes. Then there are rehearsals of full sections with me or whoever's conducting; then half of a double choir and then maybe full choir. In the full-choir rehearsals, every session is different from every other. Mornings start slowly and carefully and build, we hope, to something emotional and strong at lunchtime. Late afternoons are gentle and not too demanding, while the blood sugar is low. But involve lots of left brain and learning and marking in scores. Evening rehearsals, when the adrenaline is high, can be anything from focused and spiritual to crazy and wild.

What I like to think the rehearsals have in common is that the singing is physical; there's often physical action going on as well to reinforce the music. There will be lively and involved active listening for people who aren't singing at the moment. In other words, they have to be ready to answer a question about those who are singing, whether it's effective, or whether something could be improved – anything to keep people on their toes and to reinforce the rehearsal.

Singers will have an objective, be it to learn the next thirty-six bars, or to memorize, or to get inside some pronunciation difficulties, or to put a piece together. We don't allow repetitions of a piece or phrase without giving a reason to do so. That could be simply to memorize or to establish a way of singing, but could equally well be to get certain passages right, or information marked. I think it's important that these young singers learn to learn music quickly. For that reason, we have to keep reinforcing different aspects of the music, which is what I call being a "sheepdog": looking at words, vowels, consonants, pitch, blend, harmony, rhythm, round and round again each time.

JS: Whose choral work do you admire?

MB: I mentioned Eric Ericson before and bracket with him anybody who has that ability to make wonderful sounds without appearing to be stressed about it. A great friend of mine, and someone who has influenced me more recently, is Gunnar Eriksson from Gothenburg. He has an uncanny ability, with very little apparent effort, to inspire very large numbers of people to incredible musical feats. He hates the ceremony of concerts and loves to ambush audiences by having his choir sing in the middle of them or start singing while people are talking or change a concert program in mid-stream. To me, that is what music is all about. I don't want to bore you with a long list of all the people I admire because it's too long, and I don't want to leave anyone out.

I'm excited whenever I hear someone molding a choir into an exciting performing unit, which consists of people who have an understanding of the music, both intellectually and spiritually. That's quite a rare thing and easy to spot when you hear it. I suppose I would call myself right-brained in that I would rather have magic with flaws in it rather than craftsmanship with safety.

JS: How do you approach score preparation?

MB: I would do the things you are supposed to do, namely go through a new score, looking at the overall shape: first, speeds, pauses, changes of mood. Then, in more detail, I would look at the rhythm and harmony as well as the melody and gain an overall shape of the phrases and sections. I would do all this without a piano. After a run-through with the choir, I would take the score again and then double-check aspects like upbeats, fermatas, and corners needing careful conducting. The choir then goes away and works in detail, after which we assemble the music, as I said earlier. I absolutely don't learn dynamics early in rehearsals, and in fact we would rehearse them with varying dynamics. On about the third rehearsal, we would settle on dynamics and gain general approval for what is on the page, or we might change some things, depending on the style. If we're looking at Renaissance music, we spend a lot of time looking at internal rhythms, hemiolas, threes within four and so on, and particularly the rhythm of the verbal phrases and their relationship to plainchant.

Some aspects can be done efficiently early on, like placing final consonants on rests and working out consonants at commas. As I've said, I'm very committed to deconstruction: to using different bits of the brain at different times, to learning the music separately from the words, making games out of the rhythms, out of the harmony and difficult bits of the melody, and playing games with the words, too.

I ought to add that we are very much involved in the training of new singers in the pure joy of the physical act of singing. This applies particularly to getting boys involved. We try to maintain a reasonable choral ratio of boys and girls, despite having, I would say, a ratio of four to one, girls to boys, in our field of applicants. We do tend to find that the boys who have the courage to come along are those who are sufficiently interested in singing to withstand the slings and arrows of their classmates. Somehow we have to find a way to make singing socially acceptable again in the mixed-gender school. This is where, in workshops for example, the importance of world music comes in, rhythmical, vital, and physical music. As for the National Youth Choir, I would summarize that we are trying to provide a wide experience of singing repertoire from many times and cultures in order to enable every chorister to develop as an individual. We hope the immediate tangible product will be a higher and exciting performance standard. And the long-term results are far-reaching, ranging from sending people out to conduct their own choirs to joining other choirs.

JS: How do you view the controversial topic of girls in cathedral?

MB: I should mention that David Hill, a student of mine many years ago, was a pioneer in introducing girls into cathedral singing, and he's at Winchester. His neighbor, Richard Seal in Salisbury, established a girls' choir several years ago which is achieving great success.

To summarize, I think that young children sing best separated by gender, and to have a girls' choir and a boys' choir is wonderful. And if ever we founded a children's choir within the National Youth Choir, we would look very carefully about having segregated genders. There is a National Children's Choir, just started, which is mixed, and is really at a very early stage.

One issue, which is not an issue for me, is the sound of boys and the sound of girls. There is a slight difference between the well produced girls' sound and that of the boys, but it has been demonstrated that you can't actually tell the difference. My main concern, really, is that we do keep boys singing to produce the tenors and basses of the future. One personal angle is that I have four daughters who wanted to sing in my local cathedral but weren't able to at that stage. But now that cathedral has a girls' choir which is doing very well. Incidentally, those four daughters are all singing happily for me in chamber choir now, so it's all worked out well. But it's a difficult situation for the cathedral artists to manage because of the fact that it isn't a simple question to answer. I do think the way forward is to have separate choirs of girls and boys which combine on special occasions. Then, of course, they can eventually move on to youth and adult choirs where they all happily sing together.

JS: How do you view the use of vibrato among your young singers?

MB: My chief aim in teaching singers is to give them control of what they're doing; that includes vibrato as much as anything else. In a workshop, for example, I would ask singers to make a sound which is rich in vibrato and then gradually reduce it to try to sing with no vibrato at all. This method also works very well with existing choirs of older singers. As with instrumental music, vibrato is used for effect, and to a different degree in different styles, so that's where the control comes in. In the National Youth Choir, we try to sing Renaissance music with less vibrato and Romantic music with more.

I think my main challenge in working with young people is trying to release their inhibitions. I've just finished a series of school workshops in New Zealand where it's taken a great deal of energy to release the young people from their shells and get them using their whole bodies to sing, opening up, and communicating. I always feel a great thrill when that point is reached in a session, where everybody is resonating together, having a lot of fun, and filling the room with sound. After that, anything is possible. I believe strongly that it's much easier to refine a big sound than it is to create something from a little. I think taming a lion is an excellent occupation if you're a choral trainer. In the National Youth Choir, it's wonderful when we achieve the right kind of creative tension between exuberance and energy, and focus and concentration. Naturally enough, for much of the day we're simply quietly getting on with the job of learning things. But those great moments of release we can channel our emotional excitement into the music in a way that makes it all worthwhile.

JS: Any closing thoughts?

MB: One final point I want to make, which is important to me, is the question of empowering people to make choices, to give them the control which they need. This is why, I suppose, we spend so much time on vocal games, and on questioning why we sing in a certain way. By that I don't mean keep analyzing in rehearsals, but by holding a principle whereby we would learn a phrase, let's say by singing it three or four times, each time singing it in a different style so that the note learning is going on while the mind is being encouraged to accept that there is more than one way to do something. Then when we come to the performance; we try to choose the way which is most appropriate or most authentic for that music. On the way through, it's very important to do inappropriate things to give the context for that kind of end product.

I find that running a large choir at national level is very exciting because the singers have enormous potential, and vastly different background and experience. We have the job of bringing that all into one unit in a very short time.

Peter Broadbent

Born: 1947

Joyful Company of Singers

Education: Northern School of Music, Manchester

Interview: January 14, 1999, The Barbican, London

Peter Broadbent began his conducting career as Chorus Master and Assistant Conductor of the Manchester Opera Company, and for several years he was director of St. Angela's Singers, the Esterhazy Singers, and the Enfield String Players. However, it has been since his founding of the Joyful Company of Singers in 1988 that Broadbent has gained acclaim through that group's innovative programming, well received recordings, and by winning a number of international choral competitions. He is in demand as an adjudicator for choral competitions in Hungary, France, Spain and Italy.

The Joyful Company of Singers have won numerous national and international competitions, including Sainsbury's "Choir of the Year," the *Grand Prix*, and four major prizes at the *Floriliege Vocal* in Tours, along with the title "Choir of the World" at the Llangollen International Eisteddfod, and the *Citta di Arezzo*. The choir, which fluctuates in size, is made up entirely of amateur singers. The JCS sings repertory of most style periods but specializes in twentieth century music, notably that of Kaija Saariaho, Giles Swayne, Alun Hoddinott and Jonathan Harvey.

Website: www.jcos.co.uk

Peter Broadbent

Peter Broadbent
Joyful Company of Singers

JS: Please tell me about the Joyful Company of Singers.

PB: The Joyful Company is quite unusual in terms of most British amateur choirs, because it is very professionally organized and professionally run. We do something like twenty-odd performances a year. We have a pool of about one hundred singers rather than "a choir" as such. We normally sing with between twenty-four and thirty-two, but because we do so much we need a big pool. Having said that, we're doing the Strauss *Deutsche Motette* at the Bath Festival this year, and we'll be taking fifty-eight to sing that. Our repertoire ranges right across the board, and, I suppose, our principal interests are *a cappella*. I believe very much in the Eric Ericson theory that you must do at least seventy-five percent of your repertoire *a cappella* to have a good choir. We do a fair amount of orchestrally accompanied work for other conductors and with me. We record and perform quite a lot with Richard Hickox – we are his favorite choir! My and the choir's interests are very wide, so we enjoy singing everything, but we do sing a lot of twentieth-century *a cappella* repertoire.

JS: Do you have any professionals?

PB: We have professionals who sing with other choirs, but they don't get paid when they sing with us. They are happy to sing with us for nothing. We have some people who commute from Leicestershire, 200 miles round trip, and someone from Southampton, but they think it's worth it. It's a very high-quality choir.

JS: Is there an "English approach" to choral music?

PB: I'm probably the wrong person to ask, but I think there is, and I don't like it. I would not describe our choir as being typically English; in fact, very few people would. It's much more like a European choir in terms of its sound and its approach. On the other hand, I do benefit hugely from the fantastic tradition of sight-reading that has come up through the cathedrals. But I hate the traditional sound of English choirs because I think the English cathedral tradition – while valuable in terms of repertoire, teaching of technique and sight-reading – has been very damaging in several ways. I think the blend of the English cathedral sound becomes very bland. I was a great admirer of George Malcolm who used to be Master of Music of Westminster Cathedral in the fifties, and that choir still does, or once again, sounds the way it did under Malcolm – very much like a Spanish or Italian Choir. The boys are trained to <u>sing</u>. He put it very nicely in an article he wrote in a book of tributes to Benjamin Britten on the composer's fiftieth birthday. He was asked to write an article about boys' voices and said that the typical English Cathedral sound of a boy's voice is very, very beautiful as an acoustic phenomenon, but it's got absolutely nothing to do with a little boy! It's this awful, white, head-voice sound. The reason I dislike it so much is that mixed choirs with women try to sound like that. I suppose there is a repertoire from the end of the nineteenth and early part of this century for which it works very nicely. On the whole, music comes alive when you give it some color. We had a delightful review of a recent program of Renaissance and contemporary Spanish music. Hilary Finch in the *Times* gave us a lovely review saying, "The Joyful Company sings Renaissance music in a way which would make Peter Phillips and his ilk cringe! They sing with a full-throated, full-hearted sense of joy, with the color the music deserves." I find this English, etiolated approach to Renaissance music quite frightening.

We were singing Palestrina in Arezzo in Tuscany, and I've always believed in singing that music passionately because I think it is passionate music. We were in a little village nearby and had just been to see the *Resurezzio* of Piero Della Francesca. We were having a meal after our concert, and this little fifteen-year-old girl who was serving could have stepped straight off any one of those Piero frescoes. I thought, "The faces haven't changed; the weather hasn't changed, the colors haven't changed – why do people think that, in the sixteenth century, people sang without vibrato?" I don't believe they did because I don't believe the Italian voice has changed over the centuries, any more than anything else has changed. Palestrina believed in what he was writing passionately. But even in Italy, The Sixteen and The Tallis Scholars are held up to be a prime example of how to sing Renaissance music, but they are not because they sing it without color; they sing it with this white, blanched approach.

JS: How do you select singers?

PB: I'm looking for vocal quality, good intonation and pretty good sight-reading. Ideally, brilliant sight-reading. I always tell them to bring something they enjoy singing, in whatever style. If I like their vocal quality, then they stay for half or all of the rehearsal. I put them next to somebody whom I trust, and I get feedback from them as well. I tell them that, from their point of view, they may as well sit through a rehearsal because they might not like the way I work. A lot of our singers come through recommendation, and sometimes if we're short, I might not audition a person at all if they've come highly recommended.

There is a type of approach to professional singing that some have in England which says, "I don't smile in rehearsal, and I don't smile in performance. Impress me." Those who have that approach sing for me only once because they are uncomfortable, and I'm uncomfortable. I make a lot of jokes in rehearsal, and while I don't expect people to laugh at my jokes, I don't expect them to be affronted by the fact that I am making jokes. I don't like an atmosphere in a choir where someone is sitting and reading a newspaper in rehearsal. It's a professional thing that must be part of the Protestant ethic where, if you're being paid for a job, you're not supposed to enjoy it. In many British orchestras, you have a high percentage of players who appear to sit there and go through the motions. There was a very interesting interview with a fine, young Italian conductor, Daniele Gatti, in which he was asked the difference between English and Italian orchestral musicians. He said that with an English orchestra, at the first rehearsal ninety-five percent of the notes are there and by the last it's one-hundred percent. But with an Italian orchestra, at the first rehearsal you're lucky to get seventy-five percent of the notes right, and by the last rehearsal you're lucky to get ninety-five. But the difference comes in the performances because the Italians will give 120 percent, but the English will give exactly what they gave at the last rehearsal. This approach drives me mad and it's not only the professionals. Quite a lot of amateurs have this attitude.

JS: Do you get large audiences?

PB: Getting audiences in England is terribly difficult. People sing in choirs in England; they don't like to go and listen to them. If we do contemporary *a cappella* music, we no longer promote concerts in London. There's no point because nobody comes.

JS: Do you do anything at all to develop London audiences?

PB: We have a newsletter, and we do lots of different types of concerts, so we are attracting different audiences. We did our own series of popular choral classics at St. John Smith Square to build up our following, but it costs a huge amount of money.

JS: You mentioned that blend can mean bland. How do you approach blend?

PB: I believe blend is achieved through the same approach to vowel sounds. The danger of the word *blend* in England is that what it means is *blend down*. What happens is that you listen to the voice next to you and try to match it, and then everyone ends up blending down to the lowest common denominator. What you can end up with is colorless. When I talk about this with my singers, I tell them to blend up and leave it to me to tell them if they are too loud!

The breakthrough for beginning to get the kind of sound that I was looking for was when we were working on the Russian disc. I remember a wonderful phrase from a Russian conductor who was being interviewed. He said he liked very much the English choir – "that blend, that blend" – but he said they don't do that in Russia. They go more for a "bouquet" of sound. I remember vividly where I first applied this idea. It was in a phrase sung by the sopranos in the Rachmaninoff *Sacred Concerto*. I said to them, "You're on your own. You're on the apron of the Bolshoi, and you're singing a Tchaikovsky aria. Don't think about anyone but yourself. I want color; I want vibrato. I just want you to be a soloist and leave it to me to tell you if it's too much." They started singing the phrase, and everyone sat up. It was incredible. These people come along with wonderful voices, audition with an aria, go off and sit in the choir and disappear. I have to keep on them all of the time to encourage them to do this because their natural tendency is to be careful and make sure it's safe. I'd much rather go for danger!

JS: Do you use this approach with all repertory?

PB: I think, to some extent, it does apply to all repertoire. If we are singing Palestrina, I don't want a big vibrato, but I don't want it colorless. You must be very Italian with the vowels. A lot comes from the language. Tonight we are rehearsing Poulenc, and even in the Latin, in sacred music, I shall still want it to sound like French because that's the sound he had in mind.

An awful lot of both blend and tone quality I approach through the particular music we are singing. I don't have any particular way of getting it. It's more a question of focusing on particular moments for a sound that I want. More than anything, I encourage them to sing and to let me make the decisions.

JS: How do you deal with intonation problems?

PB: Well, you can't sing Russian music in tune. If you are, you're not singing! I have no approach, and I suppose it's the weakest part of my choir-training abilities. I tend to deal with intonation problems as they arise and when they are noticeable. But I'd rather give a good performance that drops a semitone. Some conductors are so paranoid about intonation, they never get to color. It's important, but I'm not obsessed with it.

JS: Are you always talking style?

PB: I think that my strongest quality as a conductor is a sense of style. I have a highly intelligent choir, so I don't have to spend a lot of time talking about it. A lot of it's done with gesture. You know, you don't conduct Bach the same way you conduct Bruckner.

JS: How do you choose repertoire for the JCS?

PB: When we began, one of the things we wanted to do with the choir was to educate. I'm a great believer that you can lead people into real music and even contemporary music if you set about it the right way. We've often done programs which have readings in them. We have a very fine actor who is a marvelous reader. He hardly works in the theater any more and gives only solo recitals, so he's book-able. I've done lots of different sorts of programs grouped around a theme of some kind, including quite a few funny readings. It's a marvelous thing that when you get people laughing, which they normally don't do in a concert hall, then they listen in a completely different way. I've had them listening to quite difficult contemporary music and loving it because they're relaxed.

JS: What is an example of this kind of program?

PB: One called "Full Fathom Five" was based around the sea. We used all sorts of settings, not only by Shakespeare but everything "sea-worthy." Those included Stanford's *Songs of the Sea*, which are quite jolly, and also Giles Swayne's *Shakespeare Songs*. People will listen to anything once they've had a good laugh. One of the passages we used was from a very funny book by Jerome K. Jerome called *Three Men in a Boat*. It was so funny, the choir could hardly sing. This kind of program breaks down barriers and also gives the choir a rest.

I'm also very conscious of program shape and coherence. Even if it is not obvious to the audience, if it works for me, I know it will be successful. However, there has to be some sort of build.

JS: What is this?

PB: I have a very, very strong feeling that, whether you're working with professionals or amateurs, music is to be enjoyed. That's one of the reasons for the name of the choir. It's also, in many ways, probably one of the reasons for my relative lack of success in certain fields. Some don't take you seriously if you smile or if you don't throw your weight around as a conductor. I never shout, and I'm never rude to singers. If I have to say something to them that's hard, I always do that just before the interval so that I can rebuild afterward when they're a bit more relaxed. I never leave a sour feeling at the end of a session. Everything you do in music should be enjoyable while you're doing it, and if it isn't, then something's wrong.

JS: What is the role of choral music in England?

PB: It's not a spectator sport. People go to the same works – *Messiah*, *The Creation*, whatever, again and again. They don't really like to go and listen to choirs. When we go to France or Italy, we get three or four times the numbers of audience we get here. We have a problem with concert-going in this country since people are so conservative. If they don't know it, they won't go. If you put on a program here at the Barbican and you did a Mozart Overture, a Beethoven piano concerto and Brahms symphony, you'd fill the hall. If you did Schoenberg and Barber, you'd take away about twenty percent, easily.

JS: How do you get away with performing so much contemporary music, like Jonathan Harvey?

PB: We don't do it in London is the short answer. We gave a concert recently with *Figure Humaine*, paired with the Smirnov concerto as part of an educational project. The financing for the concert came out of the project through a grant and through the school that was involved. We had an audience of, I'd say, thirty-eight to forty people. At least ten were members of The Joyful Company of Singers who weren't singing for that concert. Eric Ericson gave two concerts across the street at St. Giles Cripplegate as part of a festival given by the BBC and the Barbican. I was there for one of them, and I think there were forty-eight people there. I think I knew about twenty of them, mostly conductors.

JS: So what is the short answer to the role of choral music in English culture?

PB: It is a participative sport, not a spectator sport. You do better outside of London because there is just too much going on here.

JS: What is the balance between professional and amateur choral groups in England?

PB: There are very few professional choirs. The BBC Singers is the only full-time professional choir in the country, not counting opera choruses. They used to have the BBC Northern Singers, but that no longer exists, as such. There's a group in Birmingham called "Ex Cathedra" which is sort of semi-pro with a mix of pros and amateurs.

JS: How do you define groups like The Tallis Scholars and The Sixteen?

PB: You'd describe those as choirs, I suppose, but you wouldn't call The Hilliard Ensemble a choir, would you? The thing is, they do very little work in this country. If they get good recording contracts, they'll be all right, but most of the work comes from abroad. Some years ago The Tallis Scholars produced a disc of arrangements of English folk music. In Japan it was number two on their classical hit parade, but it wasn't even released in England. There was no point. The professional choirs hardly work here.

JS: Do all school children have singing experiences?

PB: The short answer to that is that "they are supposed to" but the correct answer is "no." There was a very, very dire time when there was a huge increase in practical and creative music making in the schools, which is a good thing; but it all went very instrumental, and teachers lost sight of singing as a creative element. This is one of the reasons we go into the schools doing educational projects because it's amazing what you can get children to do with their voices. They hadn't thought of that. The children sit there at these keyboards, and they "compose." They don't know what they're doing, of course; I know that from teaching. So we try to get them to use the voice and compose for each other's voices. We get some wonderful stuff from them. The thing is we have a national curriculum now, so every school should be following the national curriculum; but lots and lots of primary schools don't have a music specialist, and many of them don't have anyone at all who is confident in delivering a music lesson.

JS: Forgive my naiveté, but why not, if it's the national curriculum?

PB: Because they are not trained, and there is no support for them. But there are some people who do tremendous work in it. There is a group called The Voices Foundation led by Susan Digby. They go into a school for three months, and all of the school has to sign up; the head and all of the staff have to say "yes." She's got a huge training program running, not only here but also in South Africa. It ought to be running in every primary school in the country, to be quite honest, because of the confidence it gives. What it gets non-musician teachers to teach is incredible.

JS: Who underwrites this program?

PB: They have quite a big underwriting, I think. Susan's husband is a banker, which might help. She is a real live wire. She got a Churchill Foundation Scholarship and went to the States and to Hungary to study choral training. The approach, it seems to me, is so right: getting into the schools and training teachers how to do it there, with the kids there and giving the teachers confidence. It's fantastic, and it ought to be running everywhere, but it's not.

JS: Who have been your greatest inspirations?

PB: My biggest hero is Sir John Barbirolli – not a choral conductor at all. As I was growing up in Manchester, he was the conductor of the Hallé Orchestra there and was a very, very great influence on me. In choral terms, I've been impressed by choirs from Eastern Europe, more than any, in terms of their color, excitement, precision and wonderful, if sometimes overly regimented, discipline. I'll never forget the first time I heard a Bulgarian choir. In those days, the "Iron Curtain" days, only the good ones got out! They were a fabulous choir. I learned all sorts of things from watching these choirs. I didn't learn a thing about conducting until I was in College. You know, there are no choral conducting classes in England. We're starting one – it's my personal crusade!

JS: Please describe a typical rehearsal. For example, do you do warm-ups?

PB: I do nothing. I expect them to warm-up before rehearsal. I hate wasting rehearsal time.

JS: Whom do you admire in the choral world?

PB: A wonderful Bulgarian choral conductor who is now dead, Vasily Arnoudov. He conducted two fabulous choirs in Bulgaria. Eric Ericson I admire as a trainer, enormously, for what he has done in the choral world in general and in Sweden in particular.

JS: How do you select repertory for recording?

PB: Basically, whatever a company will take.

JS: How do you find so much interesting, rarely-performed repertory?

PB: I used to spend a lot of time looking through things in libraries and publishers, getting ideas. I have found that, since we've become relatively successful, composers send me things all of the time; publishers are constantly bombarding me with stuff. There is not much I throw away, and when it comes to programming, I've got a very good memory for what I've seen and have kept. Also, my choir is very good about suggesting stuff, and then I've been on juries of competitions in France, Spain, Italy, and Hungary. I've got a wealth of Hungarian music I want to do; I adore Hungary.

JS: How do you learn a piece you are going to conduct?

PB: I heard a great, underrated Scottish conductor, Bryden (Jack) Thomson, being interviewed by the BBC on his recordings of the Bax symphonies. The interviewer asked, "How do you set about preparing these works? Do you start off with an analysis of the overall construction?" Jack said, "God no! I sit down at a piano, and I hack my way through it till I got the feel of it." That's exactly my approach. I do rely on my choir a lot because they are such wonderful musicians. It's a very collegiate atmosphere in that regard.

JS: Where do you fall on the vibrato spectrum?

PB: Too much is too much, and none is too little. It's got to be natural. I just ask my choir, "Can I have some vibrato?" if I wasn't getting any. There's a difference between vibrato and wobble.

JS: How do you fund your various projects?

PB: Our chairman deals with all that side of things. She is a very successful businesswoman. We get very little in terms of commercial sponsorship because we're not big enough to fill the Festival Hall regularly. We run these educational projects, and it's quite easy to get funding for things like those, which then pay some of the costs of a concert. But we want to do these, anyway. A lot of orchestras have got into the education business just to raise money. *Outreach* is the word now, but we've done it because we want to. It's as difficult to get bookings and sponsorships now as it ever has been, and it's not going to get better here in London.

JS: What is your ideal size for The Joyful Company of Singers?

PB: It depends very much on the repertory. Twenty-four is lovely. We do the *St. Matthew Passion* with about forty; *B Minor Mass* with about thirty-six. Orchestral and double-choir repertoire takes more. If it gets too big, it loses that chamber-choir quality. Singers will stop listening, and then they will slip back into the "big-choir mentality."

JS: Everyone seems to have a choral niche in England. What's yours?

PB: That's our problem – we don't have one, not in commercial terms. We love doing twentieth-century music, but then the London Chamber Choir – James Wood's group – does the hard-edged stuff all of the time, so it's not exactly a niche for us.

Ken Burton

Born: 1970

The London Adventist Chorale
Croydon Adventist Chorale

Education: University of London

Interview: January 20, 1999, Royal Festival Hall, London

A singer, pianist, organist, composer, and arranger, Ken Burton is the leading
gospel choir conductor in England today. His choirs have performed frequently
in London's most prestigious venues, and he is increasingly active as a clinician
around the world. Burton also directs the Chamber Choir at Goldsmiths'
College in London.

Under Burton's direction, both the London Adventist Chorale and Croydon
Adventist Chorale have won numerous awards. Since 1991, both have been
finalists in the Sainsbury's "Choir of the Year" Competition; the London
Adventist Chorale won the prestigious award in 1994. The choirs have been
heard internationally on BBC Radio and Television, and appear in major festivals.

Website: www.kenburton.com

Ken Burton

Ken Burton
Croydon Adventist Gospel Choir
London Adventist Chorale

JS: Will you comment on the gospel choir movement in Britain?

KB: The gospel movement is growing and has been growing, especially in the past five years. Much of the gospel music here still comes from choirs that started in the 1970's. The blacks living in Britain at the time are from the Caribbean, but the Caribbean doesn't really have its own choral background, so to speak. They sing, mainly, music of the Anglican Church or gospel from America. Choirs over here tend to do American gospel music and have been doing so since the 1970's. In the 1980's we started seeing a lot of community gospel choirs which were formed by different churches bringing their best talent together. The longest running one is the London Community Gospel Choir, which has done quite well.

JS: Please describe the choirs you work with.

KB: I direct two: the London Adventist Chorale and the Croydon Adventist Gospel Choir. We've been around for about twenty years, but unlike many of the other gospel choirs, we do a broader range of gospel music. We do spirituals arranged by people like Hall Johnson and Jester Hairston, along with the straight, three-part *a cappella* spirituals.

JS: How do the singers learn their music?

KB: Strictly by rote. Most will buy an album and listen to it and imitate it. A lot of the gospel directors over here don't have much schooling in music. They play very much by ear, so learning is a case of sitting around with a tape recorder and listening and picking parts up like that. In the choirs I work with, we have a lot more people who read music, so that enables us to do music of a more complex nature.

JS: Do you make your own arrangements for them?

KB: Yes, I do. I do a lot of compositions and arrangements or adaptations. I write a lot of the music we do, and we get a lot of it from the States. We also do music by Walter Hawkins and André Crouch. A lot of pop musicians are using gospel choirs in their recordings.

JS: Has that been an opportunity for your choirs?

KB: I don't mix pop and gospel with my choirs. We don't do pop music at all.

JS: How many members do you have?

KB: In each choir, it fluctuates between thirty and thirty-five.

JS: Are all of your singers people of color?

KB: Currently, yes, though not by policy. They are Adventists from the Seventh Day Adventist Church. The Adventist congregations that you tend to find within the city are black.

JS: How many gospel choirs would you say are in the city?

KB: It's a growing number because gospel music has risen in popularity over the past five years. A lot of people have started their own choirs, and from those choirs you get offshoots. So for some strange reason, we've been getting community choirs popping up all over the place. There are probably about thirty different community gospel choirs around London, and you'll see about five or six, regularly, on TV.

JS: Is it a church phenomenon?

KB: It is very much a church phenomenon. There have been blacks in London for centuries.

JS: Why has the gospel choir movement taken off in the last five years as opposed to, say, twenty years ago?

KB: I can't put my finger on the reason, to be honest, but I can speculate.

Have you heard of Kirk Franklin? He's an American gospel artist. He's absolutely massive as a gospel artist. He's not a singer. He talks and the choir sings. He writes songs with commentary in between the lines, almost like a preacher. He's become very, very big with his choir, and it's rubbed off over here. He mixes soul and R&B and funk with gospel, which has gone down well with the young people.

JS: How do you audition for your choirs?

KB: First of all, I look for the ability to perform, not just to stand there and sing the notes, but to actually perform and be a part of the music. So I always get them to sing a prepared piece. It could be a hymn, a Christmas carol or an aria. Secondly, I play a chord and have them sing the upper, middle or lower notes. I have memory exercises where I play something and have them sing or clap it back. And I'll do something to trick them. For example, I'll have them learn a phrase and then I'll play an accompaniment designed to throw them to see if they can hold their part. I test them also on their ability to respond to instructions. I give them a phrase and say to sing it staccato and legato, with crescendo and diminuendo. I test their ability to be able to vary their tone of voice from heavy to light, back or forward tone so that they have the ability to blend with the other singers.

JS: How do you deal with intonation problems?

KB: It is often a problem. With my gospel choirs, I've done works like Vivaldi's *Gloria*, and Handel's *Messiah*, with orchestra. Obviously, string players always play slightly sharp whereas, to get the warmth of sound, we are slightly on the flat side. Those are the kinds of conflicts we might have, but we are able to fix that.

JS: How do you work on pitch in rehearsal, or do you?

KB: I do. I think it's important to work with a piano, an instrument that's got absolute pitch. Lots of singers respond to tactile feedback as opposed to auditory feedback, so they do memorize how a song feels. If I can get them used to singing it in tune, they get used to feeling it tune when it starts getting low; it feels low to them. I also get them to respond to my hand gestures, indicating to sing slightly sharper or flatter.

Also, it's very important to sing scales as an exercise. People are increasingly finding it more difficult to sing a scale dead in-tune. You find that coming down a scale, the semitone intervals will be slightly flat. I also use semitone scales for this purpose too.

JS: How would you describe your approach to tone?

KB: It varies depending on the style of music. I prefer very much a full tone, an equalized tone, a tone which has enough backward placement to make it a full, rich sound and enough forward placement for it to carry. A lot of British conductors like a lighter tone, but I go for the American choral sound which has more depth. I went to a boys' school so I was used to hearing the very pure, traditional sound. A lot of university choirs use this sound too, but it is not the one I prefer.

I always try to do exercises that encourage singers to use the open throat, to help get the fullness, power and control, and also to get the sound in the mask. I also prefer vibrato in this music.

JS: Is intonation affected by the encouragement of vibrato?

KB: The forward placement tends to help with that. In close-harmony, jazz-type pieces, I try to get them to keep away from vibrato.

JS: Do you address blend?

KB: I certainly do. My choirs would say, "It's Ken's thing." There are several ways I approach it. I try to make sure I know the singers' voices individually by doing annual vocal assessments just to see what the voices sound like. If I know that a singer has a particular type of voice, then I will place him or her next to singers who have voices which are very different to try to get them to balance and find some equilibrium. If I think the basses are important to the tuning and blend of a particular piece, I may place them in a specific formation. I also do a lot of work getting the singers to make different mouth shapes and to bring out different types of sounds and get them aware of the fact that the voice is capable of an infinite number of sounds. Once they get that working, I can ask for a particular sound, and they can blend toward that image.

JS: What is the disposition of the choir?

KB: Tenors are rare in gospel choirs in England. Generally, you'll find the choirs to be female-heavy, too. The ratio would be usually something like two to one, women to men: ten sopranos, ten altos, five tenors and five basses. Within those categories, we have soprano one and two, alto one and two, etc.

JS: If one were to hear several recordings of gospel choirs, how would he or she identify one of yours?

KB: My stamp is what I call a cross-cultural approach to singing. I think the American sound as I know it, in terms of gospel singing and the college choirs, is a lot heavier. The British sound is a lot purer. So with my choirs, you would hear something which is somewhere in between. It would have a slight heaviness that would sound black, but not black American; lighter than black American, but heavier than white English.

JS: How would you describe the role of the gospel choir experience for society in general and in people's lives in particular?

KB: If you're looking at the history of gospel music, going back to spirituals, it was a way for people to express their sentiments at the time. It's a very personal and immediate music. Especially within the churches, you tend to find that as people sing, others can identify with you. You have an experience in your life and you go to church and you sing about it. It's very difficult to do that when you're singing an impersonal song. I think it's an important part of society, because gospel music is a "message" music, a ministry music, and it can send a lot of positive messages in the community and society. When we put together programs, it's more about what works musically. We also think about what we think the needs of our audiences are. In addition to concert halls, we do a lot of work in prisons. The needs of prisoners are specific, and so you would sing songs of comfort. We try to get them singing with us so they can have something they can take away. Many prisoners have written to us saying, "Remember that song you taught us? We've been singing it in our cells and it's been a tremendous comfort." In fact, we've started a whole prison ministry. So it's more than just an entertainment thing; we feel it's very much a way to bring change in people's lives.

JS: How do you finance the management of your choirs?

KB: They are all-volunteer. Within the choir, we have a number of people who volunteer their services in whatever way towards the choir's management. With both choirs there are individuals who have varying skills, from computers to public relations, and they help support the choirs. For most performances, we charge a fee that builds-in our expenses. It's a business project, but we do a lot of volunteering as well.

JS: Who or what have been your influences?

KB: The American gospel musicians have been the greatest inspiration, I think. There's a choir from Oakwood College in Alabama that came over in the early 1980's. We borrow a lot of stuff from their library since it's so hard to get printed gospel music here. So almost anything they have sung, we sing also.

One of the people who has been an influence is Mark Shanahan. He was a conductor at my college, the University of London. He conducts a lot of opera, and his approach is different from many. His whole approach and influence is the bringing together of drama and physical movement with the classical choirs.

JS: Where is gospel music headed?

KB: I'm working towards making it as popular an idiom as other musical styles. As I said from the beginning, it's growing and becoming more popular. In fact, the young people like the style, and you are now finding it in schools. A lot of schools are recently calling people like myself to do workshops. Often I will go to a school and do a one-day workshop; they like it and then will want to start a gospel choir of their own. I see it coming into the school curriculums.

JS: When you do one of your school workshops, what sorts of things do you do?

KB: I will give a little bit of history, discuss the differences between gospel and spiritual, and then take them through some simple pieces of the gospel repertoire. Most of them just want to get straight in and sing. I try and make it interesting. With a lot of people who are classically trained, there is some snobbery towards gospel music. I try to change people's perception of that, to show that there is a gospel discipline.

JS: How do you describe the difference between gospel and spiritual?

KB: Spirituals are earlier and are associated more directly with the slavery experience. They are unaccompanied and much more sorrowful and reflective in nature. Gospel is urban, accompanied, more positive in its themes. For this last reason, you find that a lot of the gospel choirs nowadays, both in England and America, are forgetting the spiritual roots or completely rejecting them.

JS: Do you see a market here for gospel arrangements and compositions?

KB: Sure. I do that myself. I have publications out through Faber Music. My first published piece came out two years ago, called "Feel the Spirit." I have one coming out this year for upper voices.

Andrew Carwood

Born: 1965

The Cardinall's Musick

Education: St. Johns' College, Cambridge

Interview: January 17, 1999, near Brompton Oratory, London

Andrew Carwood is active on many professional fronts: first as the Director of London-based Cardinall's Musick and as an author and lecturer on various aspects of early music. From 1995 to 1999, he was director of Music at the Brompton Oratory in London.   As a singer, he has performed with nearly all of England's early music ensembles and has a growing international solo career as a tenor.

The Cardinall's Musick was co-founded in 1989 by Andrew Carwood and David Skinner while they were lay clerks at Christ Church, Oxford. The professional consort comprises of nine singers. Part of the Cardinalls' mission has been to uncover neglected choral masterpieces from the English Renaissance.   In 1991, the group issued the first of a series of recordings by Nicholas Ludford, and it has been ranked with the most elite of England's early music ensembles ever since. In 1995, the Cardinalls received the Gramophone "Early Music Award" for the first volume of their Robert Fayrfax series. Co-founder Skinner remains involved with the Cardinalls by preparing fresh, scholarly performance editions.

Website: www.cardinall.demon.co.uk.aboutcm.html

Andrew Carwood

Photo: Gerald Place

Andrew Carwood
Cardinall's Musick

JS: How do you audition your singers for the Cardinall's and the Brompton Oratory?

AC: In a sense it works in the same way. A lot of people come to me with some previous experience already. So a lot of it is by word of mouth. I've never actually auditioned anyone for the Cardinall's Musick. I've always done it through seeing them work in other groups or singing for me at the Oratory, and then inviting them to sing in the Cardinall's Musick. At the Oratory, we have a procedure in which I expect them to sing a piece of their own choice with which they feel entirely comfortable, whatever that may be. I tend to steer them away from Wagner and Puccini. Then, I always give them a piece of sight-reading, which is usually a piece by Lennox Berkeley because he is the great "secret weapon" for sight-reading. Nobody knows very much Lennox Berkeley! Then I talk to them for a while to find out what their interests are. It's quite important to learn what the character is like. That's the process.

JS: How do you view choral blend?

AC: I hate the idea of choral blend as being matching your weakest singer. I think it's a slight English disease that you make a small noise. Because I'm a singer myself, I like people to sing out. So I very rarely talk to them about blend. I think blend is something they create when they get used to themselves. In the case of the Cardinall's Musick, there is a very well-blended sound, but you can hear all of the individual singers, which I think is much more interesting. I think what I go for is a uniformity of approach in their vocal technique and their phrasing; that creates a blend.

JS: What do you mean by uniformity of vocal approach?

AC: There are two things which I like: open, well-supported, deep sounds and clarity of text. I'm always encouraging singers to open their mouths, in the same way that I'm often encouraging string players to play with long bows. In terms of uniformity of approach, that really has to do with the way they sing the text more than anything else. I talk to them about the text, about the color of the vowel sounds, about how the composer appears to be interpreting the text, through his choice of harmony, melody or scoring or whatever, and how we can best amplify that in what we are doing. That's how I try to achieve uniformity of approach.

JS: Is intonation an issue to be dealt with in a group such as the Cardinall's Musick?

AC: Very rarely in the Cardinall's Musick – hardly ever. More often with the Oratory, because we have to sing at a quarter to ten in the morning and we have to sing Vespers when everyone's had lunch! So there are always practical problems.

To be perfectly frank, I don't have the best ear in the world, so I don't spend hours and hours tuning every single chord. There are things you can show them about tuning in the way that you conduct; by the way you stand and the way you encourage people to sing, it often affects the intonation. James O'Donnell is very good at this. If someone is singing flat, he will alter what he is doing in order to encourage the boys to sing in a slightly taller sort of way, sharpen the which will quite often sound. I'm a great fan of that attitude.

JS: You've already touched on tone quality – anything else to add?

AC: Big, open singing noises. I'd rather tell people to be quiet than tell them to sing out. I'm not a great fan of the style of singing, which says everything must be perfectly blended and equal. I don't think polyphony is like that, by which I mean that each strand is equally important, but each one needs to be heard in a colorful and individual way. Having a sound where the boys dominate as you get in the cathedral style of performance is wrong. I think all of the parts should be heard equally.

I don't think you can sing expressively unless you are singing well. I don't mean to say you have to be a Caruso or Pavarotti, but you have to sing well, to breathe well and produce the sound properly. If you're doing that, then, by necessity, you should be making a good, vibrant noise because that's the inevitable off-shoot. I think this opens up new vistas in choral music in terms of sound – things which we've kept for Romantic music and not used for polyphony much.

JS: Do you do anything in rehearsal to develop ensemble?

AC: Again, I find this comes from the uniformity of approach. Obviously, you've got to get the tempo right for the building and the piece, but once that's set I rather like to let people get on with it. I find that if they're phrasing uniformly, if they're thinking about the piece of music in that same sort of way, then the ensemble sort of happens.

JS: Does The Cardinall's Musick sing only Renaissance repertoire?

AC: We do some twentieth-century stuff, and we're doing some Bach in Athens this summer.

JS: How do you shift styles with singers that are mostly singing Renaissance repertoire?

AC: Again, there are certain things which are important to me, whatever we're doing. The text is always the most important to me. And although I'll not always rigorously impose it to the detriment of other things, I always like to have the text first; text first, then the music. There are exceptions, of course, like Gombert, where the text just isn't that important; you can't impose it. So I will always talk to them more about the text and the context to start off with and then we go into style. A difficulty can be that there is a certain sort of professional singer's approach to music-making which means, "We're here doing our job, so we sing and get the notes right. That's all we have to do." Sometimes you have to work a little bit harder to make them dig away underneath the piece and find out what it's about – all the things I've already talked about. I don't like this idea that music sits on the page. I think you have to get hold of it.

JS: How do you select music for a program?

AC: At the moment we're sort of stuck because everyone wants us to sing Byrd which is wonderful but a bit restrictive! I think you need to challenge the audience when you're putting a program together, both for a CD and a concert, without exhausting them. They always need to hear something new, either newly written or which they haven't heard before. You've also got to think about what the singers can do. When I was at Cambridge as an undergraduate, I did a terrible concert which consisted of *Spem in Alium*, another forty-part piece by Striggio, three motets by Gabrieli in twelve parts and the Bruckner *Mass in E minor*! They did it – I don't know how, but it was a terrible thing to expect a choir to do, so I don't do that anymore. I try to strike the right balance.

I don't have qualms about mixing different periods together, providing there is a reason behind it. Some people like to keep it strictly one period, but I don't have a problem with mixing, providing it makes sense.

JS: Can you give an example of the kind of program you might design?

AC: I've just had to prepare four programs for Athens, and they wanted contrasting programs of the Renaissance and Baroque, so I've done a mixture of things. The first program is Byrd, so I've done a variety of things to show his different styles. There are some heavily political Latin motets; there are some lighter things to do with the Mass, and there is some English music. So there's a sort of an overview of Byrd's writing. For the Baroque programs, I've based it around countries, so we've got some Bach, some Monteverdi and some Purcell and then one or two little odd things by people like Allegri and Grandi and some things that I've dug up that I don't think people have heard before. And another thing is the plans for the Proms, where we've been invited to sing in the next two years. We've been asked to put together some modern and some ancient music, so I've been looking at things like Josquin and Poulenc, which I find a quite interesting juxtaposition – Byrd and Lennox Berkeley and Rubbra, too.

With the recordings it's been rather different because we've had the luxury of a record company which has been terribly supportive. They've wanted us to do series of discs of individual composers. So we're about to finish the complete works of Fayrfax, and we're in the middle of this Byrd project at the moment. There, it's just a matter of putting the right pieces together, which ones work, lighter and heavier pieces and so on.

JS: Did the record company contact you first?

AC: I contacted them in 1993. I went to them with a CD which we'd made for Meridian Records, and I brought along some ideas. That was a time when the record industry was booming and everyone had more money. We had a long chat, and they liked our ideas and our approach, and they said, "Yes. Let's see what happens."

JS: Who buys something as esoteric as a Fayrfax CD?

AC: A very good question! Obviously, someone. I think there are certain people who like to collect series of things and some who love early music. Part of the problem with the record industry at the moment is that it seems to have exhausted its markets. They have flooded the market, particularly with this sort of repertoire. So I suspect, actually, that it's a rather narrow band of purchasers. I think average classical record sales are now around four thousand. That's really not very many. But we get nice e-mails from all over the world, so I know there are people everywhere who buy them. The Japanese market is very strong.

JS: How would one know they were hearing one of your choirs?

AC: I hope it would sound like a group of singers singing very, very expressively, and I hope you would be able to hear every single word. And I hope they would sound like a group of people who knew what they were singing about, not just from knowing what the individual words mean, but knowing how it relates to the context of the period and the subtext, when that's appropriate in a composer like Byrd. Also, how the music relates to the lines and why a phrase is of such-and-such a length and why it lies the way it does in the voice. So I hope the singers are well informed and very expressive.

JS: Could you describe more specifically what this expressiveness means to you and how it might be audible?

AC: We can use two examples, perhaps. If you're doing a strong, happy piece like *Exultate Deo* by Palestrina, which has got a good, strong tactus and is quite fast , because of the way Palestrina set the word "exultate," you've got to do things with the consonants and the vowels, which make the fizz happen and give you the feeling of what he is after. That's one form of expressivity. The other example I'd use is something like *Ad Dominum Cum Tribularer* by Byrd, which is a deeply plangent, mournful piece about the state that Byrd finds himself in as a Catholic in sixteenth-century England. Every single phrase has got something to say, and the expression must come from the way you sing the words – the way you sing "plorate." There's a wonderful word that starts the second half – "Heu mihi." Some people sing it as "hugh." I think it is a lost opportunity to start this terribly beautiful section, when you've had a lot of noise and anguish beforehand, with the word "hugh." It comes as a solo alto and should be sung as "Ay-oo mee-hee. " If you're singing "hugh" you lose the expressive quality entirely. So I encourage them to think about the color of the word and the weight of the word. That's what I mean by being expressive.

JS: How would you describe the range of English choral styles?

AC: I was an undergraduate at St. John's College, Cambridge, with George Guest, and before that I had another choirmaster who was a singer, so I am very used to this expressive style. I went from St. John's, Cambridge, to Westminster Cathedral via Christ Church, Oxford. This is quite an expressive tradition and the one I've most tapped into. The blanket phrase that used to be used to describe this was the "Continental tone." This is opposed to the style of the place down the road at King's, which was always described as the archetypal English sound which, I have to say, in its purest form, I've never had very much time for. Some of the recordings of King's under Willcocks from the 1960's I find very difficult to take. I think them bland and inexpressive. It's like hearing a beautiful, white sound, like the walls of King's are themselves: they are beautiful to look at, beautiful to listen to but, ultimately, cold because you can't actually get close to them. However, I can provide numerous examples of English choir trainers who stress a good, strong, honest, open-throated sound. Things are changing all of the time, though. Look at the people you've got now: you've got James O'Donnell at Westminster, John Scott at St. Paul's, David Hill at Winchester and Barry Rose, who is retired now.

If you want to compare and contrast two different styles of singing, the old way and the new, there is a re-issue of a disc of music by Peter Warlock. Brought out by EMI two or three years ago, it is a centenary album and is a hotch-potch of things. On it is Guildford Cathedral Choir with Barry Rose, a few years after it was founded, singing *Bethlehem Down*, and it has Westminster Abbey with Douglas Guest singing *I Sing of a Maiden*. The difference in styles is just huge. One rather bland and breathy, and the other full of color and very word-based. For me that sums-up the way things used to be, but it's changed so much now, really. I think it's partly to do with the increasing awareness about singing amongst those who are organists and are running choirs. For example, James O'Donnell knows a lot about singing; David Hill knows a lot about singing. It is now considered essential that you understand how the voice works and how you get boys to sing with good technique. It's not unusual now for boys, and now girls, to have singing lessons as part of their regular routine.

We are going back to my earlier point now. By increasing their technical facility, they are inevitably going to sing in a more open way. That covered, English "hoot" is not natural; that is not the noise that children make. George Malcolm always used to make the point that when you go into a playground and hear kids playing, they use their chests; they shout.

JS: Where did the conception of the "hoot" come from?

AC: I don't know. I know they used to have it at King's. There's another interesting comparison – there are some old recordings of King's under Boris Ord which have come out recently doing Gibbons, a choral evensong and some other things. It's a very, very different choir from Willcocks' choirs; it's much more gutsy and rough edged, whereas the later King's sound is terribly refined. But David Willcocks was making a sound for that wonderful building with its shimmering echo. That was the sound that he heard there and that was what he wanted, and he did it to perfection. In many ways, he is the founder of the perfection that we now expect in our choral music. I think so. I'm sure all sorts of other people would say other things. My heart is in St. John's, and I think George Guest has done a huge amount for music-making in this country. But in terms of the perfection, that is that you must sing in tune and you must sing together and that this is expected, that comes as much from Willcocks as anyone else.

JS: What role does choral music play in society and culture in England?

AC: It's a vital part of the culture, but I don't think it is a vital part of the society. I think England has a problem with the arts because for years and years, art was considered a class thing. You only liked art if you were upper class or middle trying to be upper class. We now have this terrible situation where giving money to the arts is considered an inappropriate use of funds by many. As a part of our culture, though, it's vital. It's a major part of our history. Obviously, I think it's important because I'm involved with it. I think perhaps in this age, when people seem to be searching for a spirituality which is not in organized religion – they want their Arvo Pärt and their John Tavener and their Gregorian Chant – I think it's probably even more important that choral singing keeps going because it can provide part of that.

JS: How do young people get singing experiences in England?

AC: There has been a big change in the English system. While I was in school, and always before then, children learned music through singing. You gathered around a piano and you sang songs. We've had a change now because that is considered elitist – some people can't sing. Therefore, now everything has got to be creative music, so now you bang chime bars or rattle tambourines because everyone can do that. I happen to believe everyone can sing, actually, but not everyone shares that belief. So there has been a definite decrease in the general amount of singing that goes on in schools. This means that chorister applications are down, I think, across the board. It's not to the worrying stage, but if you look at the last thirty years, you notice a decline in chorister applications.

Of course, the new thing is that girls are now getting a chance to sing. I like the way David Hill is setting it up at Winchester Cathedral. The girls there are going to sing on Sundays. They have three services at Winchester on a Sunday – a Matins, a Eucharist, and an Evensong. One week the girls will sing Matins and Evensong, and the next week they will sing Mass. So every other week the boys will have Sunday afternoon off, which is good for their parents, and the girls have a chance to sing one or two services per week at a very high level.

JS: Who have been your greatest inspirations?

AC: I have to say that all of my philosophy of music-making comes from my time at school and then at St. John's, Cambridge, with George Guest, without a shadow of a doubt. At school and at church, I had a wonderfully informed and talented director of music, Frederic Goodwin, who developed my love of music, my singing abilities and my love of language. Then George Guest who made such a deep impact with his intensely expressive, word-based performance at St. John's. Then I had a wonderful time with Stephen Darlington at Christ Church, Oxford. We worked on a lot of things we did not cover at St. John's! Then I spent five years with one of the most professional, most polite, most wonderfully musical gentlemen I've ever met – James O'Donnell at Westminster Cathedral.

JS: Whose work do you admire, today?

AC: I wouldn't hold up every recording George Guest has made as being good, but his recording of the Britten *Ceremony of Carols* is, by far, the most fantastic recording of that piece. Again, James O'Donnell at Westminster, and I also have to say that I have huge admiration for Andrew Parrott of the Taverner Consort. I'm a great fan of his work and his approaches. Roger Norrington changed my perception of the Brahms *Requiem*.

JS: From what to what?

AC: From a rather stodgy, overly slow approach, to realizing that this is a work of a young man and what his emotional concerns were at the time.

JS: What is your position on the "girls in the cathedral" controversy?

AC: I don't share this view that girls or women are not as good or appropriate as boys. There was a very naughty comment about the Salisbury Boys' Choir and Salisbury Girls' Choir a few years ago. Classic FM had set up a competition in which they played some excerpts of the same piece, first with the boy's choir and then the girl's choir singing. They didn't tell you which was which. People were invited to ring in and vote for which they thought was which. The answer was inconclusive. It wasn't clear to the listeners who rang in which was which. There was a letter in *The Times* which said that there was a very good reason why nobody could figure out which is which, and that is because the Salisbury boys have sung like girls for three-hundred years! This was very mischievous, rather tongue-in-cheek and not true. Richard Seal did wonderful work at Salisbury.

Children will be what you make of them. If you went to Cambridge with Willcocks and Guest, you would have heard one group of boys, terribly English, and one group sounding terribly "continental." There's no difference in their physical makeup; it just depends on what you require of them. It's the same with girls. Of course, the noise of an entire group of girls is rather different to an all-boys' choir, but it's just as exciting and just as valid. Here at the Oratory we have a mixed children's choir, and the girls and the boys make the same noise.

There's one other issue – the thing about boys versus women. A lot of people say that Renaissance music has to be sung by boys in order to be valid, and of course Westminster Cathedral Choir sings this repertoire beautifully, no doubt. But I think that the itinerant women sopranos we have now can bring us much closer to an understanding of Renaissance music than the cathedral choristers can.

JS: What do you mean by itinerant women?

AC: By itinerant, I mean the sort of women who can go around from group to group, or place to place, singing music that is put in front of them from a very wide repertoire of Renaissance music. So they might be doing Fayrfax, Byrd or Guererro, or moving from composer to composer very quickly, and they have to be aware of differing styles. Now, boys in cathedral choir – and don't include Westminster Cathedral because their repertoire is rather different – have to sing Stanford and Howells and Wesley and Britten, and so their music-making is rather diluted by that. Of course, you could say that professional sopranos learn how to sing Wolf and Brahms and Mahler and all of those things. That's what I mean by itinerant – they have to use their brains to get themselves into the right mood and style to sing this music. They have the maturity and experience to do it. If you go back to the Renaissance period, boys sang only the music of that period. They had no knowledge of anything else. So although we can't replicate their style, we know they would have been single-minded about what they did, and one assumes they sang in a style that was 'appropriate' to the music. All we can do is sing in a style "appropriate" to the music, and I think that, probably, early-music sopranos are better able to do that than cathedral choristers these days.

JS: How do you use scholarship in selection of repertory and in perform-ance practice decisions?

AC: The Cardinall's Musick is a wonderful thing because it is actually run as a partnership. I direct the group and deal with the musical matters, and my part-ner is David Skinner who is a Fellow at Christ Church, Oxford. He deals with all of the research, prepares the editions and transcribes the music. We always have fresh editions for everything that we are working on, so that it's all been newly thought about. We make a point of including his name with my name on the front of our discs to emphasize this very point.

I do a certain amount of academic work, but it's not really on the musical side anymore. I tend to do it on the text side, so I write notes on the texts and the liturgical things, which is my area of expertise. David does all of the editions. Two heads are always better than one. So he helps plan things, discuss things, and he's around for the recordings and the concerts. It's very good to have good, clean, modern editions. There's a big argument going on at the moment about whether you should sing everything from original notation, which I don't believe in.

JS: Edward Wickham is doing work in this area, among others on the Continent.

AC: Edward is very keen on this. I think it's a very important part of the jig-saw. The danger is that it can become a substitute for having an interpretation. You can end up just concentrating on singing that notation. I'm a bit bothered by this because going back to the time when singers sang from that notation, they knew no other notation. They were completely familiar with it from their earliest experience. They knew how to read it; they knew its implications, and, of course, they listened rather than watched. When we look at a score, we watch to see what other people are doing – they had to listen. Well, here we are five hundred years later and that is not our modus operandi. That is not what we are used to. We are used to properly laid-out full scores, and that gives the people the information they need to sing the piece immediately. When we talk about things like the text or the phrasing or whatever, I have to say to them "ignore the barlines," "watch this accent," or "please listen to what is going on" – obviously you have to tweak things. But I'd rather do it that way. I worry sometimes that if you're dealing with original notation that you can spend so much time reading the notation that you don't actually find the music.

JS: How do you view vibrato?

AC: I think vibrato is a technique which you use when you want it. I think it should be something you can switch on or switch off. Again, it comes down to the size of noise you're making and the interpretation of the piece. If you're singing Wagner, you must sing with vibrato; otherwise, it would sound excruciatingly awful; you would in effect be shouting.

If you're in the middle of a phrase and you are starting quietly and you're going up to something fairly high in the range, like an F or a G, and it's an important word and it's got very long line, it's often quite attractive to use a little vibrato to warm the tone. It makes it more supple. I think there's a midway between the old-fashioned, wobbly style and the opposite extreme. We see it in soloists these days – singers like Anthony Rolfe Johnson and Catherine Wyn Rogers. String players play with vibrato, not all the time, but as a technique. I think it should be used judiciously.

JS: Is this a matter of taste, tradition or scholarship?

AC: I think it's probably all. I'm sure there are some people who like no vibrato at all. I like it for effect sometimes. But fifteenth-century music – things like Josquin, for example – doesn't really benefit from vibrato because the scale is smaller. It all depends on how big the piece is and what your taste is.

JS: What are your ideal numbers for your ensembles?

AC: For the pre-Reformation stuff, of which the Cardinall's Musick has done a lot, I like to have three to a part so that I can have a big choral sound because it's big choral writing. Then, when I go down to one voice for solo sections, they don't have to make a tiny noise in order to provide a contrast. I like to have a nice, warm, full sound and let my soloists sing at a level that is comfortable for them. I think once you go past that period, it really depends on the piece. There are some very slow-moving pieces of polyphony I wouldn't want to do one-to-a-part.

Harry Christophers

Born: 1953

**The Sixteen
The Symphony of Harmony and Invention**

Education: Magdalen College, Oxford

Interview: January 19, 1999, Central Park Hotel, London

Early in his career, Harry Christophers combined choral conducting with singing in such groups as the BBC Singers and the English Music Theatre. In recent years, Christophers has been in demand as an opera and orchestral conductor. He made his operatic debut in Sao Carlos Opera House in Lisbon, conducting Gluck's *Orfeo*. He has also conducted Purcell's *Fairy Queen* in Tel Aviv, and *King Arthur* and Monteverdi's *Il ritorno Ulisse* in Lisbon.

Harry Christophers formed The Sixteen in 1977. With over seventy recordings to its credit, The Sixteen has long been one of the world's most visible and honored professional choral ensembles. Originally known for its Renaissance interpretations, the professional ensemble has made forays into repertory of all periods, especially the Baroque and twentieth century. Among its numerous awards are two *Grands Prix du Disque*, two *Deutsche Schallplatten* prizes and the Gramophone "Early Music Award" for the first of their five-volume *Music from the Eton Choirbook* in 1992. In 1986 he founded The Symphony of Harmony and Invention as the baroque orchestra for The Sixteen. That group occasionally performs on its own.

Website: www.the-sixteen.org.uk/about.html

Harry Christophers

Photo: Hanya Chlala

Harry Christophers
The Sixteen

JS: How do you select singers for The Sixteen?

HC: The Sixteen is such that it has to contain pretty good soloists, but the basic premise is good musical intelligence. The way it all started was just getting together with colleagues, the same way most groups like ours began. To this day, I don't know how I put together that first group of people. Some were older, some younger, some from student days at Oxford; some were colleagues. The main thing about it was that the people got along incredibly well socially and musically fired each other up. Nowadays, there is a list of extra singers and if someone does more than one concert they tend to then stay on for years.

If you're going to take somebody, the ideal audition is to put them in the group and see how they'll work. Basically, I can tell that in one concert. I'll tend to try somebody out when I need a large choir; that way there is not as much risk. In addition to watching them and listening, I also have my spies – someone who is in the group and is on the same wavelength as I am. They know what I want, musically.

JS: Do you assume someone is a solid musician or do you test their sight-reading?

HC: I used to but I don't now because, by and large, the London music scene is so good. I can tell what I need to know from the performance.

JS: When a singer auditions by singing a concert with The Sixteen, what specific things are you looking for?

HC: A lot of things, really. We do quite a wide range of repertoire. I'm looking for attention to phrasing, how quickly they pick up their line, articulation, how much eye contact they have with me so that I know that the singers will respond if I do something completely different in the concert. I'm also looking for the way they interact with the audience, the way their faces light up at appropriate moments.

JS: Do you use the same singers for Victoria and, say, Poulenc?

HC: By and large I will. The thing is, The Sixteen is The Sixteen. I don't mix and match according to the program except when I'm doing a big piece like

Figure Humaine (Poulenc) where I will need more singers. In that case I'll bring in two female altos to mould the male section, for example.

JS: How does The Sixteen break down per part?

HC: The Sixteen is just the name. The choir is actually eighteen or more. So, it's six, four, four, and four. Very rarely will we do a concert with sixteen singers. In Tudor music, you'll often as not have split soprano parts, treble and mean, so I'll divide those three and three. When there are split alto parts, and they're often low, I may well add a couple of tenors to each line. In any case, I do like to have a healthy tenor and bass sound – being an ex-tenor, I love the voice; and a rich and versatile bass sound is essential.

JS: What things are audible in your performances or recordings that distinguish The Sixteen from other, similar English professional choirs?

HC: In Renaissance music there is a lot of personal interpretation that goes in. Therefore, I go ultimately to the interpretation of the words that fits my mood, really. The most difficult thing is trying to put yourself in the composer's shoes. It's so much easier in later music when the composer has made his intentions known. If you're doing the music of Victoria, Tallis, Byrd, Sheppard or whatever, you have to go on what is stylistically correct. But these days I tend to put that in brackets.

The main thing about The Sixteen is that we are not trying to be authentic about this music. We've taken the music out of its context, so already it's inauthentic in that regard. This was music to pray to. It's still for the glory of God, but we're taking it out of the church and into a concert hall. If we're doing a set of lamentations, Tenebrae Responsories or whatever, we're doing them one after another, and automatically we're stamping a mood onto the music that is instantly inauthentic. So, I think that the performance is what is absolutely paramount to our individuality. I think if people listen to our recent recordings, for example our recordings of Victoria, they will feel that. There is definite drama being created. And that's drama in the sense that it's one person's interpretation, the way I feel it should go. I do find more difficulty with Renaissance music that has English text, after Catholicism had been replaced. For example, I don't feel that Byrd's works in English have anything of the interest of his Catholic works. Some people obviously look to a Sixteen CD and hear everything one strives for in choral music – we try to do everything to the best of our ability, but I hope that won't be the end of it. I think that on top of that we've conveyed something more and given a real performance.

Often, for example, in the big Baroque works, there is too much attention by a lot of people on finicky stylistic things that actually destroy the whole of a piece. They will create each chorus, each aria, as a miniature and lose the perception of the entire work.

JS: How do you convey what you are trying to do?

HC: It has to do with timing. And the performers have to rely on the fact that I know what I'm doing – sometimes that works, and sometimes it doesn't work. One of the great things about The Sixteen is that they are absolutely with me in the performance. We've done *Messiah* countless times, but they know they can't take their eyes off me because I'll do something different. I won't do something different just because I feel like it, but there are many things that can be done in different ways.

JS: How do you approach score study?

HC: Right now, I'm working on some Poulenc. The first thing I do is go through his letters to find out what he'd mentioned about the piece. The work is in French; therefore, I have to know what the words mean. I'm not a linguist so that is always hard work. It's much easier for me when the text is in Latin since I studied classics. So the first thing I try to do is get behind the words. As I said before, so much is there in a modern score. So you go through the score and look at every detail. In the case of Poulenc's music there are many details to consider: accents, color of chords, pauses – so much is there. In a piece of Renaissance music, you have absolutely nothing. So you work with what you do know. You know a little bit about the composer's background; you see what set of publications it comes from, early or late, so you'll know a bit about stylistic requirements.

Then again, what does the text mean? You need to go through it to see how the composer has interpreted the text because they will all do it differently. Say if it's a Victoria motet, I'll look at the architecture of the whole piece. All of that music has a basic architecture, the rise and fall of phrases. Imitation should be heard clearly. I look at things that aren't imitative and perhaps exaggerate them. Are there any harmonic delicacies or bold uses of harmony? Where are the points of rest? Gradually, the whole thing takes shape in the mind. Use of dynamics and breath will then help give the shape to the interpretation. With a Baroque oratorio, say, *Jephtha*, you read the story. In that case we know, of course, it was one of Handel's late works. His sight was going, and there are certain aspects of the work that meant a lot to him – the anguish and the intensity. Where did the story come from? In that case, it's from "Judges" in the Bible. Looking through it you see it actually doesn't bear much resemblance to the libretto. You also look at the way in which he's dealt with the major characters.

Scholars offer a lot of information, too. We're not jacks-of-all trades, and there are people who have devoted their lives to major scholarship. Read them. You don't have to obey them, but read them. In the case of a Handel oratorio, you read Winton Dean. You don't have to agree with everything he says and you may not; but, because he is an excellent Handelian scholar, what he has to say should be taken note of. Once you've done that, in the case of a Handel oratorio, you need to make decisions about what voices you use. Again, one should go back to the sort of voices Handel had in mind. It's important when you come to female altos and male altos. In certain roles in Handel oratorios, that is of major, major importance. Sometimes it doesn't matter, and sometimes you have the feeling that when he started writing he had a female in mind and by the end he was writing for a male.

JS: In terms of your choral preparation, how do you convey phrasing? Do you mark scores for the singers beforehand?

HC: With The Sixteen I won't necessarily mark all of the breathing in. If you're working with a big chorus, perhaps you need to deal more with those aspects of phrasing things. With The Sixteen, they already know the basic stylistic requirements; the rise and fall of the phrase, how to articulate semiquavers. I will have guideline dynamics in my score. I will mark in my score a phrase that carries through against the norm – certain kinds of ornaments and articulations – then I will run through all of those indications before we rehearse it. Dynamics are always a guideline, but we will use them to shape a performance.

JS: Who or what have been the strongest influences and inspirations for you?

HC: I was a chorister at Canterbury, which was fantastic for me. I was terribly lucky to go there. Allan Wicks was there then and got a lot of the young composers of that day writing for the choir. Even as a little kid I was taught the sense of a phrase. I remember one day he gave an example of a line by throwing a Psalter, for what seemed to us a mile. We came to get a thrill out of singing a line. That remained in my mind. He introduced us to the music of

Purcell and Tallis and all those fantastic composers. One of the most beautiful things about singing that you can convey is this sense of line.

And there's another thing I learned from Allan. At Canterbury, we had three men on each side – an alto, tenor and bass. They'd come in each day after work and on weekends for the numerous services we'd have to do. For these guys, it was their relaxation. They loved doing it. A service could be going along, pretty ordinarily; there may have been a catastrophic mistake in the Magnificat, but Allan would never give in. He would always turn on some little piece of performance magic and send the choir and congregation away with a wonderful experience. That's a real artist, and it was special for me.

Allan has followed my career. A few years ago we had just done a Purcell CD and he phoned me up and said, "I always knew his music was great, but you know, in our day we didn't know how to perform it."

Later on when I was at Magdalen College, Oxford, Bernard Rose was my tutor. Bernard was one of these real unsung heroes of the English choral tradition and a reviver of Tudor church music. He was very idiosyncratic and had some bizarre ideas, but one of his great strengths was allowing us to love music. He was a terribly strict man and put the fear of God into us sometimes, but in a rehearsal he would always encourage questions – not to the extent that the whole thing would turn into a big question-and-answer session, but he would always pose little problems. If the question or answer was banal, he would never ridicule us. We learned so much about the shape of the music. It's hard to actually write these things down. You know, I went up to Magdalen not really knowing anything about Tudor music. I went there loving Liszt, Brahms, Bruckner, and I came away from Magdalen loving the music of Tallis, Sheppard, Victoria, Stravinsky, Poulenc, Tippett, Webern and Schoenberg.

I was very lucky early on in my professional music days. I started life as a singer. I was at Westminster Abbey for six years and also in the BBC Singers, and I also had the great fortune to be in English Music Theatre Company which was the new name for the English Opera Group, Britten and Pears' creation. That was under the baton of Steuart Bedford and producer Colin Graham. I learned a lot about Britten's music from working with Pears. I have to say that my days with the BBC Singers was a means to an end for me – a way to pay the mortgage and a way to get my conducting going. But its big bonus was that it introduced me to many pieces I never would have come across. And it also gave me the chance to look at really great conductors. We worked with Boulez;

we worked with Ozawa, Dorati. This gave me a look at music away from choral music for the first time. It was fantastic.

You know, choral conductors have a lot to answer for. Nine times out of ten, they conduct very badly. There's a lot of affected rubbish that's done. One of the funniest things to watch is how eighty percent of choral directors, world-wide, end a phrase. To see the economy of gesture in someone like Gennady Rozhdestvensky is a memorable, formative experience. Unfortunately, he hates rehearsal and lives off of fear but he's a star. He is phenomenal in performance because his whole body is expressive. Even if he seems completely still, there is a mood, a pulse you can't help but follow. He's one of that breed of Russian conductors who were absolutely convinced in what they were doing. So, in their minds, "What's the use of rehearsal? If the musicians are good, they'll follow me and I'll give them everything."

Another one is Ozawa. The rhythm that comes from his whole body – you can't help but know exactly what to do. I worked only once with Bernstein, but that was the most electric performance. He is a very, very big hero of mine. We haven't got anybody today in music of that incredible power. When you saw him conduct, he just enveloped a choir and orchestra into his body. Of course, he was an incredible showman and got away with blue murder, but at the height of all the showmanship was an incredible awareness of how that music should go. One of my favorite recordings of Haydn's *Creation* is his. His actual performance of it was not that of a Haydn scholar, probably far from it. But his innate musicianship told him where to go.

JS: Is The Sixteen subsidized at all?

HC: We receive no government subsidy whatsoever. We've had 2,000 pounds from the Arts Council in twenty years. There are so many groups of all kinds competing for the same money. For our own promotions we decide that if it's something we want to do, we may have to accept that we're going to lose money. Or we try to get a sponsor for each concert. But, in short, groups like The Sixteen, The Tallis Scholars, The Monteverdi Choir, the Gabrielis – all survive off work abroad … tours of Spain, Italy, France, Portugal and The Netherlands. Recordings are obviously very important as a useful way to say that we're still out there. The heyday of making money from making classical recordings is gone, so it's not financially rewarding anymore.

JS: Whose work do you admire today?

HC: I listen to John Eliot Gardiner a lot. I don't always like the way he achieves his results, but I am always staggered by the results. Someone else who encapsulates everything, especially for Bach, is Phillipe Herreweghe. His Bach, I think, is second to none. The work is always absolutely fabulous, beautiful, with very stylish playing, and always with interesting singers.

In terms of early music, I've always loved my old friends The Hilliards (The Hilliard Ensemble). They have a very direct approach, fantastic blend and always very interesting programs. In England, particularly, I also admire the work James O'Donnell is doing at Westminster Cathedral. I was delighted they won the "Gramophone Award." That was fantastic, especially for the Catholic Church, as well. Most of my love of colleagues' work tends to be in the orchestral world. In terms of Baroque music, I'd have to say that Herreweghe is my number one.

Stephen Cleobury

Born: 1948

King's College Choir
BBC Singers

Education: Worcester Cathedral
　　　　　St. John's College, Cambridge (Organ Scholar)

Interview: January 21, 1999, King's College, Cambridge

Today Stephen Cleobury conducts two of England's best-known choirs. After a succession of posts, including Sub-Organist at Westminster Abbey and Master of Music at Westminster Cathedral, he came to King's College in 1982. Along with these positions, he remains active as a concert organist, is a Fellow and Visiting Professor at the Royal College of Music, and is also Conductor of the orchestra and chorus of the Cambridge University Musical Society.

King's College was founded in 1441 by King Henry VI who established the daily singing of services that still are maintained by the Choir. Sixteen choristers, aged eight to thirteen, receive scholarships to provide the trebles for the Choir as they receive their education at the College School. Fourteen choral scholars and two organ scholars form the remainder of the Choir and represent a variety of academic disciplines. Every year, millions worldwide enjoy a radio broadcast of the Choir's "Lessons and Carols" service. In recent years the Choir has continued to expand its repertory with recordings of such contemporary composers as Swayne, Panufnik, Penderecki, and it frequently commissions works.

The BBC Singers trace their origin to 1924, and today it is Britain's only fulltime professional choir. The Singers are well known through their frequent broadcasts, concert appearances, and recordings. Over their celebrated history the BBC Singers have been committed to commissioning and premiering choral works from a broad spectrum of composers.

Websites: www.kings.cam.ac.uk/chapel/cchome.html
www.emiclassics.com

Stephen Cleobury

Photo: Nigel Luckhurst

Stephen Cleobury
King's College, Cambridge
BBC Singers

JS: How many singers are in the King's College Choir?

SC: Thirty – sixteen boys, and fourteen "Choral Scholars" who are undergraduates in the college: four countertenors, four tenors, six basses. We also have two organ scholars who are, in effect, my assistants. They provide the organ accompaniment at services; they play most of the voluntaries necessary, and help in the training of the choir, particularly the probationers, whom I haven't mentioned. We have six or eight of those who rehearse at school, and who have a program of their own, but don't come to the daily services while they are probationers.

JS: Do all of your boys and scholars receive voice lessons as part of their package at King's?

SC: Yes, they do.

JS: You also conduct the BBC Singers. How are they disposed?

SC: There are twenty-four full-time singers, six of each voice, and it is, to the best of my belief, the only full-time professional choir in the United Kingdom. From time to time we will work with smaller numbers. For example, last Sunday we sang the Messiaen *Cinq Rechants* (for twelve voices) in the Barbican Hall, London. Occasionally, we expand, as when we made a recording of Richard Strauss' *a cappella* choral works a few years back. There, we expanded to about sixty for the *Deutsche Motette*. There are twenty-four people, however, on the regular payroll.

JS: Do you expand or contract the King's College Choir?

SC: Sometimes the men give concerts on their own. Occasionally, I will increase the numbers of men for special works. For instance, we have just recorded Rachmaninoff's *Vespers*, and we are about to give two concert performances of that, so I brought in a few extra people, particularly low basses. But in order that we can, with a clear conscience, call this the King's College Choir, these extras are always people who are former members of the choir, usually who have been recently in the choir and who still have voices that are on a similar scale to those of our present students.

JS: Are these two groups your principal musical activity?

SC: I also conduct the Cambridge University Musical Society, which has a symphonic chorus of about 180 to 200 people, two symphony orchestras and a wind band. I also do some organ playing and outside conducting.

JS: Is there a traditional King's College sound and, if so, do you try to maintain it?

SC: The answers to those questions are, to the first, a "half yes" and to the second, a "half no." That's rather pedantic, but perhaps I can explain what I mean. When I first came here in 1982, I felt myself aware of the weight of the King's tradition. To begin with, I felt that I had to try to preserve and emulate that, to that extent I'm aware of a so-called King's tradition. But, on the other hand, if you actually listen to recordings of the choir under Boris Ord and under David Willcocks and under Philip Ledger, you will find differences. It may be that they will be, so to speak, cousins or sisters or brothers; there will be some kind of generic consistency there, so I think it would be true to say that one could detect a King's sound, even through to my time as well. Quite apart from anything else, the building lends a particular quality to the sound. At the same time, even within Boris Ord's time, I'm sure the nature of the choir changed. Concerning the second part of your question, "Do I try to maintain it?" I try to maintain what I believe to be the central things one should maintain – blend, intonation, and all of what you might call the techniques of good choral singing. Any change I have brought is probably a result of evolution and of being myself, instead of looking over my shoulder. And I think it has changed. We've gone for a more open sound. In an older generation, boys were encouraged to use more or less exclusively head voice. The changes that have come about were very much influenced by George Malcolm at Westminster Cathedral and then taken up by George Guest at St. John's. These have had a great influence on people like me, John Scott and David Hill (who, like me, were at St. John's with Guest). We have all worked through his ideas and produced our own versions of them. So in that regard, many choirs have changed. While I hate to use the term "chest voice," one is trying to exploit, develop, coax, employ, and find a greater variety of vocal color than was the case previously. At the same time, I would also say that the repertory has expanded for many of the choirs like ours, and, in a sense, that also changes the sound. One wouldn't have thought of King's Choir singing Rachmaninoff's *Vespers* even ten years ago. But after we've been immersing ourselves in this and singing in Church Slavonic, the sound does change.

JS: How would you describe the King's sound before your tenure and the values you bring that make the sound different?

SC: I prefer to answer that question in a slightly indirect way. I, for one, take good intonation, balance and ensemble as something which all of us have sought to achieve, and there, I think, we continue to have some measure of success. Then, take the question of blend. If blend is one of your very high priorities, then you may achieve that at the expense of a variety of interesting vocal colors. You know, there's this famous phrase that's bandied about that singing is a controlled form of shouting. You will hear choirs now which very often are lauded for the so-called "bright, vital, metallic" quality of the sound that they make. However, with that, it has to be said that a certain amount of shouting is taking place. Also, the concept of *piano* singing is lost. There is, of course, the risk that you also lose blend. So I suppose if you pressed me on it, what I would say I try to do is to move away from the idea that blend is such a goal that you have to go for a rather white, bland sound in order to achieve it. But, in trying to open the sound, make it brighter, make it more varied, trying for more vocal color, I have tried to be very careful not to lose blend. You might say that's a compromise, but for me it's actually a positive goal to try to achieve because, as I say, you do hear choirs now that sing with what is superficially a very bright and captivating sound. But when you listen to it for any length of time, you find that it's all *forte* and it's all one color. It seems to me that that's no more desirable than having it all *piano* and all one color.

JS: Along those lines, what are your views on tone quality?

SC: In a sense, beggars can't be choosers. When you're auditioning, you are to some extent making a compromise decision. You're looking at somebody who will have certain abilities as a sight-reader, or you'll have someone with instinctive feeling for phrasing or other general qualities of musicianship, and you'll hear varying vocal qualities. In any choir, it's good to have, at any one time, a number of people who can stand up and sing a distinguished solo. Clearly, one has to have that. But I don't discount the kind of person who has a voice of relatively modest quality in soloistic terms but who is a good sight-reader and a good musician. You don't actually need thirty soloists in a choir. The ideal voice that I like, particularly with children, is what you might call "natural." The most natural singing you will hear is when you get a two-year-old toddler or a baby lying on its back screaming its head off. That's free vocal production because there are no tensions. They're not thinking, "Oh, my goodness, I've got to sing a high note." If it's a free voice, it's usually got a natural brightness. Now, you can make kids sing with a bright metallic sound, as I was hinting earlier, but unless they are producing that naturally, the danger is that there will be an element of forcing with all of the attendant problems of intonation, blend and so on. So the natural, open, forwardly produced sound is what I like. But you also have to look at the other essential qualities they might have. For instance, there is a kind of voice that blends well in an ensemble and lends weight to an ensemble, but that wouldn't necessarily be seen as a solo voice. I don't actually discount questions of personality in a small group either. It doesn't help the general spirit to have somebody who is actively disliked by the twenty-nine other people. This is true for all three choirs I work with. The other thing I might mention is that in dealing with King's Choir, one is auditioning boys who are perhaps seven, and young men who are maybe seventeen or eighteen and whose voices have not been trained for long. One is very much looking for potential; and therefore, you are making your best guess about how their voices are going to develop. Obviously, the longer you do it, the more that guess is informed by the experience of what you've seen similar people do before. But it remains a guess in many cases.

JS: What are the sight-reading expectations among the little fellows?

SC: I don't expect anything when they come. I regard it as my job to teach them.

JS: How do you teach them?

SC: I would say if anybody could produce a patent method of how to teach people to sight-read, they could do very well for themselves. You may have seen a book on this subject by John Bertalot, who is an Englishman who worked at Princeton. Part of the job I see myself as having at a place like King's is providing the youngsters who come under my wing, as it were, with as broad a musical education as I can. This is why I try to do a wide repertoire. It seems to me, if you are taught to sight-read well at a young age, you have that ability with you for the rest of your life, and it's a key which unlocks who-knows-what music for you in the future. Of course, if you become a solo singer, or particularly an opera singer, sight-reading is not a primary consideration. It's useful but not necessary. There are a number of well-known opera singers one can think of who don't read music very much at all. But for the choral singer, it is central. In the way that the music profession is developing today, there is undoubtedly a lot of important work for people who are expert sight-readers.

One of the things I see myself doing is trying to encourage others to become as good at reading as they can so that, when they go out into the profession, as some of them do, they are well prepared for it. As to how you teach it, we give special training to the probationers and all the boys (as I mentioned, I have

86

organ scholars who assist me). During a rehearsal we might take the boys out, one by one, and give them special sessions on aural-training and sight-reading. Sight-reading is partly a matter of practice. In school, the boys are taught musical theory, in addition to the two instruments. Then, within the context of the practice with all of the boys, I will throw in work on intervals and sight-reading. Sometimes I will use a piece we are learning as a vehicle for reading practice. I will make it a bit of a game and make it a competition and start a little peer pressure going. We try to teach them theory, get them to recognize and practice pitching intervals, and we give them sight-reading to do on their own, as opposed to reading with the whole group where the less able ones can hide and copy the others. I like to think that, by the time a boy leaves here at the age of thirteen-plus, he is quite a reputable sight-reader. The trouble is, of course, that he then goes to his next school, and while the school choir may be excellent, it might be rehearsing only one or two programs for the whole term, and the singers don't get daily practice in reading. Once you've got the background and the skill, you've still got to practice it. Unless you're doing it on a regular basis, you'll get rusty.

JS: What do you do to maintain the excellent reputation for pitch at King's?

SC: In the audition process I try to ensure that a person has a highly developed sense of pitch and also has a vocal technique that enables him to sing the pitch his mind hears. We all know people, who claim to have perfect pitch, who sing out of tune because their vocal technique is faulty. I find that, for most singers, if they sing out of tune they tend to be flat. Sharpness comes usually through misplaced enthusiasm from the amateur singer and also the nervousness of inexperience. Flat singing is more common among amateurs than professionals. Among professionals, it comes from laziness, because they know perfectly well how to sing in tune. Among keen students or amateurs, it's a question of reminding them that when they sing a descending phrase, particularly a descending semitone, the tendency will be for them to come down too far, and when singing an ascending phrase, the tendency will be for them not to go far enough. You can point out the difficulties of particular intervals; for example, a descending diminished fifth is often sung too big. With a series of repeated notes on a different vowel, one reminds singers to keep on the same pitch when they switch from one vowel to the next. It's constant pegging away at it, constant reminding and not accepting anything that isn't right. I try to avoid, though, getting them screwed up about it because this can lead to vocal tension. Good vocal technique, a musical ear and constant listening are the keys. Often a particular phrase will present a difficulty; in which case you have to try to isolate the problematic notes. I think for the choirmaster, the hardest thing to do is to work out the exact point in a phrase where the problem is beginning, because it isn't always the note you first perceive as being out of tune; very often the problem starts one or two notes back. It might be to do with how the voice is placed, or any number of things.

JS: Do you subscribe to any system of tuning?

SC: Well, this is a very controversial question because when we sing with organ, it is usually tuned to equal temperament. So clearly it is no good trying to sing in Pythagorean meantone. What we have to do is to listen to the organ. Perhaps we sing fifty percent with the organ and fifty percent without. When we are without, I think what, in fact, happens is that we tend towards a more meantone, natural intonation.

JS: Does that happen naturally?

SC: I think it happens naturally. I don't say. "Come on, this is without organ, so we'll all start singing meantone!" It's natural. I remember talking to David Willcocks about the concept of having continuo organ in Renaissance music which, in an older generation, they wouldn't have done; they thought of this music as *a cappella*. But, for example, when singing Gabrieli, one should properly have organ continuo. Willcocks said, "Oh, but if you have any continuo instruments, that would inhibit you from using natural intervals. " Nowadays, with the authentic-music movement, you will often find that the chamber organ which you are performing with has been tuned to a particular temperament. We had this at the BBC just before Christmas in a performance of German Baroque Christmas music, using quarter meantone temperament. Of course, the singers had to get used to that. I got the organist to play a scale, play some chords and say, "This is the chord of A major, can you listen to where you've got to put the C sharp in this chord? It will be different from what you've got to do in equal temperament." They learned quickly because they listen carefully, which you must do. In some cases you may get a B major chord with D sharp: that can be really difficult. The solution I adopt is to have the organist omit that note.

JS: What are your thoughts about the movement toward using girls with cathedral choirs?

SC: Very positive. Obviously this is a very sensitive issue. In general, my views are very supportive and positive, but at the same time, I don't want to give any false impression about what we might or might not do here in the near future. It seems to me that the education that a chorister gets in places like this is an enormously good one. It's very valuable and something that can be taken away and used whether or not one becomes a professional musician. If it is such a good education, why do we deny it to fifty percent of the population? That's an argument that is difficult to refute. So, I applauded Richard Seal when he introduced girls at Salisbury Cathedral. I encouraged him. I think there is a debate on whether or not you should mix the boys and girls. At the moment, the policy seems to be that it is best to keep the boys and girls separate. This may be partly for social reasons and partly for musical reasons. I think that some people see this movement as a threat to the boy-choir tradition. My response to that is, yes.

If it's going to lead to a diminution in the total number of boys singing, then that would be a danger for the next generation. These boys are the tenors and basses of the next generation. It's much harder to motivate an adolescent boy if he hasn't sung before. Whereas if he has done it before, although he might well go through a rebellious period, he might still come back to singing. There was a boy who was a wonderful head chorister here who went off to his next school. He became very bolshy about singing, preferring to play rugby. Now he's gone to Oxford. He's not a choral scholar, but he's singing in a choir there and is rekindling his love of singing. Let me answer the question this way: I think that every choral foundation has to look at the question in its own context, to ask: "What is best for us to do; what can we afford to do; what can we do, and what is appropriate for us to do in our circumstances?" Now, King's is not a cathedral; we're not a diocesan church, so we don't have any diocesan responsibilities.

We have a private college chapel. It just happens that it's rather well-known, and we're delighted that a lot of people come to it, but officially it's a private college chapel. We have four to five hundred students at the college, and at the College school we have 280. So our answer to the question has been to do what we have done last year – to set up a mixed-voice choir in the college called "King's Voices," which provides opportunity for women undergraduates in the college to sing in Chapel. Now, for us, given that we have finite resources, that has been our priority.

JS: Among these singers is there an overlap with your choral scholars?

SC: No, there's a different set of tenors and basses. I insisted on that because the Chapel Choir already has a very full program. Of course, it gives additional opportunities to other male students as well. So that's what we've done, and it's been very widely welcomed. I simply couldn't predict what we would do in respect to younger girls. Lots of cathedrals are doing this, and that's absolutely great.

JS: In a hundred years do you think there will be girls singing in the King's College Choir?

SC: I have no idea. I wouldn't rule anything in or out.

JS: I read before arriving that there were six men and sixteen boys in Henry VI's original chapel choir. Were they singing in that space with only twenty-two?

SC: I guess so.

JS: Are there implications for performance, given the size of that group?

SC: The numbers game is difficult because it depends on who the people are. Two eighteen-year-olds will probably make about the same sound as one thirty-five-year-old. So I wouldn't think a comparison of that kind is necessarily helpful. This is the choir I've inherited (that is, sixteen boys and fourteen men) and that's its constitution, so what we do is to make it work in its own terms and to try to achieve a balance.

JS: Who or what have provided the greatest influences on your career?

SC: Early experiences were very strong as a chorister at Worcester Cathedral with Douglas Guest. Then, I was taught by Christopher Robinson, who succeeded Douglas Guest as organist at Worcester and who is now at St. John's, having succeeded George Guest. He's one of the finest musicians I know. Then I came to Cambridge and worked with George Guest and also with David Willcocks. I have the highest regard for both: again, among the finest musicians I have encountered.

JS: How did they influence you?

SC: I think that with George the qualities that struck me were his ability to sense the shape of a phrase and to mould the music instinctively. He had a very strong motivation towards interpretation. He would never be satisfied with anything that was merely correct. If I say that with David Willcocks one admired the sheer precision and energy of his performances, that isn't to say that George's performances weren't full of precision or that David's performances weren't full of interpretive insight. It's just saying what came through to me at that age. When I was working as a freelancer in London I played for many different conductors, quite a lot for John Eliot Gardiner, whom I admire very much. The things that came through from him were the attention to correctness of language and pronunciation, and also the importance of blend and vowel color.

JS: What is your approach to vibrato?

SC: I say this with the greatest of respect for some of my colleagues. I feel that the idea that you can make people totally vibrato-less is slightly misguided because I think that the best way to sing is naturally. I don't believe that anybody, either today or in the fourteenth or sixteenth centuries, could sing naturally without vibrato. I have to say that listening to a choir that purports to sing without vibrato is a limited experience! At the same time, it is quite clear that excessive vibrato is born of faulty technique, so I would seek to avoid that as well. Therefore, I personally would discount extremes, but that leaves the whole of the middle, and there's quite a variety of what you can achieve there. In the same way that when you listen to a string quartet playing, if they reduce the vibrato, there is a very special kind of expressive effect. Certainly, if they turn it on a bit faster, that can achieve another different effect. So there's no reason why one shouldn't be doing that. I don't run a specialist, small choir; and I don't specialize in any particular repertoire, so I'm a bit of a jack-of-all-trades, in a way. I think any collegiate or cathedral choir like ours has to be like that if we are going to present enough repertoire. So what one can do is say, "If you're singing Renaissance music, just try and keep it on the straight side," and if you're singing Puccini or Verdi, then obviously you're not going to try to do that. It's more of just nudging things in a particular direction. That's the way I see it.

JS: How would you sum up your work with King's?

SC: To imbue the members of the choir with a sense of the value and privilege of singing the liturgy in such a great building, and to give them an enjoyment of music for life through offering them the best musical education we can.

Pamela Cook

Born: 1937

Cantamus

Education: Royal Academy of Music

Interview: July 9, 1999, Rotterdam, The Netherlands

Pamela Cook has had an extensive career as a vocal soloist and is widely sought as a voice teacher. In recent years, she has gained an international reputation for her expertise in choral technique, especially with women's voices. Cook is the recipient of many honorary awards for her service to music, including Honorary Associate of the Royal Academy of Music and the Honorary Fellowship of the Birmingham Conservatoire.

Cantamus was founded in 1968 by Pamela Cook. It consists of forty-two girls between the ages of thirteen and nineteen. The group won the Sainsbury's Choir of the Year Competition in 1986 and 1995, the *Grand Prix* at the *Riva del Garda* (Italy), 1996, and the title "Choir of the World" at Llangollen, in 1997, among many other awards. Cantamus is heard frequently in Great Britain on radio and television, and has appeared with such orchestras as the Academy of Ancient Music and the City of Birmingham Symphony Orchestra.

Website: http://freespace.virgin.net/marek.kuczynski/cantamus/news.htm

Pamela Cook

Pamela Cook
Cantamus

JS: Are girls' choirs rare in England?

PC: No, far from it. There are many girls' choirs. There are more girls' choirs than young boys singing in choirs. Many of the schools seem to have girls' choirs.

JS: Please describe the girls in Cantamus and the feeder choirs.

PC: Initially, from 1968 to 1980, they were just private pupils of mine. I had fourteen girls, and I thought it would me a nice thing for them to meet each other and sing. For a number of years it was that small, but it gradually grew from girls wanting to have singing lessons. I never intended to form a choir. It came as a result of wanting girls to sing together and meet others who liked to sing. Now we sing at around forty-two members.

JS: What is the range of ages of the girls in Cantamus?

PC: These girls are from thirteen to nineteen, and they all study voice.

JS: What is the radius from which you draw?

PC: I would say from about twenty miles around Mansfield.

JS: Are there other choirs associated with Cantamus?

PC: Seven years ago we formed a training choir which starts at age nine and goes to thirteen.

JS: Do all of the girls study voice?

PC: Yes. We now have a team of teachers, all of whom have studied voice with me. The junior girls have group lessons within their own voice parts. It's all basic things like posture and breathing. As the girls get to the point that they will be moving from training choir to Cantamus, they begin to have an individual lesson.

JS: Who pays for all costs associated – lessons, travel, accompaniment and all the rest?

PC: We've been very fortunate in the last twelve years or so. Our county council, the local government people, decided they would give us a grant. It's about 10,000 pounds a year which helps with expenses. We now get paid for many of our concerts. For years, most of us did this for nothing. The girls pay for their individual singing lessons, but they don't have to pay for anything related to the choir.

JS: Since these are all voice students in Cantamus, do they have to audition?

PC: At first, we used to take them without, but since we have a training choir, we have auditions, and they must come through the training choir.

JS: Please describe the audition process for the choirs.

PC: For the training choir, we ask them to sing a song they like; we don't care what it is. Then we give aural tests, mainly rhythmic, melodic and intervals, and reading tests.

JS: Is the reading just simple tunes or intervals?

PC: No, no. Not sight-reading, just reading English to see if they can read words. If a child reads haltingly, it will ring alarms. Even if they aren't high flyers academically, you need them to be able to read fluently.

We don't do any sight-singing. Everything is taped. We encourage them to take piano lessons or other musical instruments, if they can. We don't expect them to sight-read parts. I like them to know the parts when they come in because, in the rehearsal, I want to get right to the music. Not only do I not want to waste time reading, but I also feel that when they are reading they are not singing properly. They do work on sight-singing in their individual lessons so they steadily learn to read music. For a new piece in Cantamus, the girls will bring it to their voice lesson and we will say, "Do you need a taping?"

JS: And then you plunk it out on the piano?

PC: No, we sing it on the tape. We find, though, that by the time the girls reach fourteen to fifteen years, they will be able to sight-sing quite fluently.

They all take the Royal School's examinations in voice, and sight-singing is a requirement.

JS: What is the amount of rehearsal time available to you?

PC: We have two hours per week on Friday evenings. But this year we've been very busy and also have been rehearsing for two hours on alternate Sundays.

JS: Without a group like Cantamus and the training choir, what experience would these girls receive in school?

PC: There is some music in the schools. The national curriculum requires that they have an hour a week, but there have been problems with choral music in schools. That's not a problem in Mansfield, though. Most of our girls are active in their school choirs.

JS: Do you employ any techniques for rehearsal that are unique to you?

PC: No, I don't think so. I just use what I do as a singing teacher. I've always approached it simply from the voice and the music. I can hear what is wrong with the sound and can put it right straight away. I can tell by looking at their mouths if they're tense in the jaw or producing incorrect vowels. All of the time you're looking and listening for these things.

JS: How do you approach blend with this group?

PC: I'm looking for a sound that blends together within a part. Within their own parts, I want them to be making a homogeneous sound, a beautiful sound. But I wouldn't be asking them to blend with each other throughout the whole choir. The vowels are the most important thing. I make sure the vowels are resonating properly and that they are all singing the same vowels.

JS: Do you ever approach blend deliberately?

PC: Well, I will say, "I can hear somebody's individual voice. Please listen to each other." I would not ask them to eliminate the sound of their own voice but, instead, to make a complete sound within their part.

JS: How do you develop the natural maturity of tone beyond their voice lessons?

PC: Gradually it comes. We work a lot on posture, trying to keep them free in the body and encouraging them to use their bodies properly. We talk a lot about freedom and flexibility so they can allow the instrument to work. It doesn't happen overnight. We're trying to develop the skills steadily within each individual.

I don't go in with a formula or any pre-conceived ideas. My ears will tell me that I like what they're doing, and if I don't like it, I'll fix it there and then.

JS: Having just heard Cantamus perform, I wonder how you get them to be so freely, naturally and convincingly musical?

PC: We talk about the music and releasing the sound and relaxing the phrasing, also getting them to try to pace breath so that they arrive at the climax of the phrase when the breath is most energized. We always start with the text. They love words, and they know what they're singing about, whatever language they're singing in. We wouldn't dream of singing a song they didn't know every word of, and we sing in many different languages. We invite linguistic experts in to help us with this, too. They're assimilating a very sophisticated musical and linguistic knowledge, really. The girls love it. The more you tell them, the more they want to know.

JS: Do you work specifically on intonation?

PC: It's all listening, raising the third, sixth, and seventh – hearing the chord. It's concentration.

JS: I have discovered that many cathedral and collegiate choristers are receiving vocal training now and that this is a fairly recent development. Is that your understanding?

PC: I think that it is fairly new.

JS: Given your success in the Sainsbury Competition and the publicity that it has given Cantamus, could it be that you started that trend?

PC: It sounds immodest, but maybe we've had a slight influence. I've never thought about it really. We won one of the adult sections in 1986 in the

Sainsbury Competition and two of the adjudicators (Barry Rose and Simon Lindley) asked me, "What's your secret?" I said that there was no secret, really, except that every girl has an individual lesson. They agreed that this helped to develop the sound they heard. I think that possibly it opened people's minds to the idea of individual lessons.

JS: What is your position on choral vibrato, especially as a singer and voice teacher?

PC: I would encourage them to sing healthily, which would have some natural vibrato. I don't really talk about it. If it's healthy, it's going to be there.

JS: Who have been your most important influences?

PC: People I've worked with in the singing world, teachers early on and coaches, certainly. Chorally, I was very fired by a Bulgarian Ladies' Choir who came to stay with us in 1972. Very early on that choir inspired me as to what women could do. So many girls' choirs are very uninteresting to me; the sound is very bland. I didn't want my girls to be like that because they have so much to offer, really, as human beings. So I wanted them to make the sound I knew they were capable of without forcing the voice.

JS: How can someone distinguish your choir from other girls' choirs?

PC: I would say it's a slightly richer sound than some girls' choirs. That's my choice because that's the world I'm working in and that's the sound I like to hear. I would say it's a fuller sound and more feminine, perhaps. *Voluptuous* would be a good word! Perhaps there's also a wider variety of tone color and word painting. I've tried to develop a range of sound to suit most styles of music.

Sir John Eliot Gardiner

Born: 1943

Monteverdi Choir
English Baroque Soloists
Orchestre Revolutionnaire et Romantique

Education: King's College, Cambridge

Interview: October 1999 (online response to questions)

Sir John Eliot Gardiner has been a major figure on the international music stage for over thirty years. Early in his career, he was significantly responsible for the revival of early music, and his immense reputation is acknowledged widely by his peers. Gardiner's conducting has grown to embrace repertory of all style periods, having made over one hundred-fifty recordings with the major European recording companies. He appears regularly as a guest conductor of many of the world's great orchestras and opera companies. His performances are recognized for their attention to scholarship, technical detail, and convincing, highly individual interpretations. A few of his many awards are the "Artist of the Year" from both the jury of the *Deutschen Schallplattenkritik* in Germany and from Gramophone in the UK in 1994, and Conductor of the Year from the Cannes Classical Music Awards in 1995. His recordings have routinely won many "Record of the Year" awards from a variety of sources.

The Monteverdi Choir was formed by John Eliot Gardiner, while he was still an undergraduate at King's College, for a performance of Monteverdi's *Vespers* (1610). With over one hundred recordings, many of them award-winning, the Monteverdi Choir is surely one of the most internationally recognized of England's professional choirs. The Choir can be heard on EMI, Philips, Decca, Erato, and DG Archiv. The "Monteverdis" have become legendary for their enormous projects, their latest in the year 2000. In the two-hundred fiftieth anniversary of the death of J.S. Bach the Choir, under the direction of Gardiner, performed and recorded all of the composer's cantatas. The "Bach Pilgrimage" tour took them to over sixty cities around the world during this twelve-month project.

Website: www.monteverdi.co.uk

Sir John Eliot Gardiner

Photo: Sheila Rock

Sir John Eliot Gardiner
Monteverdi Choir

JS: How do you select singers for the Monteverdi Choir? Are there any amateurs amongst them?

JEG: Getting the balance right between singers of various provenance, age and experience is critical to the successful composition of the Monteverdi Choir. Obviously, to some extent it is a question of horses for courses, in that one inevitably adjusts the internal balance of the Choir to meet the demands of the repertoire. The Choir may vary from as few as fourteen to as many as eighty-five, depending on whether it is singing Schütz motets, for example, or Verdi's *Requiem*. The line that varies the most is the alto line: with counter-tenors and falsettists generally in baroque music, the effect of the three lower voices being male is, in my experience, to render the top line more transparent than would be the case with an all-female contralto line. We tend to use contraltos for music of the nineteenth and twentieth centuries, though we have been known to include a peppering of counter-tenors in this repertoire too. The amateur element in the overall composition of the Choir, though much reduced from the early years of the Choir, is still a significant one. There are two main effects. One is to provide a testing ground for young singers who are either still too young or in the process of deciding whether to make singing their main career, and, on our side, to evaluate their potential as full-blown professionals. The other is to provide a valuable yard-stick in respect to high-calibre amateur singers of the utmost competence, who choose not to earn their living by singing, but contribute greatly by their enthusiasm and generosity of time and, to some extent also, keep the professionals on their toes!

JS: What is your concept of tone quality? Is it different for each musical period?

JEG: Tone quality varies enormously according to the idiom and language of a given composer. In the Monteverdi Choir, we have always given the greatest possible emphasis to the language of the music that is being sung, not merely in terms of its comprehension by singers and its comprehensibility by the listener, but also in terms of the particular euphony and coloration of the language in question, and how that affects the expression of the music. The Choir regularly sings in five languages: English, Italian, Latin, German and French, but has also been known to sing, for example, in Russian, Hungarian and Spanish.

JS: How do you achieve the results you are looking for in this area?

JEG: Language coaching, frequent repetition and hard work!

JS: Are there techniques you employ to develop choral ensemble? For tuning?

JEG: One of the challenges of choral singing is the basic requirement to hear as many of the other polyphonic strands whilst singing. Part of any rehearsal is given to making the singers aware of this, even if it means temporarily dividing the Choir up into smaller groupings or "scrambling" them so that they are standing next to someone singing a different part from their own.

A performance of choral music with instruments involves a reciprocal awareness: with brass instruments (in, say, Gabrieli or Schütz) of the inflection of the words and rhetoric of the music by the singers. In the case of baroque and classical, we sometimes deploy forces in two facing "banana" shapes with each facing segment of singers and players able to take visual clues from one another – singers able to incorporate the natural inflections of baroque and classical style (ictus, swift decay, etc.), the string players able to add consonants, as it were, to their style of bow attack.

JS: Who and/or what have been inspirations, influences, and models in your career?

JEG: Nadia Boulanger, my teacher; George Malcolm with the Westminster Cathedral Choir, especially in Vittoria and Britten; Imogen Holst in a range of Renaissance and Baroque music; the traditions coming out of Hungary: Bartok and Kodaly for example.

JS: Whose choral work do you admire today?

JEG: Gyorgy Kurtag, John Tavener, and Arvo Pärt.

JS: Please describe your general approach to score study.

JEG: There is no substitute to just learning it, in my case away from the keyboard.

JS: How do you use scholarship to inform performance practice and selection of repertoire?

JEG: It is a continuous process, and of course I read current journals, musicological books. For specific projects, particularly large-scale ones, I use research assistants.

JS: When one hears a recording or performance of the Monteverdi Choir, or another choir you are directing, what characteristics are audible that reflect your personal aesthetics? How would the Monteverdi Choir sound differ from another professional English choir of the same size?

JEG: This is really for others to answer!

Simon Halsey

Born: 1958

City of Birmingham Symphony Chorus

Education: King's College, Cambridge

Interview: January 13, 1999, Symphony Hall, Birmingham

Simon Halsey's reputation grew quickly and parallel to that of the City of
Birmingham Symphony Orchestra and its Conductor (until 1999), Sir Simon
Rattle. Halsey became chorus master in 1983, and now includes among his
posts Principal Guest Conductor of the Netherlands Radio Choir, Artistic
Director of the BBC National Chorus of Wales and Principal Guest Conductor
of the Sydney Philharmonia Choirs.

Under the leadership of its director Simon Halsey, the City of Birmingham
Symphony Chorus has been featured on several award-winning recordings con-
ducted by Sir Simon Rattle. Their recordings of Szymanowski's *Stabat Mater*
and Mahler's *Symphony No. 2* each won the Gramophone Award for "Best
Choral Recording of the Year," and their recording of Tippett's *A Child of Our
Time* won the *Preis der Deutschen Schallplattenkritik*. Another important
dimension of the CBSO is the 150-voice City of Birmingham Symphony Youth
Chorus, which performs regularly with the orchestra in works as diverse as
Britten's *St. Nicholas*, Henze's *Raft of the Medusa*, Mahler's *Symphony No. 3*,
and Wagner's *Parsifal*.

Website: none

Simon Halsey

Photo: Hanya Chlala

Simon Halsey
City of Birmingham Symphony Chorus

JS: How do you handle auditions?

SH: We have stringent entrance auditions (a prepared piece, sight-reading, ear test) and reaudition regularly. We take people on a variety of criteria because both of my choirs are big – they are 180 to 200 voices. Therefore, we are looking for a variety of abilities. Some people will have the most amazing minds – first-class sight-reading and a pretty ordinary voice; others will have a fantastic voice and lack some of the necessary reading skills. An awful lot of people are pretty good at everything. I should also say that it's a great deal tougher for women to get in than for men.

JS: What percentage are professionals?

SH: We have none. All of the symphonic choruses in Britain are, without exception, 100 percent amateur. There are no paid singers in any symphonic chorus in this country, partly because the way music is funded – there simply isn't the money for it, and partly because we do have a pretty good supply of amateur singers. Following the Chicago Symphony Chorus' example, we've abandoned the use of the term "amateur" here in Birmingham and we call them "volunteer professionals." That may seem like playing with words, but in fact, something like thirty to forty percent of the choir are music teachers or music graduates, and they just happened not to have chosen to use their voice to earn their living. But they are professional musicians, even if we are not paying them.

JS: How do you deal with intonation?

SH: I work to a system I learned when I was a choral scholar at King's College, Cambridge. They have a system of intonation which is very different from a lot of continental and American practices. For example, in a C major scale C, F, G and C are fixed mathematically – the fourth, fifth, and octave. Everything else, we say, is a matter of taste. The major intervals – the third, sixth and seventh – are very bright. We have the minor intervals very low: for instance, E flat is low; E natural is high; A flat is low; A natural is high; B flat is low; B natural is high. F sharp is usually high because it is regarded as the leading note away from C. This system is pretty familiar to everybody who went through that education, and the people who went through that education are pretty influential in choral music in this country. And that is, if you like, the King's College way of intonation – it's the David Willcocks way of intonation, and we all still use it. The Willcocks way is to be unimpeachably in tune (on the bright side) the whole time.

I also had a very strong working relationship with Robert Shaw. The CBSC is the only choir in Britain that he worked with, and we use all of his systems. We learned a great deal from him about the color of vowels, keeping all the vowels in a straight line, all stuff I don't need to explain to Americans brought up in the Shaw style. So there is a very big Shaw influence here.

I try to approach everything concerning intonation through technique so that everyone has a very clear idea of where they are harmonically; hence the reference to the scale and their position in the scale, even in difficult contemporary music. Everybody has a very clear idea of which are the bright vowels and which are the dark vowels; all of the diphthongs are carefully worked out. Consequently, I can say that our choirs really do sing in tune; they have a very clear idea in their own minds of what they are doing. We do a lot of warm-up exercises that focus on intonation.

JS: Intonation exercises à la Shaw?

SH: À la everyone I've ever met in my life!

JS: What are some examples?

SH: There are a lot of them based on a chromatic scale; or we say, "This is an F sharp, sing an A flat; this is G, sing me a C." So people get a very strong idea in their mind what an interval feels like. We employ a lot of "techniques" to address intonation. We also analyze vowels and then sing the text in unison on a single note to check that the text is not hindering intonation.

JS: How do you approach blend?

SH: Blend is a difficult thing. I increasingly believe in trying to build up, as much as possible, the lower frequencies. Of course, this has a lot to do with intonation and tone quality as well, but I try to make the bottom of the choir as rich as possible. We are fortunate here in Birmingham to have well over forty basses. So we try to make quite a rich sound based on a real fundamental. We happen to be light on tenor sound but not in tenor numbers. Because we don't employ professional tenors, we have to go for a very blended, light tenor sound that sits lightly on top of a very rich bass sound, and whenever possible, I divide the basses and leave the tenors undivided. We have splendid altos who are dark and rich. So the altos and basses have a big rich, fat sound, and the sopranos and tenors are light. Unlike in America, we have a taste for comparatively little vibrato, though this may have to change. We work in Germany a great deal; and, especially, Kurt Masur and Simon Rattle increasingly want a much richer palate of colors than most British choirs can give. Therefore, we're trying to learn to fatten up the sound so that we can offer a Czechoslovakian sound or a really rich Russian sound, as well as our fundamental British sound.

JS: How do you do this?

SH: A lot of that comes from very good language coaching. There was one year that we sang fifteen languages in one season. We employ a full-time singing teacher with the choir. We are trying to get better use of the vocal resources of each member of the choir. Variety of tone quality is beginning to come from the awareness of possibilities created by our singing teacher. We work on blend by getting people to listen to each other by singing in quartets. A lot of these ideas we've imported from the States. I suppose I try to make sure the voices broadly blend before we start. If we are having trouble with anybody's voice sticking out or a nasty tone color, we send them to singing lessons. We do re-auditions every year for everybody over the age of fifty and every two years for everyone under the age of fifty. Therefore, we have a pretty quick remedy if anything is spoiling the sound. We will retire people if we have to. So it's half audition process and half voice-building.

Also, we devote a lot of time to rhythm. Being an orchestral chorus we have to have absolutely unimpeachable rhythm so that we don't get in the way of our orchestra. That seems to me the most important thing an orchestral choir can do. It really sorted us out when we did John Adams' *Harmonium* which is the most demanding thing, from the point of view of needing perfect rhythm, that I've ever done. We can completely wreck a piece if every consonant and every vowel is not exactly on top of the conductors' beat. Fortunately, we've always had principal conductors – Louis Fremaux, Simon Rattle, and now Sakari Oramo – who were very interested in their choirs and demanded only the highest standards. All three help the choir but do not "spoon-feed" them. They conduct the music, and whilst they are very helpful to the choir, they won't beat bigger to get the choir in, for example. We have to be part of the total ensemble. A great deal of our work is built upon Shaw's technique of count-singing which we have embraced fully. Again, we are almost the only people in this country who do it.

JS: What personal aesthetics do you try to achieve?

SH: It sounds all very technical. Again, very much like Shaw, we build things up. We must have this absolutely fail-safe cage of rhythm, on top of which we must have the vowels and diphthongs correct. Next, we must have the most energetic diction which will always be coached by a language coach, when it is not in Latin or English. I try to build things in stages so that the final result has the most fantastic drive to it. Now, on the whole, British choirs are good at all that: they're good at drive, and they're pretty good at getting their eyes out of their copies and giving a performance. What we are trying to add is something the British are not good at: a variety of tone color and really coloring the text – one word at a time. We do try terribly hard to make sure that the notes are learned a couple of rehearsals before the end so that we can really search for what the music is about. Here, it's a slightly odd thing in that I'm always preparing for others, but I'm very fortunate to be able to choose the conductors we work for. We only work with orchestral conductors who have something to say to a choir. Here we don't have to give concerts we don't want to sing for.

JS: Who are your favorites?

SH: My favorites include Rattle, Masur, Claus Peter Flor, Mark Elder, Ton Koopman, Kent Nagano, John Eliot Gardiner and Edo de Waart.

JS: How do you view the role of choral music in English culture?

SH: It's a huge question. Ever since the Industrial Revolution, it's been enormously important and completely central. Other people will tell you about the cathedral tradition so I won't go into it. It's there and it's extremely influential because it educates many of the conductors and singers.

Then you have the industrial choirs, those that grew up in mining communities or in mill towns – the male-voice choir tradition in Wales and the big choral societies in the North were based on industrial money. If these are faltering, it is because of the decline of the sense of community. In the modern world, people are not so focused on their workplace as a place to make music. People are able to travel; we have people who travel two hours to sing with us here.

We did have good school music; we destroyed it in the 70s and 80s, and it's coming back in the 90s. There is an extremely strong youth-chorus culture that is almost new. You've seen the two youth choruses downstairs; they're world-class. There are nearly 200 singers here, but they've only existed three years. We're founding a third youth chorus next month – SATB – to foster the young tenors and basses we need for the future. Suddenly, an orchestra sees its job to foster children's choral singing! Five years ago this was unthinkable. Every town in this country has a first-class youth orchestra, but we allowed orchestral music overtake choral music. Resources went to instrumental playing, and choral music was killed off. Now the balance is beginning to shift. It's too expensive to do orchestral music, and it's a lot cheaper to do what we do!

There are exciting choral developments, too. We are a fully multicultural society. Gospel and barbershop are becoming popular. Birmingham has 200 gospel choirs. Don't underestimate gospel music and show music, because it's coming in a big way. They involve lots of people and a completely different group of people.

JS: Who have been your greatest professional influences?

SH: For me it's Robert Shaw, Willcocks, Eric Ericson (of the Swedish Radio Choir) and of course my father (Louis Halsey); also, the whole experience of having been a singer in a place like King's. Other people who have influenced me strongly along the way have been Richard Hickox (because he just makes everything such fun; people love to sing for him; it's amazing to see how much you can get out of people just by giving them a good time). Gardiner and Rattle and Masur, because they are so demanding.

JS: Please describe your typical rehearsal.

SH: Only five minutes of warm-up because we have so much repertoire to cover. By the way, fifteen years ago warm-ups were almost unknown in this country, and now they are almost universal.

JS: What happened?

SH: Among other things, until fifteen years ago we didn't have any equivalent to ACDA (American Choral Directors' Association). Now there is the ABCD (Association of British Choral Directors), and it's quite influential. It has a very good annual conference with 200 or 300 delegates who have seen people all over the world doing warm-ups. Everyone started doing them. There is also this new emphasis on quality of singing. It isn't just learning notes anymore; it's how you sing. Even cathedral choirs, most of them, are employing singing teachers to teach the boys. A lot of things have changed recently.

One of the most important things about the rehearsal is to have the breaks at the right time and the right length. I plan the time extremely carefully and never end late! One of the most important things Richard Hickox ever said to me was that you must cover nearly all the program at each rehearsal, because if you do something in too great detail early on, you will arrive at the penultimate rehearsal and the final movement will not be known. I will begin the first rehearsal by singing through the entire piece. At the first rehearsal, they are given historical notes and translations to take home. I very often start the second rehearsal at the end and work backwards so that there isn't anything lurking at the end of the piece. We also do a certain amount of sectional rehearsal. Everything is planned down to the minute.

JS: Whose choral work do you admire?

SH: The people I'm very interested in at the moment are the ones who give a singing lesson at the same time as teaching the notes. Though I am a singer, I perceive this as a weakness of mine. This approach is not a terribly British, but it is a coming thing.

JS: Who does that kind of work?

SH: My colleague at the Netherlands Radio Choir, Martin Wright, is an American from San Diego. He is a fine baritone who has turned to conducting. He has transformed the Dutch Radio Choir because he gives them a singing lesson and happens to teach them the notes at the same time!

JS: How does your staff voice teacher work?

SH: His name is David Lowe, and he's a very interesting character. He was in the King's College Choir with me. He's a Professor of Voice at the Royal Academy of Music, and he teaches all of the choral scholars in the choirs of King's, Trinity and St. John's in Cambridge. He's very influential in the teaching of seventeen and eighteen-year old boys, helping them to find their voices. He provides a sort of complete service for seventeen to twenty-five year olds.

JS: How can he handle so many students?

SH: Most of the scholars are getting a lesson a week. With us, he comes every rehearsal evening, and he just does five individual lessons. We send him twenty people per semester to have five lessons each. It's just to get them thinking about singing; then he places them with local teachers. Sometimes he comes in once we know the music well, and I will say to him, "The sopranos sound thin here. What are we going to do about it?" He always knows what to do!

JS: Why are there so few women choral conductors in England, or is that a misconception?

SH: It is a misconception. If you look at the male-voice choirs, you will find that a very large percentage of them are conducted by women. You will find that ninety-five percent of the conductors in school (by which I mean school as opposed to university) are women. Most university choirs are conducted by men, and one of the reasons that so many men are in the profession is that there is this dominance of what we call the "Oxbridge" tradition – the people coming out as choral scholars from Oxford and Cambridge. But since 1971 and, really effectively since the mid-1980's, there have been the same number of women choral scholars as men in those choirs. It will change. Also, if you go into the cathedrals, you will notice that a lot of the cathedrals are starting parallel girl's choirs. Twenty years down the road there will be a load of people who have done it. Up until now, though, it's been a male-dominated education. It is changing.

JS: How do you approach score preparation?

SH: As the years ago by I get more and more obsessive, and I also get to the stage where I get more and more frightened. I suppose you have more to lose as the years go by! Because a lot of the work I do is preparing choirs in orchestral works, I try to know the orchestral score as well. Before I begin score preparation, I will listen to recordings; it's just a way into a piece. I then abandon them and don't listen to them at all. I simply read from the beginning to the end of the score. I look at every word: every "forte," every "allegro," every "Soprano I and II," every quarter note, every half-note – I look at everything and ask questions about it – "What did the composer mean by this?" I then go through and decide whether I am going to re-score things, putting baritones on tenor lines, for example. I then prepare everything to do with where they are going to breathe. We produce our own editions; I learned that from Shaw.

JS: How do you address the copyright issues?

SH: We pay the publishers for the use of their edition and then seek permission to make our own modified edition.

JS: How have you been able to expand your own international conducting from preparing the chorus in Birmingham?

SH: When I first came to this area to be head of music at the University of Warwick, I met Simon Rattle. We were both very young. He was principal conductor here at twenty-five; I was chorus director at twenty-two. Rattle made this a very international organization, and through him we traveled a lot. Through our work and our recordings, I got invited to go and sort other people out!

JS: Do you use the children's choruses with the orchestra in things like *Carmina Burana*?

SH: Much more than that. They have a huge repertoire, including things like Henze's *The Raft of the Medusa*. For example, we've just recorded Mahler III with our senior youth chorus which is actually girls, and we simply call it City of Birmingham Symphony Youth Chorus. We have done *War Requiem* with girls, not boys. However, we recorded it with the boys of Christ Church, Oxford. That's a very important tradition to me, and I wouldn't do anything to damage it. But we have this fantastic girls choir here, and therefore we use them whenever we can. Now we'll be doing a lot of Mahler VIII's and will be recording it in the next few years, and we'll do it with all of our kids – something like forty boys and 160 girls. It's supposed to be a *Knabenchor*. We did it recently with Andrew Davis and the BBC Symphony Orchestra, and he insisted, as he's perfectly entitled to, on boys. So, on that occasion we did with the boys from the three London Cathedrals. It was wonderful, but we wouldn't do that here.

JS: What is your position on vibrato?

SH: In this country, unlike in the United States, your average amateur singers never have a singing lesson. They don't study voice. They just sing naturally, and that's bad and it's good. So, the ones who are lucky with their school music (where their directors sing naturally well) – they go on their whole lives singing beautifully. Of course, the ones who learn to sing badly spend their whole lives trying to do it better. The result is the natural sound that people expect to hear in this country. The thing they grow up with from childhood onwards is a clean alto and soprano sound, so that's what they do. Unless someone actually teaches them to sing a different way, that's what the British way will be. It's also basically what the Scandinavian way is.

JS: So vibrato-less singing is not cultivated?

SH: Absolutely not. People aren't trained! The choirs like the Tallis Scholars are trained specifically not to do it. That's a completely different ball game having to do with performance practice. But all these adult women are doing is imitating the way boys naturally sing. At the same time, however, there has been a change in fashion in the way boys sing. The sound has become richer, for example. The St. John's College, Cambridge, sound, the Westminster Cathedral sound has become more normal in this country in the last ten or fifteen years.

Something else that is important to understand is that we don't train many conductors. Until recently, there was nowhere in this country that you could study conducting. Now, you can study a one-year course, and there are a couple of three-year courses in orchestral conducting. I was the first person ever to take one of those. That gives you an idea of how recent that is. The first choral-conducting courses are beginning, but the level of education in the United States for choral conductors is much higher. In this country, an awful lot of people do it through real conviction, so there are a lot of people who have no technique at all, but actually are rather inspiring to work for. It makes for a very different choral culture.

People who do church music in the States are often paid better; and there is almost no equivalent here to the American high school choir director, or choral departments like you'd find in an American university. The only equivalent is at Cambridge, a completely different setting, which is that every college chapel has a great choir, one after the other, right down the same street – six or seven of them. Each has a choral director, but no one studies it, they just sing. That is a really fundamental difference.

Stephen Layton
Born: 1966

Polyphony
Holst Singers

Education: King's College, Cambridge (Organ Scholar)

Interview: January 22, 1999, Temple Church, London

Stephen Layton formed his professional ensemble, Polyphony, in 1986 at King's College. He has also been Music Director of the Holst Singers since 1984. Under his direction, both groups have a growing reputation and varied discography. Layton works regularly with other groups, including the Netherlands Chamber Choir, the Danish Radio Choir, and the BBC Singers, in addition to many other international engagements. He is only the fourth organist in the last two centuries at the Temple Church in London.

Polyphony is a London-based, professional group with a core of eighteen singers, expanding to as many as twenty-four. The Holst Singers were founded by Gustav Holst at St. Paul's Girls' School, Hammersmith, in West London. The Holst Singers have a core of thirty-six and consist entirely of amateur musicians. Under Layton's direction, both groups have made a number of acclaimed recordings for Hyperion.

Website: www.podium.uk.com/holst-singers

Stephen Layton

Photo: Hanya Chlala

Stephen Layton
The Holst Singers
Polyphony

JS: Do you do anything noteworthy in the audition process?

SL: With children, I always tend to look for some kind of theatricality, to see if I can get them to appear from behind a door or to present themselves in some way as if they are coming on stage in order to see if they have any performing instincts. For amateur adults, I try to get them to gradually sing stronger as they gain in confidence over nervousness in the audition. For professionals it is painfully simple; if they cannot sight-read, they cannot usually survive in a group like Polyphony because this music is often recorded on little rehearsal. Polyphony's Arvo Pärt CD, for example, was done with one three-hour rehearsal.

JS: How long is a rehearsal, and what is the going rate for a professional?

SL: For Polyphony, we would pay between 60 pounds and 80 pounds for a three-hour rehearsal. This relatively small pay is indicative of an economic situation which cannot sustain well- funded musical projects. We have a great prize in London – a collection of perhaps the best sight-readers and singers anywhere in the world. I suspect that if we were as well funded as, say, a European radio choir we could produce even more devastating results. The reason English choral music is considered to be so good is probably little to do with extravagant financial support and more to do with a choral tradition stretching back to our cathedral and collegiate foundations. These institutions have given many musicians a firm grounding.

JS: Approach to choral blend? That's amazing blend for one rehearsal!

SL: If I choose the right people, I don't have to worry too much about it. I know the market place and who is out there and whom I want.

JS: Do you have to deal with intonation problems?

SL: Yes, I have perfect pitch, so if it goes out, I stop and sort it. I don't let singers sing for very long if it's out of tune. In a recording session I would stop the moment it was going. People sometimes say that the spirit may be right even if it's out of tune. I don't agree.

JS: Do you have methods to address this?

SL: Much of my rehearsals are spent encouraging people to see where they have to adjust their pitches to make a chord come "alive." No more is this so than in Poulenc's *Figure Humaine*. On a straight forward level, I always ask singers to realize the same vowel shape, often encouraging the "ah" sound above all others – Robert Shaw of course has said all this for many years.

JS: What is your personal aesthetic when it comes to tone quality?

SL: I want thunderbolts underneath – real "rockets of sound" in the bass and tenor. On the top I prefer purity. Listen to *All and Some*, on the disc *O magnum misterium*. I like the "organ" quality, that Stokowski was known to favor, that of balancing from the bottom of the sound – plenty of bass. What can devastate performances of choral music is where there is a lack of bass and the sopranos sing with what is called "romantic passion". It isn't. It's just singing out of tune, with excessive wobble and I can't abide it !

JS: Do you use the pyramid model with more men than women?

SL: Yes in Polyphony, generally six basses, four tenors, four altos, and maybe four sopranos.

JS: How can a listener distinguish between Polyphony and other professional groups like it?

SL: That's a tricky question to ask me. Why don't you listen to some of our discs and see if there is a difference. If you cannot hear anything, then you know that you should scrap me from your interview book ! I suppose I would like to think that I go for a warm, beautiful, committed sound, but then who does not?

JS: Who have been your most important professional influences?

SL: The greatest influence on my life was being a cathedral chorister at Winchester under Martin Neary (1976-1980). I was singing in Winchester choir when we sang in Carnegie Hall, NY, in 1979. We did the first Bach *St.Matthew Passion* in German with Baroque instruments and a sermon in-between the two parts in the cathedral in 1977. We sang many things from the *Symphony of Psalms* of Stravinsky through to all of the commissions of John Tavener and Jonathan Harvey.

JS: What did you get besides inspirations from that experience?

SL: A love of music. I remember singing in the "Alleluia" from *Symphony of Psalms* as Neary just sat at the piano and ravished over it as we sang it. I've never forgotten those moments when conductors have bared their soul and showed something about the music that they felt without saying anything. I've conducted that piece twice now, and those memories are with me every time I do it.

A more recent professional influence has been George Hurst who teaches orchestral conducting. He's taught most of the serious people who have become orchestral conductors in the UK. I attended a Hurst conducting course which has been a great inspiration to me ever since.

Because of the budget limitations here in the UK, things have to be done quickly, so through some orchestral work I've learned to be efficient and am always learning to be more efficient.

As Organ Scholar of King's College, Cambridge, under Stephen Cleobury, I learned the importance of accuracy, balance, discipline, rhythm..., really all the constituent parts of music-making!

JS: Are Polyphony and the Holst Singers more performing or recording choirs?

SL: They are concert-giving choirs, more than anything. We do Passions and *Messiah*s every Easter and Christmas here at St. John's Smith Square.

JS: I don't recognize many of the singers on the Polyphony roster. Do many show up in the other professional choirs?

SL: They tend to be aged twenty-two to thirty, and, yes, they are all jobbing singers who will sing in a London cathedral, on a film sound track, or whatever. Of late, some of those singers who sang with me four or five years ago are now making it as soloists. This is wonderful to see.

JS: How do you approach score study?

SL: I put myself in the shoes of each of the performers. I just learn their parts and sing them through; it's as simple as that. In terms of preparing the score, no magic! I tend to mark things I want to come out and things I don't want to come out. I also work out the smaller phrasing, but the overall structure I tend to have in my mind.

JS: Do you use scholarship to inform your performance approaches?

SL: I read articles and literature. I'm conducting the *B Minor Mass* in a couple of weeks, and I am reading John Butt's recent book on the subject. He was a musicology Professor at Berkeley; now he is in Cambridge. He used to supervise me at Cambridge, and he's done much research on Bach's cantatas – articulation marks and the like. His book gives you an awful lot of insight into the process of the composition of the *B Minor Mass* as we think we know it – the history of the movements and their complication.

JS: Are you of the camp that suggests one on a part for this work?

SL: That's sort of a tangent! I don't personally subscribe to that idea. Of course, I try to be informed about these kinds of things, but in the end, you know, I follow my nose. I do that far more than follow scholarship. I'm a conductor. I stand up, enable the performers to give a great concert, and in doing so probably bare my soul at some point. I am not an early-music specialist, but I do conduct the *Messiah* and the *St. John Passion* with Baroque instruments every year. I love it, but I try to encourage the players to play with vibrato. I also try to encourage them to play long bows and long lines and long phrases. I try to treat a Baroque orchestra like a modern orchestra. For example, I would ask for "I know my Redeemer liveth" to be played/sung with a long soaring line, not detached and divided into small phrase units.

JS: Because of the limited time, do you have to rely on gesture exclusively to communicate your ideas?

SL: Primarily, yes, but also many of both singers and players have a common heritage of place of study or other groups they work for, or really strong influences like having sung for a strong conductor like John Eliot Gardiner. This means that automatically these players have a code, a language that we all understand that comes into play. What I often do early on in rehearsals in order to remind the players and singers as to how I'd like something shaped is to get the choir to sing for them. The "Amen" chorus in *Messiah*: I generally start *piano,* unaccompanied. So I get the choir to sing it *legato* and *piano* in the rehearsal, and then the instrumentalists will just fit into that and realize what we're after. So, in the world of oratorio, I use the voice as the maximum vehicle of expression and get the instruments to match what the singers do.

JS: How do you view vibrato?

SL: Well, I'm trying to make a warm, sexy sound in most music and particularly in the romantic things I've done, like Grainger. I don't talk about vibrato; I just sing to them how I want the phrase in my own voice (demonstrates). Does my voice have vibrato?

JS: Yes. In terms of how you train your boys and how you encourage professionals, in what direction are you pointing them?

SL: I talk of "buzzing" all of the time.

JS: By that you mean?

SL: A sound that all is always going somewhere, is always traveling.

JS: Do you have a musical niche?

SL: My area of greatest interest is late-romantic, particularly English.

JS: What is your ideal size of orchestra by period?

SL: I could give you all sorts of philosophical "ideal" answers, but, I'm sorry, it's entirely pragmatic. It's financially what's available. But for a *Messiah* or *St. John Passion*, my bread-and-butter stuff, with the Baroque, I like to have six first and six seconds because I find that the strength of the sound that Polyphony will make obliterates a Baroque orchestra of smaller proportions with the sort of full-blooded sound that I would like. I feel that the power of modern singers requires the Baroque instruments to play up. It may be that the "authentics" will say that I ask for too much from the singers and should hush them down. Every singer I've talked to tends to prefer to sing, and I try to encourage that.

JS: How about the rest of the Baroque orchestra?

SL: Two violas, two cellos and one double bass. But with modern instruments I would use four firsts and four seconds.

JS: How do you select pieces for recordings?

SL: I'm having a battle at the moment trying to find some inspiration. The first recording I made was four or five years ago with the Holst singers on Hyperion. Since then I've made about eleven or twelve. I found some Holst pieces that had not been recorded and did it with the Holst Singers. That gave me an inquiring mind for trying to find music that had not been done. That's what led me to the Grainger. Also, there are a number of twentieth-century carols by Kenneth Leighton and Peter Warlock. A lot of those had not been recorded on CD. I came to make these recordings through endless discovery.

JS: What kind of financial support do you receive?

SL: We have no financial sponsorship.

JS: Whose choral work do you admire today?

SL: I have a recording of Walton's *Belshazzar's Feast* conducted by Robert Shaw which I think is phenomenal. The chorus in that is better than anything that I have heard. Although one thing is odd: At the end, the chorus finishes about twenty seconds before the orchestra. For some reason, Shaw has the chorus sing the final chord which is terrible ! But the singing is stupendous. When I first heard "Thus Spake Isaiah," it brought home to me something that Stephen Cleobury had often talked about in my days at King's College, Cambridge, and that was introducing a little bit of diphthong. The clarity of the Shaw recording is so vivid you can almost see the singers' mouths moving for each sound – I….. SI….. AH. In some ways it's over the top, but that uniform sound is fantastic when you've got a choir that large all paddling the same way.

Richard Marlow

Born: 1939

The Choir of Trinity College, Cambridge

Education: Selwyn College, Cambridge (Organ Scholar)

Interview: January 20, 1999, Trinity College, Cambridge

Richard Marlow has directed the Choir of Trinity College since 1968, when he succeeded Raymond Leppard as Fellow and Director of Music. During his tenure, the ensemble has become one of the best known of the English choirs through its regular and extensive international touring and lengthy discography. In addition to his work with the Choir, Marlow is a respected concert organist, harpsichordist, scholar, and composer.

Trinity College is the largest of Cambridge's colleges, and like the College, the Trinity College Choir traces its origins to the fourteenth century. For centuries, the choir consisted of men and boys, the latter of whom were educated at the College's choir school, which no longer exists. The principal function of the Choir is to sing for the daily services during the university term. Marlow established today's choir of undergraduate men and women when women were admitted to the College in 1982.

Website: www.trin.cam.ac.uk/general/chapel/history.htm

Richard Marlow

Richard Marlow
Trinity College Choir
Cambridge University

JS: Please describe your audition process.

RM: Of course, the voices are quite young when I hear them, usually seventeen or eighteen years old, so you're trying to assess potential. Sometimes the voice may be quite small, but one's intuitive response to a voice is such that you can tell if it's likely to develop. Some voices are large already, and those are not voices I ordinarily will take. Very often singers can't control them, and since blend is going to be crucially important in the choir, it's important that you have singers who can blend in with other voices. Basically, in an audition one is looking for people who can sight-read fairly fluently. If you put a sixteenth- or seventeenth-century anthem or motet in front of them, one expects them to be able to essentially get it right. A fairly acute sense of tuning is important so that they can hear if they are singing sharp or flat and do something about it.

In addition to sight-reading, I have other tests like scales and arpeggios. I will ask them to hold a note, often on an awkward vowel quite high or low, and to start soft and get loud and soft again. I like to see how they can intensify the tone without losing pitch. So all of that is taken into account. They also come to their audition with a prepared piece which they have done with their singing teacher at home or their school teacher. The prepared piece is important but less important than their sheer musicality and their awareness of pitch and tuning, generally. Outside the musical consideration, I always give a lot of attention to what they're like as people, how easily they would fit in with others. It's very interesting how the way people sing is rather like driving – very often a reflection of personality. So if I sense somebody is terribly prickly and awkward, one hopes that if they're very good singers and one takes them, the choir will sort of knock it out of them. But sometimes I'm very apprehensive about taking a very good singer simply for reasons of personality. My philosophy about choir is that you can only really make music if you're making music with friends. I really don't believe that one can relax with a choir if there are one or two people that are very awkward and feel resentful all of the time, or questioning, or callous, or whatever. So, I give a lot of attention to what they're like. When they come for auditions we always have our choir there, and they get invited for coffee and can ask questions and find out what goes on at Trinity. But more importantly or as important, the choir members can find out just how easy they are to get on with as people.

This is a very complicated process and is further complicated by academic issues. The academic requirements at a place like Cambridge are just getting astronomically high. At age fifteen or sixteen, students take exams in about ten or eleven subjects; and at sixteen, seventeen, eighteen you specialize in three or four subjects which are much harder. These are given awards of A down to E, and the A's are the top. Cambridge expects everybody to have got A's in everything, virtually. Even those who will get all A's may not get in. So we are unduly choosy, and that is bad for music because there are some very able singers who are very competent academically who fall by the wayside.

JS: In the course of a student's time at Trinity, how much extra training in voice and sight-singing will they receive?

RM: The college subsidizes voice study with a teacher of the student's choice if lessons are wanted. Those who are studying music as their discipline (about a quarter of the choir) will have training in aural skills as part of their training, but those studying in other fields will not get that training. One will expect them to become more fluent at it by doing a lot of singing during their time here.

JS: How have these entering students become such good readers? Are they all from cathedral schools?

RM: A lot of the tenors and basses and counter tenors will have been in cathedral choirs. So from age eight or nine, they have been singing Palestrina, Byrd and Stanford, Parry, and everything else. They will have acquired a lot of versatility in just singing a lot of music. The girls don't benefit from that experience so much. Some cathedrals are introducing girls' choirs in addition to boys, so that's going to improve that side of things. In fact, our schooling traditionally has emphasized music and the ability to sight-read, though that is in some ways deteriorating now. So a lot of the singers have had some experience before they ever come for an interview. Among the young applying there is quite a lot of choral awareness.

JS: The move toward allowing girls to sing seems to be somewhat controversial. What is your view?

RM: I think it is a good thing. I'd hate to see the boys' tradition stop. But at Salisbury, which I think is the first cathedral to have done this, they actually run both choirs very happily together but they hardly ever sing together. They both sing with the men at different services. The success at Salisbury is by virtue of their very talented, sensible and able choir master, Richard Seal, who was there when this was introduced. A lot of girls who have sung at Trinity in the past have resented the fact that they did not have the chance to sing in a cathedral. This is now beginning to open up. As you may be aware, with regards to boys' singing in cathedrals, it's getting harder and harder to find boys to go off to choir schools. Parents, with all of their great freedoms and time that exists nowadays, don't particularly want their sons to be obligated on weekends. So some of the cathedral schools have closed down. The advent of girls coming to sing will ensure the continuation of the tradition.

JS: Do you have anything specific you do towards developing ensemble, blend and tuning?

RM: Members of our choir always stand next to a different voice. That is a deliberate decision for tuning and for their interest. I think that, if you are a soprano stuck among another eight in a block, you're far less conscious of what's going on elsewhere. If you're a soprano stuck between an alto and a tenor with a bass behind you, it's much more fun, assuming you've got the confidence. Of course, they have to have the confidence to get into the choir, anyway. You can tune; you can hear what others are doing; you just feel much more important psychologically, I think. I try to record with mixed formations, but the recording people then to like block formation much more. Our choir then finds that difficult to do; the tuning isn't as good. It's interesting.

As far as blend is concerned, that depends so much on the piece in question. If you're taking a piece of Parry or Elgar, it's such a different kettle of fish from Lassus or Victoria. In earlier music, such as a polyphonic motet, I do like contrapuntal lines to be fairly audible and etched out. In a more euphonious or harmonic piece, perhaps from a later time, the counterpoint might be less important than the vertical sound at certain times.

JS: What is your position on vibrato?

RM: Our choir basically sings without vibrato. I find that all of the girls who come here don't sing with much vibrato. They find it quite unnatural to sing with vibrato.

JS: How do they get the idea?

RM: They don't get the idea. That's how they do it, naturally. In the States, you have much more vibrato in your singing, usually. Youngsters have heard people sing with lots of vibrato, and from a very early age they think that's the way to sing. In this country it tends not to happen, particularly with cathedral choirs or elite small choirs doing lots of sacred music. They get used to a much more straight sound, and I don't mean by that white or uninteresting. But a straight sound can still be terribly intense and interesting with lots of edge and color and cleanness. You need that in polyphony. I'm not anti-vibrato, at all. I think, in fact, in later music it can be an extremely beautiful thing. But it's much better soloistically than it is chorally, or tends to be, for the obvious reasons of tuning and balance. The risk of vibrato is that it can just become the way you sing all of the time. I think that vibrato is a refinement, an ornament – expressive device. It's like a timpanist in an orchestra: if they're playing all of the time, it will get boring. But, introduce it a few times and it really tells. I encourage the singers when they are singing later music – Brahms or whatever – to perhaps put a little vibrato into certain phrases so that it gives an extra warmth and color as an expressive device. That's my basic philosophy on it.

JS: Do you have any preferences about tuning – high or low major thirds and the like?

RM: For early music, I quite like bright major thirds, that is slightly high. However, I think these are refinements which older, much more experienced singers can be more aware of, perhaps, than seventeen- or eighteen-year-old youngsters. Basically, I just try to get choirs to sing in tune. It's quite difficult, isn't it, just to get a choir to come in perfectly, every part together, right in pitch? We do quite a lot of work on just trying to get that precision of ensemble and tuning. I hate flat singing. I dislike sharp singing, but I'd rather it was sharp than flat, I think. Flat singing is always rather demoralizing and suggests people are depressed. Sharp singing does tend to suggest that at least they might be quite excited sometimes, as happens. But one has to work at it very hard, and I always try and train my choirs to learn to adjust pitch while they are singing.

JS: How do you do that?

RM: I start by practicing with them holding a chord, and during the space of, say, fifteen seconds, trying to depress it and raise it about a quarter of a tone, very consciously. During concerts, if I sense something is going, I have a simple system of signs to indicate what they need to do in terms of pitch. They actually do develop, if they work at it, a technique for adjusting during a performance. I haven't got perfect pitch, but I'm always lucky that there are one to several who have absolutely got it, spot on. And I simply look at them during a performance and have arrangements with them whereby they indicate to me we need to do this or that. I then communicate that to the choir.

JS: So this sharping and flatting exercise is something you drill on a daily basis?

RM: No, it's something one does when it's necessary. I don't have a great sort of philosophy about all this or a tight schedule of things to do. I tend to work very much intuitively and according to gut reactions to things. You don't go in with too many preconceived notions as to what you're going to do. I plan what I'm going to do in rehearsals meticulously. For example, I say to my organ scholar, "We'll be needing you at twenty-eight past five, today." And I do it as a matter of principle. And I put up beforehand exactly what the choir is going to do that day, so the choir knows where they are; they know I've thought about it and spent some time thinking about it. That has a good psychological effect on them; they respond, and we all concentrate very hard together. Beyond that, I don't have any gimmicks, really. It's all so much a question of personality and communication.

JS: What do you mean by communication?

RM: I once heard a stunning performance of a very difficult Strauss motet sung for us by an American choir while we were on tour in the States. I gather they'd been doing it for six months, and they sang it supremely well. Don't get me wrong, I thought it was stunning, but it was a brilliant circus act. It was meticulously prepared, and I sensed that if anything changed or if somebody had wanted to do something spontaneously, the thing would have just collapsed. That doesn't take away from what was an absolutely stunning performance. But they had it all by heart, of course, and our singers don't do things by heart. They have to do too much music. They get a Palestrina mass shoved in front of them, and I say, "look at it, get your notes right – we're doing this tomorrow. We've got thirty minutes to look at it." Now, I expect them to get it all right in that time, but there is no way they're going to learn it by heart. So by communication I mean for them to look up at least every other bar, regardless: to have eye contact and to have the ability to look at other parts and to be aware of what's happening, where to give and take and the rest of it. What matters is the electrical charge in the atmosphere that exists between you and them.

JS: How do you approach score preparation?

RM: I will mark a score quite meticulously, actually, because we try to and do things absolutely precisely and right with a lot of finesse. I mark the breathings and on which eighth-note rest a "t" is going to be pronounced. These things will be communicated to the singers so they have a score that is very precisely marked.

JS: Do you pass along those markings verbally or with a list?

RM: Usually I will put aside the number of minutes it takes and communicate it at a rehearsal. They always come in with pencils. Sometimes I say to them that I haven't decided and to watch me during the performance. I always cue in parts with different colors.

JS: How so?

RM: Sopranos are always red, altos blue, tenors green, and basses are brown or black. This is so that I can look at the choir and bring them in, even if it's a piece I'm doing for the first time. I try to know the piece as well as I can. If we are recording something, I always make sure we've sung it at lots of services here so that it's really in the system and everyone has the confidence to get out of the music during the recording.

Basically, we expect every choral scholar to come along to any rehearsal with his notes all learned. Note-perfect. They aren't always, because some things you simply can't get right unless you've got the other parts around you.

JS: Are all of the singers "choral scholars?"

RM: Yes, and they are all from this college, too. We may be the only college in Cambridge that this is true of.

JS: When hearing the Trinity College Choir, what will one hear that is uniquely yours?

RM: I find that quite hard to answer, really. I'm told that there has developed a "Trinity sound." People can hear singing and say, "Oh, that's Trinity." But quite what it is, I don't know, to be honest. Our performances, compared with cathedral boys' choir performances, will cover a much wider range of dynamics. You can do that with eighteen, nineteen, twenty-year-old girls. This is not damning the boys at all. It is simply stating a difference, in fact. I try not to make my girls sing like boys, and I get annoyed when someone will hear a BBC broadcast and ask, "Who is the boy that sang that solo?" I don't think girls sound anything like boys, myself. They're completely different. They say this because they don't sing with vibrato. But, in fact, they sound very much like girls to me.

JS: When you say girls, you are speaking here of college-age young women?

RM: Yes. Going on with this, I think our range of dynamics will be greater, and I try to make performances as expressive and vital and immediate as I can. I don't use the word "romantic" because I think that has a lot of wrong overtones. But if I'm doing Lassus, I want it to be absolutely charged with electricity as a performance. I do get them to cover an extraordinarily wide range of dynamics. We've actually had problems with the BBC's getting us in with the bottom end; it can be so soft, and the top end can be quite a problem for them, too. That's good.

Another thing is that I aim for a lot of finesse in performance. I like things to be phrased-off. I like consonants to be together; I like the things to be beautifully tuned, if I can get it. I work very, very hard for these things.

I think perhaps even the chapel itself may have something to do with our sound. It's a rather beautiful chapel, acoustically. It has a very warm resonance, not as long as King's. We do much of our recording in there, and the room itself may lend a color to the recordings. Beyond those things, I don't think I could tell you.

JS: With so little rehearsal time, how do you communicate style to your singers in the wide range of repertoire you cover?

RM: I don't believe in talking overly long about something, but if I think something is worth saying or something might interest or inform them about the music, I will say it. I won't go on talking about a piece for five minutes – ever. But if we're doing, say, the *Matthew Passion*, I'll certainly stop and say, "Do you realize that you've sung in that chorus only eleven 'Herr, bin ich's'?" And they will say, "Oh yes, why not twelve?" And I say, "Now listen to the next recitative when Judas comes in." They're grateful for things like this. They never forget it.

As far as style of music, if I'm doing Bach, I like my Bach to dance. So much eighteenth-century music is modeled to dance.

JS: Is it enough to tell them the style you want?

RM: I'll say to them, "Let it dance," or "Let it lilt." I will try to communicate that feeling with the arms and body.

Words can be very important in helping to create the style. They obviously help color the thing but I work very hard on the soft consonants – the "l's" and the "n's." So often we just hear the vowel going through. But if it's a vowel followed by an "l" or an "n" or something, you can very often get a wonderful resonance – not just making the text audible but a wonderful phrasing. In, say, *Singet dem Herrn*, to make it rather bouncy, you don't have to detach it by singing "Sing-et" but if you sing the "ng," – "SinNG-et" – you actually have an articulation that springs. I get them to do things like this. Words can get a nice spring and dance-like feel into, for example, Bach. But I've never thought about these things – I just do them. I always try to stress to a choir that with great music – Lassus, Bach, Mozart, whatever – the composer has sat down and contemplated these words. As Byrd said in his *Gradualia* preface, "As I contemplated these words the right notes suggested themselves to me." If they're good composers, they've got the technique to put it all in, and it's our duty to try to get into their minds and to work with them in producing a kind of authenticity. But, of course, we can't go back. I think you can get into the spirit of humility, which I think is so important: actually having the courage to say "Here is Schütz. He was a very good composer. He's thought about this. We must at least try to understand what he's trying to do in this. Why has he suddenly gone into three parts here, or why has he gone low there, or why is he speeding up the note values so much here? What's he doing? We must try to communicate this." I certainly talk to them about things like that because they find it quite interesting, especially if they are not studying music. Sometimes there may be things specifically in the music that is a response to the text. I will point out that this is exactly what Schütz or Bach is doing – trying to give utterance to a particular feeling. And the singers must know that in order that they can give utterance to it in the performance, to underline and confirm it. So I think the insights that one has, with a bit of luck, gathered over forty years of teaching and studying music as an academic, actually can inform performance a lot.

JS: Who or what have been your greatest influences?

RM: Composers, certainly. I've got great reverence and admiration for composers like Bach, Schütz, Palestrina, Lassus and so many, really. Not just because of the quality of their ideas, though that, largely, and their sheer technique. But, most importantly, the humility of their approach to music. We are so concerned nowadays about CD's and performances and the like. We think back to Schütz working in Dresden, and no one was coming along to record any of the bloody music. Day in and day out, he and Bach would just go in and get on with the thing and write their music. They were just writing music for their own context. One of the things that occurs to me about composers nowadays is that they are so individualistic and cut-off. They don't direct choirs and orchestras themselves; they're cut apart. In the old days, they always did; they were practicing musicians who wrote their music for their choirs. All of the music I write, I write for my choir and in a very humble way. I feel that I'm actually doing what Bach and Schütz did: that I'm the resident director and I can compose things quite specifically for them. I find that aspect of quietly getting on with a job something that we've lost.

I get so many composers writing me, asking if there's any chance if we can perform or record "the enclosed composition." The list is vast, but I reply almost immediately and say that there are very few I am prepared to do. Why? Because there is so much that I want to do that I know about. Something terrible has gone wrong in all of this. We've lost a connection – a thread between composing and purpose and the performance of things. What led up to all of this?

JS: We were talking about your inspirations.

RM: Oh, yes. As far as the technique of conducting is concerned, I've never had any formal tuition at all. You know our conservatories, rather than our universities, are the place where you get tuition in that, and I didn't go to a conservatory. I've picked things up from conductors and other musicians, from time to time. I suppose largely what I do is something I've just worked-up for myself by process of trial and experiment with the choirs over the last thirty-five years: seeing which things work and don't work. But I don't know that I've got any particular great role model in that respect, to be honest. I've learned lots of things from lots of people: picked up little hints on how to do things. However, it's the music which really inspires me.

One is lucky working in a context like this; to go back to Schütz and Bach, one is in a very similar sort of position, really. And I enjoy that continuation and perpetuation of a tradition in a way because I think it's become almost irrelevant and lost today, in most places.

JS: Who's work do you admire today among choral music-makers?

RM: I don't listen to as much music as I should, actually. I admire lots of different things. I'm evading this question, really, because I don't think there is a particularly straight answer to that. I sometimes hear somebody do something and achieve some wonderful effects and I think, "My gosh, that's marvelous." Vice-versa happens, too.

Among composers, I very much admire people like Jonathan Harvey. They have a very deep understanding of what it's all about. We do secular music at feasts for entertainment, but most of what we do tends to be sacred. I'm not a great religious person. I am religious, I suppose. I must be to feel as I do. I'm not a great evangelical, but I do love being involved in the idea of worship of whoever or whatever: of something beyond one's self, which has been the inspiration of so many composers in the past. It motivated them, and I feel, in a way, that some of that comes through to us through the music. We get people in the choir who have not sung in or been to church virtually ever, who get totally caught up in the idea of, "Gosh, this music was written with great love and devotion for a purpose." Something of that brushes off on them, in a way, I think. It seems to be very curious. It doesn't make them go to church, as such. It's something much deeper – it touches one's soul. That's very moving. This is where music is such a wonderful communicative thing. You can sense things between you and with a composer which we are just occasionally privileged to enjoy. Something has happened, and in a curious way, you feel you've got quite close to what the composer intended; or at least you've got close to something that he intended. It's very, very wonderful.

JS: How do you select music for recordings?

RM: That's a complicated one because it's tied up to a large extent with the recording company and their commercial considerations. We began with a company originally called Conifer. They were marvelous. They were taken over about three, four, five years ago by BMG, and it didn't work very well for us at all. Whereas we used to be able to plan out recordings up to two years in advance, they began to curtail and wouldn't really agree to plans for the advance recordings. We began to stagnate somewhat, and, with some relief, recently we have left them and joined Global Music Network. It's a new internet venture which has just been launched which actually is going to be a system whereby you can get recordings by downloading. It's not been perfected yet, but in three or four years' time it will be more readily available. All of a sudden, with joining this new company, we've been given a much more open field, and I can begin to choose things. Our first major recording venture will be this July – probably Palestrina's finest collection, his *Offertoria* of 1593. We're doing a double CD of that: absolutely marvelous music. The motets come towards the end of his life. Like the *Gradualia* of Byrd, or Beethoven's late string quartets, they're all terribly concise – not a note is wasted. They're almost understated in a way, but are so powerful. Then at the end of that session, we're going to do some wonderful church music of Elgar. In January 2000, probably Mendelssohn, and in July 2000, we shall make a CD of four motet passions, including the Demantius and one by Longeval, dating from about 1505, with counters on the top part; and by Jacob Handl for two four-part choirs, and a very beautiful one by Leonard Lechner of 1594.

JS: How many recordings do you try to make per year, usually?

RM: Two or three.

JS: Does the size of your group fluctuate for recordings, depending on the repertory?

RM: Very little. I usually do things that will work with our standard choir of twenty-eight. I can do "Matthew Passions" with that, you see. I might get a few more singers in for that so we've got sixteen in each choir.

JS: How is the choir supported?

RM: The college supports the choir. It provides singing lessons. It provides three dinners a week for the singers after they've sung at service. Trinity is only allowed, as with the other colleges, to pay the choral scholars a hundred pounds a year. That's really a nominal sum, but it's all that is allowed. By the time all this is done, the college is paying out probably 40,000 pounds a year on the choir. They support us incredibly. The recordings and tours are under the umbrella of the college but are independent, financially. The royalties from the CDs go into the choir fund, and if we need money for foreign tours, which we do for some, then the choir fund has to help provide this. I don't get any of the choral scholars ever to pay to go on a tour, nowadays. They always get that provided. For certain tours, like the States, we have agents to look after everything. Some invitations from abroad will come from festivals where they fund everything and also give a fee.

All of the music I want is no problem. The college simply gets it. If I want to order thirty-five copies of *Dixit Dominus*, I don't have to go to the bursar and say, "May I?" I simply go and order them. The college, which fortunately is very wealthy, is also very generous in the sense that it thinks these things matter, and the music library collection is important.

Paul McCreesh
Born: 1960

Gabrieli Consort and Players

Education: University of Manchester

Interview: January 13, 1999, Conductor's home, Grantham

Paul McCreesh's musical education began with study of the cello. Though his reputation was established in Renaissance and Baroque repertory, McCreesh has come to be sought out internationally for a wider range of repertory, including Haydn, Mozart, Beethoven, Fauré, Stravinsky, and Elgar. He has guest conducted the Netherlands Bach Society, the National Arts Centre Orchestra in Ottawa, the Haydn and Handel Society in Boston, and the Halle Festival Orchestra.

The Gabrieli Consort and Players were founded in 1982 by Paul McCreesh. The group is widely traveled in the USA and internationally, and is a frequent visitor to British and European festivals. While a noted early-music group from the start, the "Gabrielis" came to prominence in the early 1990's with their performances and recordings of famous musical events. Examples include *The Coronation of Doge Marino Grimani at San Marco, 1595*; *A Venetian Easter Mass*; *Venetian Vespers; Lutheran Christmas,* and *Christmas in Rome.* One of the ensemble's first efforts in this direction, *A Venetian Coronation,* won the Gramophone "Early Music Record of the Year Award" in 1990. The group has won several other European awards including the *Deutsche Scallpatten Preis* and *Diapason D'Or.*

Website: www.gabrieli.com

Paul McCreesh

Photo: Hanya Chlala

Paul McCreesh
Gabrieli Consort
Gabrieli Players

JS: Please describe the vocal sound of the Gabrieli Consort.

PM: The one thing that the press often say about the Gabrieli Consort is that it is perhaps the most un-English of all the English groups. When I listen to a choir like the Tallis Scholars, that, for me, is the quintessential English group – technically perfect, extraordinarily efficient, very clear, very clean. Much as I admire the technique, I'll be honest, it's not to my taste; and I find that kind of sound rather cold and unengaging. What I am trying to do, especially in polyphony – in which I think our choral sound is most markedly different – is to take the excellence of the English choral tradition and to try to add new sounds and sonorities. So I try to combine English technical prowess with a more "continental" sound, and to incorporate a much wider range of colors.

JS: What made you adopt such an approach?

Most of my colleagues are a direct product of the English church tradition; most were boy trebles, for example; most are singers. I was trained as a cellist and am completely outside of that tradition. I hope, at my best, to be able to query a lot of the unquestionables in the choral scene. My basic interest has always been to discover how music might have been performed in its historical context, not out of any desire to try to claim authenticity, but as a means of discovering something about the music as we perform it again today.

I have this sneaking suspicion that the English choral tradition is all part of some sort of Romantic arts-and-crafts mythology. At its worst, one might cite those who look at those sweet little choirboys at King's (Cambridge) with their Victorian hats and believe that they are part of an unbroken heritage that goes back to the days of Byrd. Well, the building is, but the boys clearly aren't. Compare the sound of King's choir today and twenty-five years ago – it changes every generation.

So the idea that there is necessarily any authenticity in the English cathedral sound is palpable nonsense. The pitch has changed; the formation of the choirs has changed as have the ages of the singers. In the Renaissance, cathedral choirs often used instruments; and yet to perform polyphony in any other way than *a cappella* (or, just possibly, with a discreet organ accompaniment) is regarded as a heresy. But we continue with such a fantasy because we like the idea of this unbroken "hey-nonny-no" school of English kitsch, like an exhibit in a Disney theme park.

One of the things that I think has contributed to the confusion is that twenty to twenty-five years ago, English choirs were viewed as *the* authentic choral sound for early repertoire because, in those days, if you were a record company, about the only decent choice was a cathedral choir. As the early music business has changed, there is a far greater range of choral sounds, but some of the most successful English choirs are successful precisely because they are a Rolls-Royce professional version of these cathedral choirs in sound and make up, even to the extent of trying to make the women sound as boyish as possible.

JS: So how would you define the English cathedral choir sound?

PM: Well, I suppose it has to start with the composition of the choir and a crucially-related area, especially in polyphony, the pitch at which the music is to be sung.   In my opinion, and I know that I'm not alone in this, too many conductor-scholars have created fantasy-musicology to justify the sound of their choirs, which they evidently like. Certainly the desire to transpose music upwards for ever-soaring trebles, in-your-boots falsetto altos, light English tenors and light baritones (who are never allowed sing below the stave) has defined a particular vocal sonority (not to mention an extraordinary part of English culture). It's not that such an approach is without beauty; it's simply that I don't believe the music was ever meant to sound like that.

Something we do in the Gabrieli Consort that is very much apart from the English tradition is transposing music to its proper historical pitches. For much of the continental repertoire, it is more appropriate to use a choir of falsettists, high tenors, baritones and basses, which means we've ditched the entire English music tradition of sopranos, counter-tenors, tenors and basses, which is an a-historical one. But even when we do English repertoire, with boys or women on the treble parts, it is more likely that the normal boys' range was more that of a "mean" (low soprano). Only occasionally was the high treble voice used, and even then the range was not as stratospheric as a good many recordings would have you believe. And I'm really pleased to note that more and more choirs are beginning to follow suit!

JS: Can you elaborate on your thoughts about the alto voice?

PM: It does seem that until at least the start of the eighteenth century the real voice for the altus part is what we would call a light tenor voice. That particular historical argument led several people like me and Andrew Parrott and some others to use high tenors on alto parts. Getting rid of this silly, croaking alto voice we called the countertenor has been a big shift. The falsetto voice did exist, without doubt, but it seems to have been used mainly as a soprano, often as an alternative to the *castrati* in choirs. Even in Purcell's time, in the 1680's or 1690's, the diarist Samuel Pepys talks about a new Italian high falsettist. It's quite clear that there were two distinct voice-types. Purcell actually writes in his scores, "For ye countertenor" and "For ye high countertenor," and the range of one is the standard tenor's range and that of the other is the falsetto voice, up to a fifth higher. Moreover, the clefs are always different.

I'll give you one other example. I don't know the answer to this, but why does Handel nearly always write his alto parts in tenor range and, when he writes the occasional B flat or C, he often writes a lower *ossia*? Look at *Messiah*'s "Hallelujah" chorus "and he shall reign"; he puts in a bottom D. They're in the original autograph. There's no clear answer why, but could it be that they still had these very high tenors singing the alto part, but they obviously couldn't sing that high?

JS: In what other ways might the listener recognize your choir sound?

PM: Well. I've mentioned my concern in forming the choir to match the historical demands of the repertoire. But as you might expect, there are plenty of other obsessions with which to drive my singers mad!

I'm very concerned, for example, about the rhythmic shape of vocal lines, the way that instruments and voices might articulate, and above all else, an obsession with text: I want to move away from the English tradition of choral sound as being the be-all and end-all. Composers don't write a tune and then put the words underneath. This is of course crucial for baroque music, and I want my chorus singers to color the text with every bit of vocal art that one might expect from an expert *lieder* singer. But even in vocal polyphony, which can be the most abstract of musical forms, the text, the rhythm of the text, and the syntax of the text all help shape the line. This is something that I've been working hard on, and I hope my choir to do it better every year.

JS: How large is the Gabrieli Consort?

PM: There is no fixed Gabrieli Consort. My choir for a Bach project, if I use a choir at all, a Victoria project or a Handel project will be very different in composition. Of course, there is some overlap of personnel, but I am absolutely specific about the particular sound that I'm working towards for each project. So there is no single Gabrieli Consort sound, I hope.

JS: So the size of the Gabrieli Consort fluctuates, depending on the repertoire?

PM: Yes. That's the great advantage and the privilege of running your own ensemble. But that's also one of my big problems. I've just been asked to guest-conduct a well-known choir that wants to do an Italian program with me. The problem is that I don't really like doing this repertoire with SATB choirs because it doesn't work; the soprano parts aren't high enough; the alto parts are really tenor parts, and the tenor part is too low for tenors. So I shall probably turn it down. Integrity costs!

JS: Do you derive the sound you're looking for from the stylistic requirements of the period?

PM: Absolutely, I try to, but with a great caveat. Most people involved in "early" music will tell you that what they are doing has a historical justification. I would argue that most of them are living in a fantasy world. However we are immersed in research and period style, what we do is not sixteenth or seventeenth century; it's at best a twentieth-century reflection of those centuries. This obsession with authenticity says more about us in 2000 than it does about any period whose music we try to re-create.

JS: How do you select singers for your projects?

PM: People come in and sing for me, often by recommendation. I ask them to sing something, and it's almost a matter of policy to ask them to sing it again in a very different way, simply because I'm interested in a quick musical intellect. I don't even bother with things like sight-reading. If you can't sight-read, you won't survive the first ten minutes of rehearsal, unless you are a high tenor, in which case you might make an hour!

JS: When you ask that something be sung differently, what do you mean?

PM: I might say specifically, "That was good, now could you sing it again with much more reflection on the text?" Or "could you sing it taking care to match your use of vibrato to the shape of the phrase." This may not go down too well, but so be it! An audition is the first step of a long, on-going relationship. Someone might audition for me three times before I take them on, and sometimes I will wonder why I didn't take them earlier. And sometimes I will book them immediately and regret it. We all make mistakes, and auditions are not easy for conductors either!

Another thing to consider is the social aspect of choir singing. You have to have people who fit in, not in a free-love-and-sex way, but in the sense that the energy and focus needed for performance cannot be dissipated by bad behavior or lack of awareness of one's colleagues. Touring is ultimately very hard work, and a choir that is happy in the bar will almost certainly work as a better unit on stage, providing those things are in the right order!

JS: Are there techniques you use to develop choral blend?

PM: I don't have a system, beyond being very specific in whom I book. Creating a good choir sound is very much a matter of knowing individual voices, and my choir is never booked by numbers. You would not want to be my choir fixer!

I remember John Alldis running a choral workshop when I was a student. I thought his choir sounded quite unblended, and I said, doubtless with all the arrogance of a student, "Don't you find the sound is too diffuse?" And he said, "When I have a choir, I want it to be the composite of all its ingredients, and I don't want people to have to sing up or down or blend to some average level." This is a very good maxim for a choir. While I might not have wanted that particular blend of voices, as a concept, it is so much more interesting than this very clean, white sound so typical of many choirs.

JS: What is your concept of tone quality?

PM: I like the sound to be quite throaty and full-voiced. I want to feel that the singers are singing one hundred-ten percent, not seventy percent. I can't bear niceness or prissiness. I want to feel that there is a real energy and commitment in my singers, and so I think that my choir sound is quite up-front. In terms of that directness of approach, I have to acknowledge the work of John Eliot

Gardiner, in the past, although I feel our own sound is far more "liquid" in terms of phrasing. I don't have a particular tone quality in mind for the choir because it should always vary with the text. I don't like aggressive, *marcato* singing, which I find very ugly, and I don't like choral tricks which are impressive for five minutes and deeply boring thereafter. And I try to preserve some sense of vocal freedom; you can impose choral discipline to create a state of chronic lack of musicianship. My ideal, not withstanding the need for some unanimity of approach, is that choirs should communicate with all the technique and emotion of a good soloist. I want my choir to rip people apart emotionally, not disappear into a mire of technical conformity.

JS: What is your position on vocal vibrato?

PM: A natural warmth and color in the voice is great, but inflated, unsupported wobble is the kiss of death. I probably have less tolerance for wobbly vibrato in soprano voices than I do the men's voices. It has been noticed that this is probably sexist, but that's the way I like it! I like to work with sopranos who have the ability to sound like a boy treble, if they want to. To have that resource as a singer is tremendously useful, but most of the time I'll want them to sing with adult passion. So vibrato is both a big issue and a non-issue. By definition, you can't sing without vibrato because the very process of singing is vibrating. I like vibrato to be simply a natural warmth and color which is part of the singing voice. The bottom line is that, if you're going to focus the sound so that we get a very tight control of the harmonic tension, you can't use too much vibrato without the flutter beginning to affect pitch. Once you start working in historical temperaments as we do (mean-tone and others), you need to have that degree of fine-tuning with which vibrato is not really going to be appropriate. If the ear focuses on the degree of oscillation around the note rather than the core of the note, then there is a problem.

JS: What do you focus on most in rehearsals?

PM: My singers will tell you that the thing I will pick them up about most is diction, constantly; because when singers think they are exaggerating consonants *ad absurdum*, they are usually about thirty percent of the way. Another major concern is phrasing. The temptation is for the singer to give every note equal weight because it takes much more effort to create rhythmic shaping within the vocal line.

JS: Do you mark phrasing for the singers beforehand?

PM: No. I would say, "Shape this phrase as follows," or "I want the subject to be characterized this way," or whatever. And then I would expect them to apply these general outlines throughout the rest of the movement. I expect them to get to a very high level with minimum input from me. I'm probably not known for my patience, more for an instinctive approach to the notes.

JS: With such short time for preparation, how do you convey a sense of style?

PM: Well, I'm obsessed with style. I think that's the conductor's primary job. Singers do often have to be told about it, not because I'm right and they're wrong, but because there are always many solutions to a musical problem and a legitimate variety of approaches from different conductors. On the other hand, we don't start from scratch each time, and most of my colleagues by now will know likes and dislikes.

I think you'd be quite shocked at how fast we work. It has to be incredibly fast, not just because of economics, but because sometimes we get a better perform-ance that way. For example, we did a *Messiah* tour last year. Rule Number One with *Messiah* is never, ever, ever have more than one rehearsal for the choir, because they will be bored silly! It's a piece we sing so often in this country that, if you're going to get anything special, you have to work so fast that the singers are constantly challenged to find new things; if the singers are quietly terrified in performance it's almost to the good!

JS: What is the role of choral music in English culture?

PM: The subject of a thesis, no doubt. Anyone who is writing about the history of English choral music has to view the cathedral tradition as a fundamentally upper-class pursuit. Even today, a large proportion of English professional cho-risters will come from the standard choirboy/public school (called private school in the U.S.), thence to Cambridge or Oxford Universities, with perhaps a year or two as a postgraduate at one of the music colleges, and then on to pro-fessional choral singing. Sure, there are exceptions, especially with women, but the majority of English choristers, I think, would fit that type-cast. Choral music is well known in the upper echelons of society, especially in the cities; but for most people, and especially those in a rural area like the one out here, it's no part of day-to-day life. If anyone tells you that the English choral tradi-tion is a fundamental part of English society, they're in a fantasy world. True,

141

it's an important thing for a very tiny part of society, but it has no impact in the daily life of the man in the street.

The amateur tradition is a different thing; it ranges from quite astonishing choirs who can rival the best professional choirs to the fairly basic. The history of such choirs is complex, but certainly in the past there have been many working-class choirs.

JS: What's your view of music education in England, today and in the future?

PM: It's very seriously sub-standard and often getting worse, due to a great range of problems, not least recent governments who have constantly undermined the value of arts teaching.

Again, it's something of a class issue; the best state schools and most private schools often have reasonable choirs and ensembles, and a general interest in music education, and some of these schools are extremely good.

What is deeply worrying is the much larger percentage of children who will never have any real exposure to choral music at a high level, nor receive anything but the most rudimentary participatory experience.. For your average child in an English state school, I'm afraid that the opportunities are virtually non-existent, as there is so little serious singing work going on. I find it deeply depressing, not least because I know how much most young children love singing, and what a fabulous educational resource good choral training can offer.

I don't think it's going to worry the cathedral choral foundations, because there will always be enough boys who will go through the private system, but I think it's deeply worrying for the future of amateur choral singing. We have the same problem, instrumentally. We used to have great youth orchestras here, and still have a few, but the opportunities for the average young person are diminishing.

And yet the reputation of English musical education lives on – no doubt abetted by all our excellent choirs! Often, when I work abroad I will hear, "English music education is so fantastic!" I think, "Wait a minute. Maybe it might have been once upon a time, but it's bloody awful, now."

JS: Has the lack of opportunity to sing in the schools begun to affect amateur groups?

PM: I think it's going to be a huge issue in the future. Historically, there is a great working-class choral tradition, especially since Victorian times, when choral singing was a great social event, almost a dimension of Victorian morality. To this day, there are a large number of choral societies in towns throughout the country, but I think they are beginning to suffer.

There are not enough younger people coming in, partly because of the educational factors, but also because of the stresses that many young people are under at work. There is quite a big age gap between youth choirs and the choral societies. What we really need to do is to get people singing from the ages of thirteen to thirty. Happily, there are some wonderful organizations such as the BFYC (British Federation of Young Choirs) which is doing sterling work in encouraging singing amongst young people, but it's interesting that such developments are coming from outside the normal education channels.

JS: Do you work with young people yourself?

PM: I try to do a project with young people at least once or twice a year, and for me it's some of the most important work I do. It's certainly some of the most difficult, but also perhaps the most rewarding, because children won't put up with conductor waffle! I run a festival deep in rural Northern England, where last year we invited forty children to join the Gabrielis in two performances of *Dido and Aeneas.* Explaining baroque allegory to a group of kids who have very little experience of singing anything is not easy. But to witness and share their sense of achievement in taking part, and their discovery of the beauty of Purcell's music, is worth any number of standing ovations or good reviews, or even big fees!

JS: Do you have to work to develop audiences for your concerts?

PM: If we had a geographical base, we could develop audiences, and hopefully younger audiences, but we are a professional organization and we provide a product at a price – cultural whores I suppose! We don't really have a direct relationship with an audience, although we know we have our fans and do get fan mail from time to time. Most of our time is spent selling ourselves worldwide, for concerts and recordings. I suspect the people who come along to our concerts are the same ones who would show up at a Monteverdi Choir concert or whatever. There's not much brand loyalty; indeed, I think people like comparing the various groups – look at some of the website discussions!

JS: Who have been your main influences?

PM: I haven't had a guru, really. As a string player, I have come to choral music from a different direction than most, and for all my love of vocal music, I don't regard myself as a specialist. My influences have been very wide, and I guess my personal style is eclectic.

Whilst I come increasingly to trust my strong musical responses, I've never felt embarrassed to draw on things that I like. After all, I'm probably one of the most questioning conductors on the scene, so I don't assimilate ideas without thought.

A terrible disease we conductors have is that we all want to be very original, above anything else. Every conductor will tell you they have an original interpretation. It's all rubbish because we all build on preceding generations; we all react and overreact, and there are always musical fashions. In some ways, we actually build on (or demolish) what a conductor did last week with the same singers in another choir. I am very happy to acknowledge that I could not do what I do were I not building on the foundations of a great many conductors over a great many generations.

JS: So is there such a thing as an English style?

PM: No, there isn't. There can't be! And I hope there never will be! How could one possibly speak of the Tallis Scholars, the Monteverdi Choir and the BBC Singers in the same breath? I'm sure people use the term as a shorthand for the cathedral sound which we've talked about: the expert and extraordinarily well-disciplined cathedral choirs and professional choirs. But the choral scene today is fantastic in its variety. If there's one thing that could represent the English style in a new century, it might be the English chorister's astounding ability to pop up with all the choirs on a freelance basis and make a different sound as required. That to me is the most impressive thing about English choral singing and why I feel (for all the frustrations) it's a pleasure to work here.

James O'Donnell

Born: 1961

Westminster Cathedral: Master of Music
Westminster Abbey (since January, 2000)

Education: Jesus College, Cambridge (Organ Scholar)

Interview: January 15, 1999, Westminster Cathedral, London

During the assembly of this book, O'Donnell took the Master of Music position at Westminster Abbey after a widely-hailed term at Westminster Cathedral. While at the latter institution, O'Donnell expanded the Cathedral Choir's repertory and reputation, adding to its extensive discography. In 1998, the Choir's recording of the Frank Martin *Mass* and Pizzeti's *Requiem* received Gramophone's "Best Recording of the Year Award." O'Donnell is equally well-known as a concert organist through performances around the world, and he received first prize in the Royal College of Organist's "Performer of the Year Competition."

Westminster Cathedral Choir was established with the opening of the Cathedral in 1903. It was led by Richard Runciman Terry who was responsible for the revival of the polyphonic repertory of the sixteenth century. Today, Terry is remembered as the editor of *Tudor Church Music*. The Cathedral maintains a choir school, which supplies choristers for participation in the daily service music provided by the Choir. The roster of distinguished Masters of Music who have served at Westminster includes O'Donnell, George Malcolm, Stephen Cleobury, and David Hill.

Websites: www.westminstercathedral.org.uk/record2.html
          www.hyperion-records.co.uk/artists/odonnell.html

James O'Donnell

Photo: Gerald Place

James O'Donnell
Westminster Cathedral
(Westminster Abbey as of January, 2000)

JS: Please describe the disposition of the choir at Westminster Cathedral.

JO: We have three categories of singers: the boys, ages eight to thirteen, are students in the school and there are twenty-five to thirty of them at any time; there are the professionals ("lay clerks"), who consist of ten men: four basses, four tenors and two altos. And then there are the "deputies": professional (paid) singers who sing in place of the lay clerks from time to time.

JS: In auditions, what are you looking for?

JO: In the boys, I'm looking more for potential than anything. At eight years, they will not be accomplished readers, but I can judge their ear. While they are students, all of the boys will study two instruments.

With the professionals, the skill to sight-read is a must, of course. We also judge their reading and their ability to contribute by asking them to rehearse with the other men. The other singers also report to me on how they fit in.

JS: Do you have specific rehearsal techniques you employ with the choir?

JO: That's a difficult question because, when you're actually rehearsing, you don't think about things like specific technique. Because I am a musician, there are certain things I like in my music-making, and there are certain ways that I look at a piece of music. Inevitably there are certain kinds of sound, approach, and style that I like, so I encourage those things. And in my auditioning I am looking to see if singers have these qualities.

JS: Would you describe a few of those things?

JO: I suppose that the boys' sound is one of the most important characteristics of this choir because it is quite an unusual sound. I like a direct, open, focused, bright sound, but with warmth. I also like flexibility and suppleness of line. What I go for is musical versatility. I like the sound of the choir to have a personality. I like music-making to be committed, not aloof, disciplined but not prissy. Most of all, I want it to be musically exciting, engaging and communicative.

JS: What techniques do you employ to develop the particular sounds most important to you?

JO: The tone quality is maintained through daily work. One of the virtues and difficulties of a choir like this is that you have a constant turn-over of boys. Every year, the top few boys leave; then there's a new group at the bottom of the choir, so membership is always rolling over. The choir changes its color, therefore, because different boys have slightly different ways of singing. But I do think that the general style of the sound does influence the boys who come into the choir; it does perpetuate itself. That's not to say that it happens of its own accord. If you have three people singing in a room, the likelihood is that they will find a way of singing together that works. And if one of those people leaves and a new person comes in, the likelihood is that they will find a similar way of carrying on. This is what happens in a choir like ours, I think, writ large. The boys train each other; the younger ones see the example of the older ones. My job is to see that the example provided is what I want and that's a constant business; I'm always working on it.

JS: How do you approach intonation?

JO: As far as intonation is concerned, correct vocal production and singers listening and being musically aware lead instinctively to good intonation. But there are certain dangers and technical pitfalls in music that do lead to bad intonation, occasionally. I sometimes think that there are certain kinds of pieces which are written to be out of tune because of the way they lie physically in the voice, somehow.

JS: Like F major?

JO: Well, people say that about F major. We don't find F major difficult, but there are one or two other keys which are less comfortable for us. We do work on this, but I also think it's possible to get completely screwed up about intonation. What does "in tune" mean? Does it mean in tune with a piano, in which case you're singing in equal temperament, or does it mean more in tune than a piano? Do you have really good thirds, fifths and the rest? Can you sing every key perfectly in tune, much more so than a keyboard? I think you can do that! That's one of the great things about singing. So, I think intonation is an interesting concept. It's also not entirely objective. There are things which I do insist on, like making sure the octaves are absolutely in tune. If we are having difficulty tuning something, we will sing it quietly and slowly, and really listen carefully. I find that when people do that, the tuning usually settles down.

JS: Since there are more boys than men, how do you deal with blend and balance?

JO: Well, there can be problems with balance, and because we have so few men for the number of boys, they are a constant issue to watch.

Blend is an interesting concept. For me, the most important thing is that the individual voice parts cohere as a unit. I like the treble part to be well focused; I like the alto part to sound different from the treble part, and I want it to sound like a good alto part, similarly for the tenors and basses. But I don't try to make the trebles sound like the tenors or vice versa, so that the whole choir sounds like a five-octave extension of one voice. The different vocal parts have their own personality and character, and one of the great things about, for example, polyphonic choral music is that the character of the individual parts is vital to animating the polyphony. How different and how similar should these things be? I don't know. Again, it varies according to the people you have. I become concerned when I think one vocal part is sticking out in a soloistic way and damaging the overall coherence of the choir.

JS: How much rehearsal time do you have each day?

JO: I have a twenty-minute rehearsal shortly before every service. I don't have the luxury of lots of long rehearsals. This kind of timetable presumes that everyone knows what they are doing and can sing the right notes. This is how it is possible to put together performances in a short time.

JS: What do you like to focus on, musically?

JO: I don't know whether I have one thing. It depends on the music I'm working on. After all, you can do one piece one day and focus on one thing and do exactly the same piece a few days later and focus on something else. For example, we were recently on tour in America, and although we didn't do the same program twice, there was quite a lot of cross-over between programs. That enabled me to do a piece differently and work on different things. I don't have a set agenda, and I hope that all of my approach springs from the music itself. That's what I want.

JS: How do you select music for a program?

JO: Well, of course, most of the music we sing is within a very specified context, which is the liturgy. So I cannot simply put down whatever I like, but within the context of liturgical appropriateness, there is considerable scope for broad repertory.

The blankest sheets I ever have are when the choir is singing a concert. Here, my approach is to choose a program which I think communicates to the audience the character of the choir and the breadth of its repertoire. I often choose new music to do in-concert so we can actually learn something we wouldn't be able to do in the liturgical context. For example, we've sung some of the Bach motets in-concert which we've tried to sing in the liturgy, but they're not really quite suitable for that purpose. That will then give you a whole set of challenges that, for example, a Palestrina Mass or Poulenc motet wouldn't give you. In a concert program, I would try to sing some old music, some new music, and some in-between. I would try to make it varied, but I would try to make sure that the pieces illuminated each other: try to have some sort of thread – that thread would go through the concert, whatever it was. I'd try to give some kind of indication of the breadth of our repertoire, and I would also try to program it so that the choir wasn't consistently singing the same kind of music at full-pelt. So if there was a very difficult, demanding or long work, we would either then have a break with an organ solo or we would sing a simpler, straight-forward piece.

JS: What is an example of a "thread" you might use in a program?

JO: For example, in one concert we did recently in Luxembourg, we were asked to give some attention to Gregorian chant which, of course, we sing every day. So the first half of the concert was polyphonic with Gregorian Chant interspersed in a quasi-liturgical order, linked by a Marian thread. Then in the second half we did more recent music, again a lot of it based on or inspired by Gregorian chant. So we did Jonathan Harvey's *Come, Holy Ghost* and one or two pieces by Bruckner which aren't based on Gregorian chant, but were Marian and draw on the ethos of the concert as a whole. I think you can get bogged down in trying to become very, very unified with the program, but if there is a strong logic to a program, I think it communicates itself to all involved, audience and singers, alike.

JS: Is there an "English style" in choral singing?

JO: There used to be more of one than there is nowadays. Even up to the 1960's, there were several iconic figures in English church music whose examples were universally emulated, people like David Willcocks, for example. Some people thought, "this is the way things should be done, this is the way things should sound," which of course is very flattering but also misguided in a way. I'm sure David Willcocks himself would be the first to say, "There is no 'the way'; this is my way which suits me, the place, the tradition and it suits the people I'm working with." I think that is the definition of a good style; it's like any other artistic question. There is no "the way."

I think, now, church music in this country has diversified enormously. There is still this stereotyped idea of the pure-voiced English boy treble – slightly aloof, pooching away in the rafters at Christmas time. You'd be hard-pressed to find that these days. One or two people have been fairly iconoclastic in the cathedral music world. The late George Malcolm, who was the director of music here at Westminster Cathedral in the 1950's, disliked what he called the "Anglican hoot," and he made the boys here sing in the most extreme and dissimilar way from that. It was very, very bright and reedy and a lot of people hated it. They thought that it was an affront to the tradition and, of course, in a way it was; it was deliberately provocative.

Then you've got people like George Guest, who was at St. John's College, Cambridge, for a long time, who was said to have been very influenced by George Malcolm. So his boys sang with much more vibrato and quite a different sort of sound from the King's College sound as it was then. I think that, like any generalization, to say there is an English sound or an English character, you have to have so many caveats that you end up devaluing what you've said.

JS: How do you approach vibrato with your choir?

JO: There is often a certain amount of natural vibrato in the singing voice, and our boys have that. Some of the boys in my choir have more natural vibrato than the others, and that's not a problem, provided the overall sound is coherent.

JS: Do you encourage more vibrato in, say, Bruckner and less in Palestrina?

JO: It's all the same basic vocal technique, though it might be a different style of music-making – a different approach to articulation, line, tactus and rhythm; but I wouldn't advocate singing with more vibrato simply because it is later music.

JS: Who have been important influences in your career?

JO: Lots of people. The trouble is, then, you start to name them, and you leave out lots of others. I've been very inspired by many, though. My two immediate

151

predecessors here are people I've worked with quite closely: Stephen Cleobury and David Hill. I was David Hill's assistant throughout his time here, so I saw his work at very close quarters; that was a very privileged glimpse, and I learned a lot. I enjoy listening to a great many other choirs, but I have a rare opportunity to do so, at the moment.

In the past, I was strongly influenced by George Guest. I very much enjoyed hearing the St. John's College Choir when I was at Cambridge, and I used to go to services there. I also enjoyed going to King's College, as well.

JS: Did you work with Guest?

JO: No, I was an organist, and I was in charge of the choir at Jesus College. But I was lucky enough to go to some of his rehearsals and recording sessions and get to see him work. The more I did that, the more I realized that, while you can get a lot of good ideas that way, it's finally down to you how to do it. Whether you are an orchestral conductor, choral conductor or chamber player, your music-making owes its origins to your own perception and experience of music. When you encounter a difficulty, you can't say, "How would Boris Ord have solved that?" You are the person who has to solve the problem in your own way.

JS: Do you do warm-ups? What else do you cover in rehearsal?

JO: With the boys I do some warm-ups in the morning, for a few moments, just to limber up. I try to vary that a lot and sometimes don't do warm-ups at all, just to avoid the routine. But we do standard limbering-up exercises like humming, downward scales, arpeggios.

JS: How do you select repertory for recording?

JO: The people who pay for the recording – the people in the record company – are calling the shots, really. What happens is that I tend to suggest music to the record company, and they tell me whether they're interested in recording it; usually they are because I know what they're interested in and they know what we do. In that way, it's a very good relationship. I like to record music that I think the choir would sing well but also give it a varied diet. For example, we might record some Palestrina, and I will then look for an attractive combination of pieces – a Mass, some motets which would complement it, a Magnificat, and perhaps a couple of hymn settings – a varied diet within the disc. With the next disc, we might do a French organ mass from the nineteenth century – Vierne or Widor.

JS: How does scholarship inform your performance?

JO: Interesting question. I think it's based on what you've observed, what you encounter and what you've researched; then you process it, and it then comes out in the work. I don't set out to do research on Palestrina performance practice for our forthcoming recording of Palestrina and then put it into effect for the recording. But I do set out in my daily work to be aware of performance practice issues, to keep in touch with my scholarly friends, read, listen, keep my eyes and ears open.

JS: Do you make your own editions?

JO: Sometimes, but we usually don't do our own editions. I often work with scholars in preparing editions, people like Bruno Turner. Our recordings are very much an offshoot of our daily work. I see recordings as being quite integral to the work of the choir. I think our recordings do communicate to the wider musical public the fundamental essence of this cathedral and its choir.

JS: Describe your approach to score preparation.

JO: It varies. Generally speaking, for a lot of the new music we do here, I will teach it to the boys. In the course of going through the music with the boys and in encountering it in detail that way, you get to know the piece pretty well. That's not to say one doesn't know it before rehearsals, but I think there's an opportunity that is quite rare in music-making: to rehearse, quite extensively, one section of the choir before the whole thing needs to be put together. I do stress that most of our performances then have to be put together very quickly. This pre-supposes a close familiarity with the score.

JS: Do financial considerations influence what you do?

JO: They do and they don't. The Cathedral is responsible for funding the choir, and the Cathedral is not a wealthy organization. People think that a Catholic cathedral has to be rolling in cash, but it's not. It relies on the voluntary contributions of the people who come here. Paying for a professional choir in Central London is an expensive business. Part of the rationale of giving the occasional concert, while incidental, would be to enhance the income.

JS: Do your recordings contribute significantly towards income?

JO: They do contribute, but not greatly; people don't get rich from making recordings. You'd be ill-advised to base the finances of our daily worship work on unpredictable outside work, which would necessarily mean that, at times, we couldn't do our daily work.

JS: How many recordings do you make per year?

JO: We usually make two discs a year, sometimes three.

JS: For how much of the year does the choir provide music?

JO: Some of the other English choirs similar to us are based in universities: New College, Oxford, and King's College, Cambridge, for example. So their singing terms are much, much shorter. They will sing for maybe twenty-eight weeks a year, whereas we're singing for forty-four weeks a year. The boys have their normal school holidays, though they stay here for Easter and Christmas. When the boys are away, the men sing all of the services.

JS: Are you a beneficiary of any public school training the boys have already had, or do you have to train them from scratch?

JO: With boys this young (seven to eight) it is unlikely that they are going to have reached a very advanced stage of formation before they come here. They come when they're eight, so we expect to start them off basically with every-thing. Most of them, if not all, have already begun an instrument and have some kind of music-reading ability, although that does not necessarily translate into sight-singing ability. The crucial thing that characterizes this kind of choir, as far as the formation of the boys is concerned, is the experience of doing it. By the time you've got to your fifth year as a chorister and you've risen up through the ranks – even if you weren't that promising to begin with – the like-lihood is that you're going to be a pretty competent chorister because of the experience you've gained.

JS: Where do they go from Westminster Cathedral?

JO: Very many go on to what we call public schools (which, of course, you call private schools) and most of them get music scholarships: that is to say, remis-sion of fees in recognition of their musical skills.

A typical chorister in any cathedral choir school will do his five years, get a good degree of training, and acquire good professional choir experience. He will then be snapped up by another school which will reduce the fees in order to have that person there. I think that's fine as long as the work they've done can be continued. The vital thing in this respect is peer pressure. In the best of circumstances, they would go on to a school where there was good choral and instrumental music, good peer pressure and a good musical ethos. Then they would spend five years in that school, gain some good academic qualifications, continue their musical development, and then who knows what they might do? They might become professional musicians, and many of them do. Irrespective of what they go on to do, they will be well-trained musicians and musically aware. More to the point, they will be musically literate in, and knowledgeable about, church music. What we need are people who have discrimination in church music, particularly in the Roman Catholic Church. You know things have slipped very badly in the music of the Roman Catholic Church, and that's regrettable. But I hope people will wake up and realize that it's not beyond redemption. There are very many ways, imaginative ways, of reconciling the heritage of Catholic church music with the current liturgical thinking. They are not at all incompatible. But one of the specific reasons why the Westminster Cathedral Choir School kept open here in the 1970's, when it went through a very difficult patch and was in danger of being closed down, was to give the church its future musicians. But it's much broader than that. The training they receive here isn't just valuable musically, but valuable personally: discipline and maturity. And it's fun! How many other children get to go to America for two weeks, all expenses paid, sing on television, and make recordings? And much else besides?

Another thing one sees is former choristers coming back as adult professional singers. Indeed, one of our lay clerks was a chorister here, and several others have been choristers elsewhere. So this is proof of what I have just said: in these institutions tomorrow's church musicians are being created.

JS: What is the role of choral music in English culture?

JO: The arts and music, in particular, have become rather polarized in this country recently. That is to say that the people who are already interested in them are just as interested as they ever were, but fewer people seem to have been exposed to them, particularly singing. You asked about the training that children receive in schools. I can't speak for the schools, but I gather that many schools now do not have competent people who can teach children to sing, or who will actually sing in front of children themselves. When I was in school, there was a tradition of the whole class getting out a songbook and just singing together. The tradition of everybody knowing some hymns of the church is disappearing. People don't know them anymore. Because of this decline, it's all the more important for us to continue what we're doing here and for many other people to join us. It is becoming harder and harder to get boys with any kind of experience in singing. If there's no rudimentary experience in singing in the schools, then when a teacher says to the parents, "Do you know your son has a rather good voice? It might be worth taking that further, perhaps in a good cathedral choir school," the parents might not appreciate what that means. They might never get to know the gifts that their children have because they're not being given the chance to explore them.

JS: Is the day coming when boys will be replaced by professional women?

JO: It's already happened in many churches. I hope that it doesn't happen here because it would be a tragedy to lose this tradition. I have nothing against all-adult choirs; in some places they are the only solution. Traditionally, cathedrals and the church have been founts of education and knowledge, and Westminster Cathedral is an excellent example of that. This is a place where the work of God is done: the liturgy is enhanced by the music, and children are educated. So I don't see the day when all of that would be replaced by an all-adult professional choir, because I think a vital aspect of this work would be lost.

Andrew Parrott

Born: 1947

Taverner Consort and Players

Education: Merton College, Oxford University

Interview: January 19, 1999, Amadeus Center, London

Andrew Parrott established his reputation as an authoritative voice in the interpretation of early music, both as conductor of the Taverner Consort and Players and as a writer. He is well known for his many recordings of Renaissance and Baroque music and also for his scholarly, often challenging articles on performance practice. In recent years, Parrott has come to be in demand internationally as an opera and orchestral conductor of all style periods. In 2000, he was appointed Director of the London Mozart Players, and he is co-editor of the *New Oxford Book of Carols*. His celebrated book, *The Essential Bach Choir*, was released in 2000.

The Taverner Consort was founded in 1973 by Andrew Parrott at the invitation of Sir Michael Tippett for a performance at the Bath Festival. The group's broad discography embraces music from Machaut to John Tavener, but is especially acclaimed for its recordings of Monteverdi, Purcell, J.S. Bach, and Handel.

Website: www.sonyclassical.com/artists/parrott_bio.html

Andrew Parrott

Photo: Tobi Comey

Andrew Parrott
Taverner Choir, Consort and Players

JS: As a conductor, on what do you focus in your music-making? How do we know we are hearing your group?

AP: Let me put it this way: I'm always happy if my work is perceived as being distinctive in some way, that a performance of mine does not merely reproduce or replicate somebody else's, but I certainly do not set out to create a "Taverner sound," or wantonly to make the group identifiably different from others. What I am constantly striving to do is to get closer to the heart of a particular work, a particular repertory or a particular idiom. Whether I succeed or not is, of course, another matter altogether. So with Renaissance Italian music, for example, I want to be able to start with a particular type of ensemble, a medium, palpably different from one that might be appropriate, say, for eighteenth-century French music. This unfortunately goes right against the conventional idea of a fixed-personnel choir performing a wide repertoire. In my case then, each group is a one-off, each is created for a specific project, though of course certain singers do turn up in a variety of configurations.

JS: Please describe your preparation of a score.

AP: The first requirement is for me to be able to specify the exact forces that will best serve the piece in question, always bearing in mind the hall or church where we're going to be performing. In other words, setting things up well is, I believe, absolutely critical. More generally, the aim of preparation is to enable me to form a clear idea of the musical text, of a work's structure and aesthetic language or style. But I don't like to have too fixed a view of how a particular piece "goes," even in matters of tempi, because I really want to be able to explore all sorts of different possibilities in rehearsal – and in performance too! That's what I particularly enjoy about the whole rehearsal process. This sort of approach obviously works better with smaller, hand-picked groups and when time is not unduly limited, but I always like to see what arises naturally from a group of performers and to continue exploring ideas in partnership with them. So, in one sense, while I undoubtedly come to rehearsal with a very clear view of what I want, with all my own preconceptions and prejudices, I also purposely come with an open mind as to how a piece might evolve during rehearsal.

JS: So is your interpretation collaborative, in part?

AP: I hope so. At least, I like to kid myself that I'm not merely imposing a pre-planned interpretation on my valued colleagues!

JS: Is that how you get to the "heart," as you said, or do you find the "heart" in your own study?

AP: Getting to the heart of certain fundamental principles – especially historical ones, which fascinate me – is definitely done in my study and over long periods of time. But the process of discovery almost inevitably carries over into the realm of rehearsal and performance, when these ideas are turned into music.

JS: You are well known for using scholarship in your work. Please describe how you approach musicology as an aid to performance.

AP: For me it's essentially all one process, despite the familiar separate compartments. My broad aim is to find out as much as scholarship can possibly tell us about how performances worked in past ages, and then in performance to draw on that information as need arises. Musicological work need not be a self-contained exercise that comes to an end once a composition has been transcribed, edited and discussed; it's a vital tool for establishing and refining many of the principles and conventions which we adopt when we perform. Necessarily, as performers we also rely on intuition and instinct and on pragmatism; scholarship can only go so far. But these two worlds – scholarship and performance – seem often to stand much further apart than they need to, and indeed are institutionally segregated for the most part. What I'm interested in is how the two can fruitfully interact, how they can feed each other.

JS: How do you approach blend in the ensemble?

AP: Primarily through the careful selection of singers. In fact, I'm rather wary of the concept of "blend." But perhaps my problem lies with the word itself, which too readily evokes *bland*-ness! It seems to imply an undue annihilation of individuality. Of course, with large numbers of singers, individuality tends to disappear quite naturally into a collective personality, and indeed this is the very beauty of the large (and usually amateur) choir. But whether this approach has any real historical or musical relevance to choral literature from before the nineteenth century, which was predominantly for relatively small groups of professionals, I'm not so sure. Ensuring that one voice doesn't overbalance others is one thing, but I know of no early source suggesting that singers should consciously "blend" tonally with others. And, entirely subjectively, I don't want to lose the distinctiveness of the individual singers I have chosen. I prefer the admittedly more dangerous route of mixing different colors, distinctive ingredients, together, as an imaginative chef might do in cooking.

JS: So what do we know about tone quality from before the nineteenth century?

AP: Not as much as we should like to, of course. It's a very intricate subject which I couldn't begin to do justice to in a short space of time, and much of it has to do with the characteristics of different languages as they were spoken. But there are some clear pointers. For example, the idea that singers might intentionally modify spoken vowels does not seem to have arisen. Yes, we claim we always want to hear singers' words, but actually we're often more interested nowadays in an evenness of tone, which we achieve largely by minimizing the differences between vowels. By contrast, there are many early writings which insist on the very clear differentiation of vowels. To me this is an important principle. When you listen to a viola da gamba, for example, it seems almost as if the instrument is speaking, as if each note has its own vowel. This is quite different from the very even string tone we cultivate today. So in a sixteenth-century piece of vocal polyphony, I want all vowels to be very distinct, so that there is a continually changing kaleidoscope of sound rather than a single, all-pervading sonority. After all, words are precisely what make the voice the supreme musical instrument, and it is perverse to disguise them intentionally.

JS: How do you approach vibrato as a scholar?

AP: This is another very tricky area, not least because of the terminology. Some writers inveigh against it, sometimes associating it with older singers and faulty technique, while others describe it as a basic component of good vocal production. Are they referring to the same thing, or are they simply expressing different tastes? Some may be thinking of pronounced fluctuations of pitch, others merely of fluctuations of intensity with little or no perceptible effect on pitch. Wide pitch vibratos are something we often encounter nowadays in our frequently over-large opera houses where solo voices are routinely pitted against big and loud orchestras, but singing on such a scale has few parallels in earlier periods. We must also distinguish between solo singing, where vibrato is a valuable ornament to be employed judiciously, like any other, and ensemble singing. But in both contexts it was always unacceptable for a vibrato to jeopardize precise intonation. In any case, to be able to sing in only one way, whether with a conspicuous and unvarying vibrato or with a relentlessly straight tone, is a technical and musical limitation in almost any repertoire.

JS: What is your view for tuning Baroque music?

AP: Most of us have grown up with the piano's equal temperament as the unquestioned model of "correct" tuning. Other historical tuning systems have mostly been thought of as harpsichordists' territory. But equal temperament is extraordinarily difficult to sing in, at least in unaccompanied music; all semitones, whole tones, and so on, may be theoretically equal in size, but the price paid is that every single interval, except the octave, is in fact out of tune to some degree and literally "unnatural." Thus, it is virtually impossible for a singer to gauge with total precision. And, as often as not, the resultant uncertainty leads to further problems, not least to a more general instability of pitch. Most important of all, though, a simple chord sung in just intonation, with all intervals truly "pure," will have so much more ring to it, so much more natural resonance. (The modern piano works the other way around, creating its own particular resonances through the "beating" of its slightly out-of-tune strings.) For singers the most critical interval, perhaps, is the major third, and this is where we most need to re-educate ourselves, to learn to think and listen differently. Contrary to what most choral directors around the world seem to preach, a *pure* major third is distinctly *lower* than in equal temperament and, for good acoustical reasons, noticeably sweeter because it locks smoothly into the overtones of the note to which it relates. This sweetness of tuning is vital to all Renaissance vocal polyphony, in my view, and is also a defining feature of one quarter-comma meantone temperament, which most accompanying instruments adopted in the early Baroque. Monteverdi, for example, never writes in "remote" keys like F minor or F-sharp major, which equal temperament would have facilitated; instead he sticks to a limited number of "home" keys, all of which can be well-tuned without compromised thirds. And in the later Baroque, too, when increasingly flexible temperaments were often required, there was a far more sophisticated general understanding of tuning than we have today. Equal temperament, which tends to iron out differences between keys and other subtleties, was but one of several options; to explore others doesn't cost us anything today, just a little time and mental effort!

JS: And pitch standards?

AP: Quite apart from their implications for the vocal scorings we adopt, it's vital to have a reasonably precise understanding of the various pitch standards in use at different times in the past, in different places and in different repertoires. If, for example, we're performing a Bach motet a semitone higher than he intended, we're likely to be introducing a tension, through problems of stamina and tessitura, that his own singers would not have experienced – as if the music were not difficult enough already! It may prove possible to "solve" those problems in some fashion, but they remain problems that we, and not Bach, have created. Why not simply avoid them in the first place? This may mean that an accompanying (*equal-tempered!*) organ has to transpose, but such things are possible.

JS: So a half-step down from a; = 440 for Bach?

AP: Yes, at least for the vast majority of his Leipzig church music.

JS: You will be conducting Handel's *Dixit Dominus* in a few days with fifteen singers. Is the number of singers based on financial considerations, or did Handel use only three to a part?

AP: It's definitely not based on financial considerations, and the orchestra is quite big; in fact, Handel may well have used fewer singers, and he almost certainly would not have required more, though I must admit that I have not yet researched the point as thoroughly as it deserves. As a general rule, though, we tend to assume that there should be larger numbers of singers than of instruments; that's the most familiar arrangement nowadays. But in the later Baroque, we almost invariably find the opposite.

JS: Is that because the instruments were weaker then?

AP: It is indeed partly to do with that, yes. Also, singers were normally positioned in front of instruments up until the nineteenth century. That becomes a problem once choirs begin to exceed a certain size. But when instead of a choir, in the modern sense, there is just a "consort" of four or five singers, then to have them in front makes perfect sense, with the instruments around and behind them. And, indeed, it's becoming increasingly clear that in Baroque Italy and Germany a great deal of choral music was in fact intended primarily for groups of solo voices, selectively reinforced perhaps by one or even two similar groups.

JS: Do economics, therefore, never determine your maximum numbers for a choir?

AP: "Small" choirs are easily perceived as the product of economic limitations, which may often miss the musical point. I think it reasonably accurate to say that most medieval polyphony was originally sung one to a part – chant is a different matter, of course – and that even a great deal of Renaissance polyphony, which we take to be quintessentially "choral," would have been considered no less appropriate for one voice per part than for several.

JS: Up to how many?

AP: On the whole, numbers are not especially critical for Renaissance polyphony, perhaps, though for concerted music from later on, from Monteverdi to Bach, it's a different matter entirely. In the sixteenth century the biggest choral establishments were thirty-or-so strong. But those are very much the exception; most institutions would have regarded half that number as ample. And these statistics can be deceptive: aside from individual absences, for illness and so on, there were rota systems in operation at, for instance, the Sistine Chapel and England's Chapel Royal, which meant that the full complement of singers was heard only occasionally.

But it would be wrong to imagine that "small" choirs necessarily lacked impact. In terms of sheer acoustics, a lot of our familiar preconceptions are rather suspect. For example, if we ask the question, "how many singers (or violins) does it take to produce twice the volume of a single voice (or violin)", most of us might instinctively hazard a guess at a total of two or three, whereas the immutable laws of acoustics dictate that there must be roughly eight. That is, eight unison voices (or violins) are perceived as sounding only twice as loud as one. And so the critical sonic difference between one singer per part and several turns out to be a matter not of volume but rather of color.

JS: What is the maximum number of singers per part we can use for Baroque music?

AP: I'm not going to generalize because it very much depends on exactly which repertoire we're talking about. But for most people the biggest surprise undoubtedly concerns the music of J. S. Bach. I would say that the implied maximum number of singers for a typical Bach cantata is just eight singers, two per part: a quartet of concertists, who sang both solos and choruses, and a supplementary quartet of ripienists who would double the concertists in some, but not necessarily all, choral writing. See my three recent articles for *Early Music*! [A subsequent book by Andrew Parrott, *The Essential Bach Choir* (2000), is published by Boydell Press/University of Rochester Press.]

JS: So Joshua Rifkin's theories about the *B Minor Mass* are not so extreme after all?

AP: Not at all; the principle is scarcely more extreme than that of having only four players perform a string quartet. And it applies not only to that one great work of Bach's but to his entire choral output, and to that of most of his Lutheran contemporaries. Joshua Rifkin's findings have been pretty comprehensively misunderstood, and I think it's high time that choral directors started to get to grips with them. Even if one then chooses to perform Bach's music with larger forces, college choirs or whatever, there is so much to be learned that can inform and benefit any approach to this repertoire.

JS: Finally, what guiding principles help shape programming?

AP: This is where financial considerations really do come into play! In all its twenty-five or so years, my Taverner group has almost never been in a position to fund a major concert, yet alone a series or season of concerts. Instead, it remains dependent entirely on invitations, from festivals, concert promoters, record and broadcasting companies. Some offers are very specific, say to perform Monteverdi's *1610 Vespers*; on other occasions, I may be asked to come up with a proposal tailor-made to the chosen theme of a particular festival or concert series. But, ultimately, the programming and our acceptance of an invitation will always depend on the appropriateness of the intended venue, on the availability of key performers, on a budget that allows for adequate preparation and rehearsal and, not least, on the nature of the musical challenge itself.

Peter Phillips

Born: 1953

The Tallis Scholars

Education: Magdalen College, Oxford

Interview: January 18, 1999, Conductor's Home, London

In 1973, Peter Phillips made a bold decision to form a choir that would specialize in Renaissance sacred music. The tremendous success of the Tallis Scholars later enabled him to establish a record company that would give them the freedom to explore less familiar parts of that repertory. The fact that Josquin, Tallis and Isaac are readily available on record today can be attributed, in part, to this decision. Phillips is also a noted author, writing regularly for *The Spectator*, and his first book, *English Choral Music, 1549-1649,* has become an important contribution to the study of choral music history.

The Tallis Scholars were formed in 1973 by Peter Phillips at Oxford University. Since then, they have become one of the most enduring of all of England's early-music groups. The group became professional in 1984, and in 1998 they gave their 1,000th concert, at which time nearly a fifth of those concerts had been in the United States. Their recordings have won many awards, including the Gramophone "Record of the Year" in 1987 for the Josquin *Missa Pange Lingua* and *Missa La sol fa re me.*

Website: www.gimell.com

Peter Phillips

Peter Phillips
The Tallis Scholars

JS: Please describe your audition process.

PP: I don't audition at all. It's been about twenty-six and a half years, twenty-seven years in November, 2000, since the forming of the group, and the system now runs itself. My regular group has two voices to a part, which is one of our basic principles of operation. Ideally, there are going to be five parts in the music, so there are usually ten of us, but we can adjust up or down. But ten is the optimum number and the most practical number. I'd like to have two voices on a part, whatever we're doing; but five-voice pieces are optimum in terms of a touring budget. If someone can't make a job, I ask the other person on the part whom they would like to sing with, thereby neatly handing on the responsibility to them for blend and general acceptability. In the end, singers of this caliber and professionalism know better than I who's best to do the job. I'm not interested in auditioning thirty people every six months to try to find a startling, new voice. As time goes by, I will inevitably get to hear about the really good singers. And I don't want them fresh out of college, anyway. They need to have got five or so years under their belts in the professional system in London.

JS: Why just two to a part?

PP: It can be authentic to have no more than two voices to a part. If you look at the cathedral lists in England, you can see that there are four singers on each part, but they are *decani* and *cantoris*, so they are divided down very often to two to a part. The boys, being children, tend not to be such strong singers, so there have to be more of them to balance up. But actually, in the end, only about three of them on each side are leading the sound, and the younger ones are just training up until they get to be the oldest. Our line-up is quite close to the cathedral model. And Byrd's recusant community, for which he wrote all his later Catholic music, was clearly a small ensemble which included women. Some of Byrd's music, especially the Anglican and English-texted music, was written for the Chapel Royal which had boys. But once he got fed up with London and Protestantism, he sort of retreated, more or less with Elizabeth's permission, to Stondon Massey in Essex. A lot of his music, the *Gradualia* and some of the big pieces, was written for a group that had women: women sopranos and probably women altos.

JS: So you do not subscribe to the principle that it is easier to blend three voices than two?

PP: The proof of the pudding is as you hear it on our recordings. Every single record we ever made has had two voices to a part as a matter of basic policy. There may be a piece or two with one to a part, but never with three or more. I can only say that I don't agree with that analysis. It's perfectly possible for two singers to work together. We sing a lot, and my singers get used to each other's mannerisms. On a very slow cycle of about six years, I think they get used to each other, and then they begin to drift slightly apart again. At that point I tend to split them up and rearrange the mosaic a bit. But three voices to a part is simply no better at all. You just get three voices beating against each other. The problem then is that the two on the outside of the threesome will not be able to hear each other properly and so will not communicate as a group as well as two.

JS: So do you still work on problems of blend?

PP: Essentially, we sorted this out a long time ago. Everyone knows very well what the parameters are, even the youngest members who were hardly born when we started. Because of the recordings and many broadcasts, the style is very well set in people's minds. I set that style between fifteen and twenty-five years ago, and I now can't exactly remember what I said. Obviously, we care very much about blend and tuning; they are very much basics. The whole style is based on group blend and group tuning, but it's not necessary to discuss most of that anymore.

JS: Are there any specific things you do in rehearsal to ensure the blend and quality of intonation you demonstrate?

PP: Let's talk about the two separately. Blend is going to be affected by the timbre of the actual voices present, so it's very important that I don't employ someone who really doesn't stand a chance of mixing in. There's nothing I can do if someone has a raspy voice or a "vibrato-ful" voice or an out-of-tune voice. We just have to grin and bear it and don't employ them again. But I still tinker all of the time. It's like tinkering with an engine. If a voice is sticking out because it's high for the particular part, I might say, "Those top notes are throttled," or "It's not really flowing." But I want people to sing fully. I don't want any mezzo-voce; I want really straight-between-the-edges singing, but it does depend on the voice being able to do this without distorting. So I'm relying quite a lot on the original choice of a singer having been a good one. As for tuning, it's really the same thing. We have quite a lot of discussion about thirds in particular, especially where the major thirds should be. The sopranos tend to end up with the major thirds that the listener can hear, so we tend to discuss that quite a lot among ourselves.

JS: Do you like sharp or flat major thirds?

PP: In theory I like flat major thirds and sharp minor thirds. I'm essentially following the traditional mean-tone system, but I am very undogmatic about it. We adapt it a lot. The strict mean-tone major third is a flat note to my ear. When major thirds are doubled and clashing, the answer is always to flatten them, but there comes a point in strict tuning when it is too flat. I've had some singers along from other, much more dogmatic conductors like Andrew Parrott. They've been trained and trained and trained, and they've got a blind-spot about it. To my ear, these major thirds can be just too flat. They make a dull, disappointing sound, and I have felt obliged to try to undo that mind set.

JS: Do you have the singers mark their scores with arrows up or down to indicate the quality of third you want to hear?

PP: I don't feel myself to be a very dominating figure in this outfit. Basically, I let the singers get on with it. I want them to work it out. I may not know the answer anyway. I don't feel that I know more than they do. What I do is conduct and make interpretations, and they have to follow that. It's my job to bring the music alive; it's their job to get the tuning, to get the notes right, to get the blend. They are very professional people – quite a few of them are older than I, much more qualified at what they do than I am at what they do. So I expect them to get it right, and they expect to get it right. If I just stop the rehearsal and say, "That chord was absolute hell. I don't know what's the matter with it but let's just do it again," and leave them to talk about it a bit, especially between the two singers on any given part, it may well sort itself out. I can help by telling them which part is flat or sharp, or what very often happens is that it is a split note, neither of them singing it quite in tune. Then the conductor has to be very careful because I could mislead them and not help with the answer. One has to have such fine hearing to be able to pick out the split note in a six-voice texture. What I tend to say with a split note is, "One of you is one side and one the other," or "One is right and the other isn't, but either way it's not working. Let's just try it again." I think my job is to help them to find the answers rather than be dogmatic, give them an answer, and perhaps be wrong.

Basically, the English system is to get things as right as possible as quickly as possible and go home. I'm not in the least bit interested in being right all the time. I dislike rehearsals – we all see them as a necessary evil. We just want to get the music absolutely as right as we can and then knock off and wait for the performance. Then we can let rip and enjoy ourselves.

JS: Where is tuning most important to you? For example, linearly or vertically?

PP: Cadences are important to me. If the chords are in tune, I tend to hang on to them. We have long last chords. If they are not in tune, I'll stop them pretty short, and the singers will know very well that something's gone wrong. I rather like the last chords, especially in Flemish pieces where the counterpoint has been involved and slowly works itself out. The last chord is probably the only point of repose in the whole piece because the cadences are always being stitched-over. So when we get to the last chord, I really sit on it, and if it's out of tune, it is deeply disappointing. It leaves a bad taste if the last thing to be heard is out of tune.

JS: What are your ideas about the specific tone quality needed for the Renaissance repertoire in which you specialize?

PP: I hope that the tone quality we produce has come out of what the music needs. All we sing in the Tallis Scholars is polyphonic music, and once you get into the workings of it, it is very complicated. To my mind it is crucial that the detail of this counterpoint is presented clearly. So right from the start, I wanted to produce a sound which was as clear as could be. When we record, we aim for the greatest possible clarity between the voice parts, and so we tend not to use buildings that are very reverberant. The buildings we tend to record in do not have traditional "church acoustics" at all, but have the sort of clarity which a string quartet would need, for example. So all of the detail is clear. Tuning and blend contribute to this clarity too. There is vibrato in our sound, but if there is a distorting vibrato, which by definition is out of tune, the clarity is going to suffer. So those are the elements of clarity which allow for the lines to be very clearly etched.

My teacher at Oxford, David Wulstan, who inspired me to start this group with his Clerkes of Oxenford, went in a slightly different direction. He went for a rather white sound: as vibratoless as possible, quiet, pure – a sort of mini-sound. He also wanted his singers to let rip when the music got exciting, but I found when the Clerkes sang flat-out, the result was beautiful, and beautifully formed, but still slightly miniature in sound. I work for something just brasher, larger and very bright. I like a strong, pingy sound from the top to the bottom. And I want an agile, very flexible legato with a sort of brilliance on top so you can hear the overtones.

JS: I think many Americans will be interested to learn of these approaches to tone.

PP: I think it's very important that your readers listen to the difference between the Tallis Scholars singing a piece by Tallis and a cathedral choir, for example, Kings College, Cambridge, singing a piece by Tallis. There is all the difference in the world. It's a very interesting difference, I think, because we did start in the cathedral tradition; most singing groups in England do. It's an amazing tradition and gives a wonderful starting point and fluency in vocal music. But King's College Chapel has a big acoustic, a mushy sound, the hooty boys, and imbalance written all over it. You've got sixteen boys there plus a handful of undergraduates who don't really have to learn to blend together because the building does most of it for them. There is a payoff, which is that you can't really hear the detail very well. It's just a different approach altogether. The King's Choir, of course, is very famous and they have a wonderful tradition, but there is still a nineteenth-century vision there. Probably the undergraduates are no longer expected to sing in the woofy voice of fifty years ago. Still, they can sound meaninglessly weighty.

JS: What do you do to create ensemble?

PP: One thing that commentators have said about us is that we have created an instrument, as it were, like an organ. They call attention to our blend and agile, lively sound. It's almost as if I am playing on an organ when I conduct. In fact, it's more exciting than playing an organ because there are ten lively minds there that are able to do different things from one performance to the next. The Tallis Scholars can sound like an organ being played because the sound is so reliable, but it's more sensitive than an organ.

JS: Do you have to work on style, or is everyone so experienced that it's never discussed?

PP: I think most of us have actually done a certain amount of reading about what choirs sounded like in the sixteenth century. I've got some very good scholars in the group. Sally Dunkley and Francis Steele have edited some of the music we do. But, in the end, no one knows what a Renaissance choir sounded like. I'm rather reluctant simply to take up the latest academic theory.

I don't think we need that. What I am doing is trying to make Renaissance music come alive for modern people. I do take into account as much serious evidence as there is. There isn't very much, really, except the music itself, and I think the music tells us a lot. That's not to say that I think our way of doing it is the only way. It's a point worth stressing, actually, because we've been at this quite a long time, and our recordings have sold very well. And if it seems as though we're saying, "You've got to do it like this; otherwise, you're nowhere." In fact, we sing it the way we do because we believe in it, and I wait with great interest to see how anybody else will perform it. Indeed, I sometimes conduct foreign groups, especially in Italy, and often hear something different, and I think it's equally valid. There's definitely a move at the moment that the French and the Italians and the Spanish are beginning to catch on to performing Renaissance music within acceptable stylistic limits. They used to be outside those limits, but recent developments have been exciting.

JS: How do you create an overview of a piece?

PP: First, we sing it through, because we can't get anywhere, any of us, until we've actually heard it. Every composer of any ability at all had a sound world of his own, and with a really good composer, each piece will have a sound world of its own, which will not be apparent by bashing it out on the piano. I'll look at it and try to hear it. What I've got to do in order to get a start on the piece is set the speed. That's really my job. I pick up the new piece, make sure we've got a good edition of it, and make sure that somebody has sorted out the ficta problems. You don't want to spend hours arguing about ficta; get an academic to sort it out.

JS: You don't do the sorting out yourself?

PP: Not if I can avoid it. My job is to produce an interpretation of that piece in front of an audience in a concert. I don't think it's my job to argue with the singers about ficta. I want to get the edition right, which is more likely if an expert has looked at it. We want a consistent answer from somebody who has sat down and worked it through.

JS: You have those kind of people in the group, don't you?

PP: Yes, it can be people in the group, which can add a great deal of fire to any argument in the group which might start about ficta, for example. But I know some highly-qualified academics who like doing this sort of thing. You must start with a copy that's not in funny clefs and that everyone can read easily. You must assume that the lighting is going to be in some way unsatisfactory in the concert – it often is in churches – so you've got to have as clean a copy as possible. And don't transpose the music either, if you can help it, because the tuning always suffers from that. My job is to get the speed, and sometimes I get it wrong. We'll go through it, and someone will say, "It's too fast. I can't sing it at that tempo." So we'll sing it again, and then someone might say, "It's too slow. I run out of breath." By then we've learnt all the notes, though, and then I have to decide how much longer we need to get to know the piece well enough to give it a first performance.

JS: Would you say that in some ways a Tallis Scholars' performance is a collaborative interpretation?

PP: Oh, yes, it certainly is. Very often, if it's a highly imitative piece, the way that the first part sings the point is picked up by everybody else. I don't have to say anything; everyone just hears it. The great thing is not to over-rehearse because, if you do that, musicians of this experience will just get bored. That can be a problem with recordings sometimes. Because of outside noise, or whatever reason, especially if we're recording a piece we know well, and have to sing it repeatedly, these can be the worst recordings because we all get sated with the music. I can't make them do it. Lively minds can get bored easily.

JS: What characteristics distinguish the Scholars from other groups? How does the listener know it's you?

PP: I want every line that we sing to stand a very close scrutiny. I'm looking to have the whole line covered from top to bottom with a *cantabile, legato* sound. It doesn't matter how dry the building is because we sing in dreadful places; or how big it is – we sing in vast places. We sang for three thousand people the other night in Vancouver. By comparison, Harry Christophers, with The Sixteen, records with bigger voices, with more of them, and in roomier acoustics. Their microphone isn't as close, and the detail doesn't come over as reliably.

JS: From where does this great interest in Renaissance music come, even in such places as Japan? What is in this music?

PP: I've thought a lot about this. I think a book could be written about it, and maybe I will write it. It's almost like a modern art form now. It's become deracinated. I mean, we're not singing in church services, and a lot of us don't believe in much of what the words have to tell us. That partly explains why the

Japanese can like it. It's not a specifically Christian event anymore.

You've got to ask: if it were performed in a different way, would it have the same effect? In the old days, when I was growing up, there were the recordings of King's College, Cambridge, which were the best of what there was available. But so many performances then were based on fundamental misconceptions of what polyphony really was.

JS: I remember when I was in high school, breves were interpreted as whole notes and beat in four, so everything was at least twice as long as it is now. We hated it!

PP: Exactly. That's exactly what I'm referring to. The old Tudor Church Music edition published everything at the original, written note lengths. I did a radio program on this recently using some old BBC Singers' tapes for illustration, and they sang unbelievably slowly. They sang Tallis like opera. After listening to this, I concluded that if we turned up in Vancouver and sang like that, we wouldn't get three thousand people to come to hear us. Not a second time anyway. So, yes, it is something to do with the way we sing it. It must be. And obviously, there is something in the music. When the music is revealed to people clearly in the way that I have described, there is something in its almost mathematical perfection that listeners perceive. I have heard people say it acts like a drug on them. It may take about ten minutes for an audience, which is not familiar with polyphony, to realize what's going on. They'll sit down, many of them will be hearing this kind of music for the first time, and they'll audibly shuffle around a bit until it gradually seeps into their brains. After about a quarter of an hour, a lot of people out there will wish that it wouldn't stop. It is strange because polyphony has become so uprooted from its original purpose. Church performances of it in the eighteenth and nineteenth centuries would not have sounded anything like the way we perform it.

JS: Do you do anything specific to develop audiences for your concerts?

PP: We just give good concerts and consistently sell our records! Historically, we haven't done much in the way of mailing lists. There is an "American Friends of the Tallis Scholars." I don't know how many names are on it now, but it's been running for nearly ten years.

JS: Where does the money come from to pay your singers, your salary and all attendant expenses?

PP: Entirely from concert fees. We've budgeted it so that everything is covered. I'm not on a salary but paid by the concert, so we know how much each concert is going to cost to put on. We've never had any government funding. Very occasionally, the British Council, which is a sort of indirect government agency, pays for our airfares if there's a country the Council particularly wants us to go to promote British culture. It's pretty rare, but it does happen. We've had no direct grants from the government, and we don't have a sponsor board. All we do is charge what it costs to put us on. So long as we get a minimum number of concerts a year, I think it's thirty-five or forty, we're in the clear.

JS: Who were your important influences along the way? You've mentioned David Wulstan.

PP: Yes. He was the only one, really. He was my tutor. It's a simple story. In 1972-73, I heard the Clerkes sing, having previously only heard King's and John's and the BBC Singers. I liked polyphony. And when I heard the Clerkes sing Tallis in Magdalen Chapel, late in 1972, that was it. I had never experienced anything like it, and I fell in love with the sound immediately. It was a real falling-in-love-with-something sensation. Being a rather stubborn-minded person, I just said, "I'm going to do that." In the end, what it took was inviting some of Wulstan's singers and using some of his editions, and essentially setting myself up to duplicate what I'd heard. He didn't like that much, and that was the end of that relationship. I haven't seen him since.

JS: So just that exposure is what got you started?

PP: It was actually just one performance of Tallis's *Gaude Gloriosa;* then I got the recordings. Wulstan was intrigued by my interest, and he fed me with the big pieces that nobody ever did in those days. What I've been doing ever since is trying to re-create the sound I think I heard that night. I actually wonder what it was I heard.

JS: Among your contemporaries, whose work do you admire?

PP: I very much admire Philippe Herreweghe's performances of certain things. I was lucky to conduct his group once. I like his versions of the Lassus *Lamentations* and especially his Bach; he's supremely good at Bach. All that discipline and counterpoint in Bach is exactly the same as in lively Renaissance music. But for Bach, the singers will need a more "modern" technique, and we've never gone that far in the Tallis Scholars partly because Philippe is so good. I just can't see the point of doing yet another version of the Bach motets. Jordi Savall is wonderful with what he does with Hesperion XX. They don't do very much Renaissance music, but Savall is such a wonderful interpreter. Whatever he touches seems to come to life.

Amongst the English groups I've been rather rivalrous with my immediate contemporaries. I don't like the way they do things, to be perfectly honest. I think the Hilliard Ensemble, who are older than us, are terrific. I admire the fact that they've been around so long at the top. Whatever it takes to do that gets my respect. And John Eliot Gardiner the same, though he's in a different field. I don't like Parrott's way of doing things, even though my wife sings for him. But there are some really good, young groups in England coming up at last. I would have thought that it might have happened ten years earlier than this, but there are now some young groups, for example, the Clerks' Group, conducted by Edward Wickham, and the Cardinall's Musick with Andrew Carwood. There are some very good cathedral musicians too, like James O'Donnell at Westminster Cathedral (at Westminster Abbey, January, 2000).

JS: Please describe your ideas regarding women versus boys in Renaissance singing. I know you feel strongly about that subject.

PP: Well, I do because people just don't listen. The preference for boys in some quarters is just traditional nonsense. The boys' choirs are not so very good, and even when they are acceptable they would have trouble functioning with the touring conditions we experience. The oldest singing boys are young these days, their voices breaking as young as twelve. You just can't produce a professional ensemble with children. But anyway, even when they are relaxed and at home and singing well, though it can be an attractive sound, I don't think it would ever have the brilliance, the strength, the resilience to match the rest of my ensemble. So I've got no problem with using adult women at all.

JS: How do you view vibrato?

PP: This is really a question of taste on the part of the singers, I think. I employ singers who sing big solos in later music, in which they use vibrato fully. When a singer has to project their voice, for example over an orchestra, that's what produces vibrato. Yet when they sing polyphony, they have to cut much of it out. Still, as I say, I don't want them to sing half-voice. In the end, they certainly don't cut vibrato out completely. That white sound which I describe

Wulstan as having encouraged, I don't want. I do want warmth – vibrating, colorful sound which is in tune. It's up to them, really. I will sometimes say, "The vibrato is too much now. I can't really hear what that note is." It is when the tuning really goes under that I have to say, "Stop that." It's a very fine line.

It's important when a singer hits a note that they hit it right in the middle, straight-off and then sing through it. As it grows, the tone will open up, and the vibrato should just touch the sound as the note gets towards the end of its trajectory. I was talking to a friend in Montreal, when we were on tour there recently, who told me, "The difference between your group and my group is that our singers will hit the notes all right, but the notes don't go anywhere. They haven't got the training, or whatever it takes to make the notes move and have your *legato* throughout the line." So I deduce from what he hears in my singers is the ability to open up, to sing through the line, to have a sense of the shape of the line down to the end. It's that *legato* which is important in stylish Renaissance singing.

JS: How do you choose repertoire for recordings and concerts?

PP: Composer-led recordings have always seemed to me to be the way to go. Gombert is a composer we've been exploring recently, and we'll probably go on to record some more Josquin. Sometimes, for concerts, we'll be asked for a particular kind of program, all-Spanish, for example. I plan the programs very carefully. It's an instinctive thing. You want variety, but not too much. You want a big piece in both halves. You want to end with something fairly upbeat, and each half lasts about forty minutes. The end result will be a mosaic of pieces which I think will follow each other well.

JS: Do you use new editions for everything?

PP: There are many editions you can pick off the shelves of any good music library in the western world. But it can be important to go back to the sources.

Every time we make a record we start from scratch. I don't trust the older editions. We need help from modern scholarship in all kinds of ways: for example, the mensuration signs, and the speed relationships implied by them in Josquin and his predecessors. For our Ockeghem record, we invited an academic to interpret these things for us. We had some speeds that were very odd, but I trusted him. He could stand up and argue the toss with anyone, which I can't.

Nearly everything we perform now is in a fairly new edition. The way the copies look now has changed so dramatically from how they looked thirty years ago. We don't have piano reductions anymore because we don't expect to learn anything by playing polyphony on the piano anymore. The ficta and editorial signs keep changing as the years go by; whether to use barlines or not, it matters. A young singer picks up a copy and immediately feels at ease if the layout is familiar in general outline.

JS: What's the most important thing for a choir to know about singing Renaissance music?

PP: They need to get a basic discipline in place. The sound needs to be reliable. So they will have to do a lot of work on blend and tuning, and achieve a sort of fluency. I would advise groups to specialize. If they want to sing Renaissance music properly, the worst thing they can do is rush off and sing nineteenth-century music, or even Handel and Bach. It's the *notes inégales* of later periods that mess up the correct singing of Renaissance music so completely. The best thing a choir can do is to sing chant and then sing polyphony and stop! This might sound rather prescriptive, but I know that the bad performances of Renaissance music are those ones where polyphony is mixed in with singing later music, which requires a fundamentally different style. The lengths of the notes in Renaissance music must be respected absolutely so that the quavers are meticulously in the right time slot. If you then go off and sing Purcell in his French mode, or Lully, you will need to make the lines sound more like embellishments: anathema to polyphony.

JS: Has the scope of your repertoire expanded in all of these years?

PP: We just sing Renaissance music. That was the novel thing when we set out all those years ago. Lots of choirs were doing Renaissance music, but always in the context of other music to boost up the program. People didn't think you could get an audience for a concert of nothing but polyphony.

JS: To specialize in Renaissance music was a gutsy thing to do.

PP: Yes, it was.

JS: Why haven't you branched out like other choirs?

PP: Because we didn't need to. I stuck to my guns, and I think the reward of that was to get a performing style that was not cluttered up with anachronisms and the needs of later music. When we sing anything else, and we occasionally sing John Tavener, we sing him in our Renaissance style. He seems to like it, so that's all right.

JS: Why do you do Tavener? He's not a Renaissance composer!

PP: I like him, and he likes our way with polyphony which has inspired him. In singing his music we haven't had to compromise ourselves. I've never been very interested in choral music of the nineteenth century or even the twentieth century. When I started out, I liked polyphony. I loved the sound that came out of it, and I liked unaccompanied voices in polyphony. I liked the intellectual context of polyphony, if you like. I just wanted to do this, and I'm stubborn. I wasn't going to do anything else, and I had no idea whether it would succeed or not. For a long time, it didn't – a very long time.

JS: What did you do to make a living in the meantime?

PP: I taught at Oxford as a graduate student, and I taught at Trinity College of Music, and eventually at the Royal College of Music in London.

Vivien Pike

City of Sheffield Girls' Choir
Cantores Novaes

Education: Royal Manchester/Royal Northern School of Music

Interview: July 12, 1999, near the Hilton Hotel, Rotterdam, the Netherlands

Vivien Pike began her education in Medical Sciences at Sheffield University and later undertook musical studies at the Royal Manchester/Royal Northern College of Music in singing, violin, and piano. In addition to her responsibilities with the City of Sheffield Girls' Choir, Cantores Novae, and as a voice teacher, Pike has remained active as a soloist, clinician, and adjudicator. Ms. Pike now devotes her full energies to Cantores Novae.

The City of Sheffield Girls' Choir was founded by Vivien Pike in 1979. Only five years later the Choir won the Sainsbury's "Youth Choir of the Year Award." Since then the Choir has won prizes at festivals in Vienna, Riva del Garda, Gorizia, Llangollen, Sligo and the Melbourne International Choral Festival.

Cantores Novae was formed in 1992 and consists of members of the Sheffield Girls' Choir, and former members. Since its founding, Cantores Novae has won prizes at Riva del Garda, Llangollen, and at the Sainsbury's "Choir of the Year" Competition.

Website: none

Vivien Pike

Vivien Pike
City of Sheffield Girls' Choir
Cantores Novae

JS: Please tell me about the choirs you work with in Sheffield.

VP: I started twenty years ago in Sheffield as what we call a peripatetic singing teacher within the Sheffield Education Authority. That means I went around to schools teaching teenagers how to sing. And I decided twenty years ago that these people ought to have a choral opportunity as well as a solo singing opportunity; therefore, I formed a choir for my students to belong to.

JS: Were there no choirs in the schools for them to belong to?

VP: There were some choirs in some schools but not in every school. The teenagers whom I taught felt that the vocal standard of the choirs in the schools were not what they wanted; they wanted something a little bit more advanced and developed. That's really the reason why I formed a city-wide choir. We started with twenty-one students and within a year it became forty-one students, and within two years we were up to fifty. I had to put a limit on the number of members because, when we tour, the busses in England have fifty-three seats. So if there's space for me, the accompanist and a parent, then there is only room for fifty girls.

I work in five-year plans, so within five years I wanted to have the best upper-voice choir that I could in the whole of England. We started in 1979, and by 1984 we had won the Sainsbury's Youth Choir of the Year Prize. That's the best we could be in the British Isles. After that there were hordes and hordes of people wanting to join the choir, and it wasn't possible to have them all in, so we had to form a junior choir as a training ensemble for the girls. So we had a junior choir of mixed boys and girls for about two years. It grew until we had sixty or seventy, and then we split them into a junior girls' and a junior boys' choir. Within six years of the inaugural choir we formed, we had three choirs, and we still had pressure for places in the top choir. Some of the girls who wanted to get into the top choir were not quite advanced enough for the material I wanted to work with, so we formed an intermediate choir as well, which was also for boys and girls. This, then, involved four choirs with one hundred sixty to one hundred seventy children.

The majority of girls in the Girls' Choir at that time were having singing lessons in school with me. But those were group lessons in twos and threes because there was so much pressure with time.

JS: Does the school pay for those lessons?

VP: The Authority provided the lessons until I was made redundant in 1994. I was made peripatetic because the Education Authority could no longer afford the cost of the teachers. I continued to go into the schools on a private basis, and from 1994 onwards, parents had to pay for singing lessons and instrumental lessons, too. I now go into three schools: one private school and two big state schools.

JS: What is the range of ages in these choirs?

VP: We start the junior level at age seven, and they stay there until about eleven or twelve. They can audition for the intermediate choir from about the age of ten. The junior choir is a non-auditioned choir where we do some voice training, some sight-reading training and training of repertoire.

JS: How do you handle auditions?

VP: They sing a piece that they know. Hopefully, they will show me, if they're not too nervous, what their voices will do, especially if I don't teach them singing. I look for some evidence that resonant tone quality is developing. If they don't have lessons with me, I look for some evidence that they are breathing properly or supporting the sound. I ask that they should be able to read a simple piece of sight-reading. That piece of sight-reading might be about eight bars long and it might modulate, and it won't be just crochets and minims, but it's not difficult.

JS: Presumably they have learned to read in the intermediate choir?

VP: Yes. And they will have learned some of it in a school, because some of them come from schools where they do a reasonable repertoire. Also, I look for a quickish ear so that I know that they are not going to be struggling for weeks on end with difficult repertoire; that, in the end, they can cope with anything I might give them to do.

The audition for the intermediate choir is very straightforward. It's a very easy audition. We try to put them at their ease and just have them sing a piece. We try to hear the range of the voices, where they are at that time because, of course, the teenage voice can change quite considerably. The boys go through the change while they're in the intermediate choir. So the intermediate choir has students who are ten at the youngest (though it will have to be a quite exceptional ten-year-old because there are social skills involved) up to about the age of sixteen.

Girls can audition for the girls' choir from about the age of twelve. For that group, I am looking for developing voices, not developed voices; good, but not exceptional, aural skills and some sight-reading. I will accept a less mature voice from a good sight-reader or a mature voice from an average sight-reader because there is only one way to learn sight-reading, and that is to give them music and let them do it. In the Girls' Choir I do quite demanding repertoire from Elizabethan pieces to works we commission.

JS: How much do you work with older boys?

We have tried to have a youth choir for the boys but we haven't really succeeded yet, and we don't really know the reasons why, but it hasn't. We do help the boys a lot, but we now suggest that when their voices change that they go back to school and sing with the school choir because the schools need them. So we do voice training until the voice changes, and then they go and sing in the barber shop choirs and gospel choirs in the schools, along with the ordinary school choirs. They don't stop singing, generally.

JS: Do the children have to pay to sing in your choirs?

VP: Yes, they do. In the early days they didn't have to, but they had to pay since about 1991 because the Authority had its funds reduced by the government. Therefore, music and art programs suffered badly.

JS: This will be a surprise to many, since England seems to be a kind of choral "Shangri-La."

VP: It is in the church and cathedral school systems, but in the state-school systems it is not "Shangri-La." There are many schools in England, particularly at the primary level, where there is nobody on the staff who reads music or has any musical skills whatsoever. So although it is part of our national curriculum to teach the children music, there are schools in England where there is no one qualified to do so. Those primary teachers have to go on special courses to try to learn some music skills, and there are now some choral amateurs and district class music specialists.

JS: Is it working?

VP: Sort of. There is a lot of enthusiasm, and there are courses they can take. The days of the music specialist in the primary schools are long gone.

JS: Please summarize the choirs you are working with.

VP: The top choir is quite selective, girls only, aged between twelve and nineteen. They have developing voices. Quite a lot of them have singing lessons with me, but not all. The singing lessons are mainly in groups of two with some having individual lessons.

The next choir level is the intermediate choir, which consists of about sixty boys and girls. Some of those children have singing lessons in school. We now have another teacher working with the children in the schools, and he is actually going to take the intermediate choir this fall (1999). The number taking lessons, however, is small. They are right at the very beginning of their technical learning.

The junior choir is seventy-strong, aged between seven and twelve, and I don't think any of them have singing lessons. All of the training has to be done in the choir practice.

Another thing I do is teach teachers in vocal skills. I've been doing that for a long time. At one time it was provided for them, and they used to come in droves but there isn't money for that any more. But I still have several teachers I will give singing lessons to so that they can pass that skill on to their students.

JS: Is the practice of making a choir out of your voice studio – as you and Pamela Cook have done – common practice in England?

VP: No, it is not extensive at all. Besides Pam, I can think of only one other person who has gone down that road, in the whole of the country. There may be others which I don't know about, of course.

JS: Who is that person?

VP: Jean Stanley Jones in Wales, although she has changed direction now.

JS: There seems to be a trend among the cathedral-school choirs and universities to offer lessons to the singers.

VP: Most of the cathedral choir schools have singing tutors, as the choristers need to use their voices well, particularly as there is so much singing to do. Without technical expertise, the voices would not be strong enough to cope with all the demands of the services.

JS: Do Education Authorities generally provide singing tuition as part of their peripatetic music services?

VP: It's fairly new. When I started to teach singing in schools in 1971, I was perhaps one of only two in the whole country. It's gradually growing, and it's been a very slow process. Now that the authorities don't run the peripatetic services in the same way that they used to; they have much more flexibility. Now that the parents pay for the lessons, the authorities can afford to go down different roads. More and more, there is some sort of voice work going on in the schools.

JS: Is it too much to say that, given your and Pamela Cook's successes with your girls' choirs (in, for example, the Sainsbury Competition), that you have had an influence in starting this trend?

VP: Well, I wouldn't like to say it as strongly as that, but I think there must be some influence there, yes. I think it's rather in the back of people's minds rather than in the front. So I think it's more of a kind of drip effect. There may be the attitude that, "If some people can do it, why can't we?" It's more like that, rather than actively going out and saying, "They are doing it; we must do it." Gillian Dibden in Berkshire is doing a lot of good work with choirs now, and ten years ago Berkshire didn't have that.

JS: How much do you rehearse with your choirs?

VP: We rehearse for maybe thirty-five weeks of the year. The juniors have an hour, the intermediate choir has an hour and a quarter and the girls' choir has an hour and a half each week. It is a struggle to get all of our concert program in within that time.

JS: In that time, how many concert programs do you learn?

VP: The juniors will have one or two every term, so that's six or seven a year. The intermediates will have maybe two or three, so that's nine or ten every year, and the Girls' Choir will have three or four every term and maybe ten or twelve concerts a year. At Christmas and in the summer, we have festivals where we put all of the choirs together.

JS: How are all of the expenses associated with the choirs, including your salary, met? Does the tuition that they pay to belong cover everything?

VP: A big N-O! In Sheffield, children who are in the choirs pay an annual fee to the Education Authority which administrates the choirs. After that annual fee, the conductors are paid a very poor hourly rate to run their choirs. We are paid for our rehearsal time only. It does not pay us for our preparation time; it does not pay for our concerts; it does not pay us anything toward the rehearsal venue where we rehearse (and that costs about 1,600 pounds per year). It does not pay for any music; it does not pay for what we wear, and choirs of our standards have to have uniforms. It does not pay for trips to festivals or concerts outside Sheffield, and yet they are very happy to accept the fact that we represent the city in various parts of the world.

JS: So where does the money come from?

VP: We have to raise it. All of the choirs together have a parents' committee that has charitable status and is a limited company. In the United States it would be incorporated. The parents work quite hard to raise money, and the choirs themselves keep all of the concert receipts. The Girls' Choir is able to charge a fee for their appearances, but we feel that the other choirs are not able to do that, except on a very limited basis. We have jumble sales where we hire a church hall where we all bring our unwanted goods and sell them. We have coffee mornings; we have cake stalls; you name it. It's an ongoing thing; and it's extremely hard work. Both parents in many families go out to work, and we're finding that parents do not have the time to support us the way that they want to or that we would like them to. I have to admit that we are struggling. It's so everywhere.

JS: Please describe your typical ninety-minute rehearsal with the Girls' Choir; do you use warm-ups, for example?

VP: I don't do a huge amount of warm-ups with them because lots of them have the technical expertise from their weekly lessons which last only twenty minutes. When they come to choir, they already know something about technique. So I don't do an extensive warm-up. I combine a physical and vocal warm-up for about ten to fifteen minutes. I will take technical difficulties out of the music and create a warm-up that will help. The warm-up, then, is not the same as you call it.

JS: How many voice teachers are working now?

VP: Two. Another gentleman and I. He doesn't teach any of the girls in the Girls' Choir. I teach about thirty-two of the thirty-nine girls.

JS: How do you get the girls to learn so much music in so little rehearsal time?

VP: Well, the fact that they sight-read reasonably does help. Yet, I do try to push music into them at quite a rapid rate because I feel that I am there to educate them about music that is available for them to sing. Very often we don't manage to learn things by heart. It's important to learn things really well, but I don't think by memory is essential, especially for the difficult, more modern pieces we sing. We just batter away. I do ask them to work at home; some of them do and some of them don't. We have to teach commitment these days, I think. We have to make people feel as though they must give of themselves because they are letting the others down if they don't. I tell them they're not in this choir only to enjoy themselves; they've come to make music and make it properly. They need to have a real commitment to the choir to keep the standard high.

JS: What do you do to develop intonation?

VP: Intonation, in my opinion, is dependent purely on technique. If the intonation is incorrect, it is not usually because of the ear. It is usually because they are not supporting properly or not placing the voice properly. So we have to work at getting the voice placed and supported properly. I do quite a lot of work on that.

We encourage each singer to think about what they are doing with the body and the muscles. For instance, when we start in September with a lot of new people, they quickly learn that if they are caught singing with crossed legs, they may be fined fifty pence. By Christmas, we have nobody singing with crossed legs. We try to make it fun, but it does impress on them that they must not sing with crossed legs. The placing of sound, I think, is terribly important.

JS: How do you approach blend?

VP: As far as blend goes, because the majority of the girls have lessons with me, they make the same type of sound. They don't make the same sound, but it makes blend easier because they understand how to place the sound well.

Also, I will move girls about in the choir. For instance, I do not put girls with big voices next to girls with small voices because that can be intimidating. Within each row of the choir I try to position the singers so that the voices are in a peak with the big voice in the center.

JS: How do you view vibrato?

VP: In my opinion, if the voice is placed correctly it vibrates freely. Vibrato is something one has to be careful with, particularly in the young years that we're working. If we allow the voice to vibrate too much, too early, it becomes a wobble, but all voices should vibrate.

Young singers will tend to imitate what their teacher demonstrates for them. I myself have a voice that has not got a big vibrato. If you are an operatic sort of singer and you have a voice with a big vibrato, you will get young singers copying this, and they will sound perhaps a little uncontrolled at an early age because they think that's the way you have to sing.

So I think a voice should vibrate naturally with good placing.. It should not have a created vibrato. "Vibrato" is a word that I used with great caution. I will approach the sound that I want from a different angle. Rather than say that I want vibrato, I will say, "That sound is white and cold. I want you to warm that sound. I want you to support that sound; I want you to position it better and let it vibrate." They know what I mean.

We need to be able to vibrate more, perhaps, for the Romantic period than we do for the Elizabethan period. So I encourage them to make a warmer sound when we're singing Mendelssohn, for instance, than when we're singing madrigals. The overall effect is that the vibrato is slightly greater for Brahms and Mendelssohn than it will be for Weelkes and Gibbons. I am very cautious, indeed, of "developing" vibrato below the age of twenty.

JS: How do you develop ensemble with your girls?

VP: We work at it. Sometimes I will mix the singers up to let them hear what the other parts are doing. Sometimes I will make all three parts able to sing each other's lines so that they understand the structure of the piece we're singing; therefore, they can think about the ensemble, think about how the phrasing should be in each part, etc.

JS: Who or what have been the most formative influences on you?

VP: That's very difficult. I have always been very interested in what goes on at the level at which I am working. I will quite often go to an international festival so that I hear what is going on – what I detect is good practice. And I might go and talk to those people whom I think to have good practice.

But I expect the only real influence is my own wish to achieve the best I can from the singers that I have to work with. I don't try to copy anybody, and I don't try to create what is impossible to create. I don't strive beyond the ability of the group I have. The level of the group changes from year to year so it's important not to try to achieve something you did five years ago if the level of students is different.

JS: How would a listener be able to distinguish the sound of your choir from others?

VP: Well, people say I have a "Pike sound," but I've never thought of it that way. Hopefully it will be a focused, bright, vibrant sound. I hope it is as good a sound as we can get for the age at which we're working and for the time we have available.

JS: Is there anything you would like to add?

VP: I really do wish that we had more moral and financial support from the educational institutions because singing for young people is very, very important. It teaches them so much else: posture, good breathing, social skills, the group dynamics we talk about in sport. I just wish that we could make more impact with the plusses we have teaching young people to sing chorally. It's a long, slow road.

The thing about choral singing and singing generally that you will not get from the instrumental side is that, in many parts of the world, wherever they live there will not always be an orchestra they can belong to, but there may well be a choir. They are learning something for life.

nota bene: Since the interview, Vivien Pike has relinquished her post as Director of the Young Sheffield Choirs. She is now concentrating on her own Cantores Novae, which is privately organized and financed. The choir consists of girls from the age of fourteen, and includes some university students and ladies as members. This mix of youth and experience is continuing the previous success of the choir both in the UK and abroad, and they have completed a very successful tour of the Northwest United States and Canada.

Paul Spicer

Born: 1952

Finzi Singers
Birmingham Bach Choir

Education: New College, Oxford

Interview: January 18, 1999, Royal College of Music, London

Paul Spicer is perhaps best known through the many recordings he has made with the London-based Finzi Singers. His versatility, however, has kept him in demand on other fronts: Artistic Director of the Lichfield International Arts Festival and Abbotsholme Arts Society; recording producer; composer; and biographer of Herbert Howells, his composition teacher. Spicer is also the Director of the Chamber Choir at the Royal College of Music, where he serves as Professor of Choral Conducting.

Founded by Spicer in 1987, the Finzi Singers specialize in twentieth-century English choral repertory. Their size generally ranges between eighteen and twenty-four voices. The Finzis' extensive discography is heard on the Chandos label.

Website: www.finzi.org

Paul Spicer

Photo: Keith Saunders

Paul Spicer
The Finzi Singers

JS: How do you select singers for your groups?

PS: Of course, the approach varies from group to group. With the Finzi Singers, which is a professional choir, the emphasis is on reading ability. As you can appreciate, there is very little money around in the UK for funding professional groups or any other sort of group, for that matter. It's terribly important that people are not only able to sing nicely (in a sense one half takes that for granted with the kind of people that would apply for a group such as this), but it's terribly important that they read well because of the limited amount of rehearsal time we can afford to have, in relation to any given work. Every disc that we ever recorded has been rehearsed in two prior rehearsal sessions. That's the way things go in this country of ours. It is very sad, and it would be very nice, indeed, to have more time, but the important thing to me is that not one person there should waste anybody's time in terms of his or her ability to read. So all of that three-hour rehearsal session can be devoted to interpretation without having to sort out notes.

JS: What does your sight-reading test look like?

PS: It's a home-grown exercise which I have written, so it is definitely sight-reading. It is a single, unaccompanied line, and there are two tests. One is what I call a warm-up test, which is of medium difficulty; the other is a bastard! If anybody can get near getting through it and just keep going, then they're pretty damn hot.

JS: Is it more pitch- or rhythm-intensive?

PS: I don't bother terribly with rhythm. I find that if someone can pitch clearly with great clarity of ear, almost everybody else will fall into line.

Another aspect of the audition to consider is choosing a group of people who will work as a group. However large your pool may be, I suppose we've got about sixty singers on the list; and we always go to the "A group" first and work down it. The corporate personality is as important as the individual. For me personally, it is of vital importance as I believe that a group of people who get on well together makes infinitely better music. This may be a very obvious thing to say, but it needs saying. So often, professional work includes backbiting, infighting, jealousy and all the rest. I believe, however, that if everybody is pulling in the same direction then the chances are, with all those other things in place, you are going to get an absolutely fantastic result. On the whole, I think the chemistry-thing is something which comes across. Even on the recordings, it's often something which critics note.

JS: How might a critic describe this "chemistry-thing?"

PS: It's quite difficult to say. I think it has something to do with a kind of warmth of feeling. What is often said is that the Finzi Singers have a particular kind of approach to repertoire which seems to come from within and is not so much imposed from without; that must have a lot to do with the way people homogenize. Of course, I have to say what I want, as any director does, but on the whole I think that the way people interrelate can help.

JS: How large is the Finzi Singers?

PS: It varies between twelve and eighteen. I'm not so keen on twelve because that just leaves two altos and two tenors in the middle of the group because we do four-two-two-four. So if you try to do double-choir repertoire, it becomes a strain on those singing one-to-a-part. One of the things singers know is that if they're booked for a Finzi Singers concert, they're going to go away from a rehearsal absolutely exhausted, partly because of the kind of repertoire we do, but also because I work very intensely. There's a lot of raw emotion that goes into it. The repertoire we do is always a big sing, and it's tough on the voice.

JS: What do you mean by "big sing?"

PS: The repertoire we focus on, mainly, is twentieth-century British; that was always our brief, right from the start. We do other repertoire from the nineteenth century and a certain amount from earlier periods like Bach and Purcell. But on the whole, our focus and all of our recordings with Chandos is twentieth-century British. That's my area of speciality and the music I've always felt closest to. Even what might be regarded as the best-written of this repertoire is so tough, with long lines and high emotion, with a lot of full voice and imagery. It's tough and it's tiring.

JS: How would you describe the musical characteristics your groups demonstrate?

PS: The very first thing I start with is the words; I love literature and poetry. A lot of British composers were similarly very fired by fine poetry; some of them weren't but managed to make marvelous settings to second-rate texts, some of which Elgar did.

But first I try to get into that state of mind. Why was the composer fired to that poem? I look for colors in words, which can be brought out in any way, even before you get to a note of it. I'm also a composer, so there are ways I look at it from that standpoint and wonder how I would treat a word or whole text; then it is lovely to look at what the composer has done. I often say, "Wow, that was his solution!" So there's a good deal of word color but also an approach to singing a text, which gives the text room to speak. By that I mean, that the whole issue of breathing and lengths of phrases are intensely personal things which I believe color a performance as personally as any other choral trademarks that you may have. I like to give music lots of time to breathe. It's never "tick-tock" in any sense. So I think the approach to the text is one of the ways in which the way I interpret music might be different from others.

I spend a lot of time with scores trying to fit sense-to-color-to-mood, and all of the things that flow from that. Beyond these things, I like to focus on balance and texture. The Finzi Singers are a group which I encourage to sing in a rather full-blooded way: very opposite I would say, from a group like the Tallis Scholars.

JS: Speaking of early music, what is your approach to vibrato?

PS: Vibrato is a very thorny issue with British choirs. I almost encourage it, without going as far as, say the BBC Singers, which is a sound I dislike. For me, that sound is too ripe and mature, but they are a superlative choir on a technical level.

But there are two things about this that I feel strongly about in terms of sound quality. One, I don't like a male section which is overripe; and two, I like sopranos who are encouraged to give more of a chest register.

JS: By that do you mean non-"hooty?"

PS: Certainly not hooty, God forbid! There are, of course, moments in music when you want to be pure, but I believe that the purity of sound is better set up by allowing people to sing freely and by encouraging them to use their voices naturally. For professional singers, using vibrato is as natural as a violinist allowing the note to spin. I would always encourage that because I believe that singers who are not using vibrato are actually having to rein-in in some way. Therefore, it's always going to be a more controlled kind of sound. Now, when singing a huge, double-*forte* passage, you have to be very careful. But, on the whole, I audition that out so I won't be employing a singer who has an overripe vibrato in the first place.

JS: When you say "overripe," are you referring mainly to vibrato?

PS: Yes, but also a voice can have varying degrees of "plumpness." I like a clean, rich voice which has a natural vibrato which doesn't affect the pitch of a note but can help give added richness to it, as proper vibrato should do.

To go back to the string analogy, if you have a violinist playing a note without vibrato and then the vibrato is brought in, the additional color which that brings is just so beautiful that you can't imagine doing without it. To me, it's just the same in singing.

I think I'm right in saying (it's been said to me, anyway) that people enjoy coming to sing in the Finzi Singers because they are encouraged to sing in this way. Unlike some of the early-music choirs, they are encouraged to use their voices more fully, and they don't have to rein-in in the same way. It helps that the kind of music I in which we specialize needs this kind of fullness of sound.

JS: With this full-throated singing you encourage, is blend an issue you must deal with in rehearsals?

PS: Blend will always have to be dealt with in rehearsal.

JS: Do you mix people up into quartets or use other methods to ensure blend?

PS: I tend not to do that and that's probably a weakness in me. I've always tended to be slightly traditional, so I prefer people standing in parts. That is something, actually, I ought to try to do more because I think it can be hugely successful. Quite often, the reason I don't do it is because of the limitation of rehearsal time. I prefer to get people there, get on with it, and deal with the problems if they come along. But in terms of blend, I think that is a matter of ear and a question of description and of encouraging people to listen more – pointing out things in the score they can look for and listen for.

JS: How do you deal with intonation problems?

PS: I have some *bons mots* which I encourage people to think about. I use them often with the Birmingham Bach Choir because, as an amateur choir, they need it more. I often point out that where there are repeated notes, the emphasis should always be upwards. I find that, universally, a repeated note always tends to slide. I ask people to inflect pitch upwards, to physically feel a sharpness, and I find that, usually, this is a very successful way to get singers to fix problems. Another danger is coming back to a note having moved away from it. More often than not, it will return flat. Once this principle is in the ears, it tends to be sorted out. Also, with the Birmingham group, we practice chord spacings, listening for brightness of fifths and the quality of thirds. Quite often we practice chromatic scales, unaccompanied, which are both very difficult and very effective.

JS: What do you mean by "brightness" of fifths?

PS: All of these tunings are very personal. For example, with a chord of G major, for me the D will be very slightly high. Sometimes that seems to anchor a chord even more than the root, so for me, the fifth is the most essential note.

JS: And thirds?

PS: It's a quality thing. I once produced a CD for the choir I used to sing in as a boy at New College, Oxford. Edward Higginbottom is the director, and I found his approach to thirds terribly difficult as it was so different from my own. Everything in my ears was telling me it was out of tune. Edward was completely happy with it, so it is an incredibly personal thing. He works with different kinds of temperament, and his ears are tuned-in to certain qualities of interval.

JS: How do you make the singers aware of your personal system of tuning? Does it involve linear adjustments, note-to-note, or is it simply a vertical tuning adjustment?

PS: It's both, of course.

JS: Do your singers know, then, to sing from a C to an E, slightly sharp?

PS: On the whole that's right, and the same with fifths. I go spare with intonation; it's a very difficult subject, partly because it's personal and partly because there is a collective will with intonation. Once one part has begun to slide, there's little anybody can do about it.

JS: Yet great intonation seems to be a hallmark of English Choirs.

PS: Yes. I think part of that comes from the backgrounds of the directors and singers of the professional choirs, particularly the men. On the whole, the boys have an advantage over the girls here because of the cathedral experience – one we're still guarding quite jealously.

JS: I understand this tradition is changing.

PS: Well, it is. I'm not at all for it!

JS: Really?

PS: It's very dangerous for our tradition for all sorts of very good reasons. In these cathedral choirs with good directors in front of them (and they're not all good), the boy's ear has been trained very early to a very sophisticated level, indeed. And the young boy working in that situation is being treated like a professional; he is an adult before his years, and he's used to treating with adults and having no quarter given at all. All of that rubs off through the system, and that is what goes through the Oxford and Cambridge Colleges and feeds the professional choirs. The basis for these professional choirs is always the "Oxbridge" choral-scholar type.

JS: What about girls in the cathedral?

PS: My view – and it's held by quite a lot of others, too – is that it's better to have girls' choirs alongside boys' choirs rather than mixed together. This new tradition is okay as far as it goes. The inherent danger comes in because of the funding of our cathedrals, which are not state-funded. Everything they do, they have to raise the money for. Music is always the most expensive item, by far, in any cathedral's budget: organ maintenance, music, the boys' scholarships, the salaries of the organists and lay clerks, administrative staff, housing, and so on. They then put alongside that a girls' choir, and you add huge costs to an already expensive item if it is done properly and run on the same basis as the boys. The girls will need scholarships, music, someone to train and accompany them and so on. They then have to have their own services in the weekly round and so, already, the boys are getting less to do since the girls are taking some of that away.

Now, take the worst case scenario where you get a cathedral roof suddenly developing serious problems and four million pounds have to be raised at almost no notice. So as a Dean, what would you do, presented with this situation? We can't do without our music, so if we can't afford two choirs we'll amalgamate them. Straight-away, the girls come in with the boys; the boys don't like singing with girls at that age, and the boys start to fall off. More serious, almost, is the fact that then you get the boys not singing through their broken voices and then we don't get the continuity through to the back rows. If the new tradition can be made to work, I'm all for it.

Everybody thinks that the central issue is the politically correct one about the girls being given the opportunity like the boys to sing in our cathedrals. Believe me, I want the girls to sing; I want everybody to sing! That is not the issue. There is, however, something very special about boys singing treble. They have only that brief moment in their lives, which then goes. It is not the same for girls who can sing soprano or alto for the whole of their lives. There are all sorts of issues here that make it a lot cloudier than people would have you think it is. I genuinely believe that there is an element of danger in our current approach to the problem and wouldn't be surprised if in thirty to forty years' time if we do not actually have very, very severe difficulties in keeping up the choral tradition as we know it. It's a big issue for me and for some others, too.

JS: Is singing an important part of a student's education, outside of the cathedrals?

PS: We have a really serious problem in our schools: there is no class singing! All of that is gone. There are some notable exceptions where there is choral singing, but singing in class went out years ago. We don't have youngsters coming through who have sung as of right at school. You can see it even here at the Royal College of Music.

We have a large group called the RCM Chorus, which is compulsory for all first-year students. I was amazed to be told by a number of these people that they've never sung a note in their lives. These are budding professional musicians! This is so tragic. So there are lots of issues to deal with which need attention from government as well as at grass roots level.

JS: How would you describe the role of choral music in England?

PS: The choral tradition was the biggest thing in English culture in the nineteenth century and into the twentieth century. It has fallen away over the decades of this century. This ties into my point about singing in schools, or the lack of it. People now coming out of schools have no knowledge of, or interest in, singing. If they are interested in music through playing an instrument and are encouraged by someone else to have a go at singing, they might give it a go. But I tend to find that, with certain notable exceptions, the age of people coming into choral singing is older than it would have been some years ago. It is quite difficult to recruit young people. The Bach Choir in Birmingham has very strong connections with the University, and a lot of lecturers sing in the choir. This is useful as they can proselytize about it to their students, but they don't manage to persuade many to come. But don't let me give you a false impression! There is still an enormous amount of singing going on here. There are a lot of choirs and, on the whole, they are probably singing to a higher standard today than ever before. The greatest issue in this regard is the singing in schools.

JS: Who have been your professional models?

PS: The person who turned me on to the whole thing when I was a kid was my choral director, David Lumsden. He is now Sir David Lumsden. He was an organist at New College, Oxford, and until recently he was director at the Royal Academy of Music. After that, John Alldis was a great inspiration. His was the very first professional choir that I heard in my youth. I remember it was in Durham Castle, and I was bowled over. It was so polished, and there was such humanity in this sound. It was the most beautiful concert I had heard, and I was so excited by the whole experience.

The King's Singers influenced me because of their impeccable blend and tuning, and their sense of fun and warmth and, again, humanity. All of those things come across very strongly. The Swingle Singers (in an earlier incarnation) for their great sense of rhythm. The King's Singers and Swingle Singers are very complementary but actually are opposite sides of the same coin.

David Willcocks was a massive influence in this country, especially to my generation, particularly when he was working at King's. He's rather dated now in some ways, but he never loses his extraordinary magnetism. For instance, the kind of vowels the King's Choir used were so distorted in those days. But he was trailblazing in Britain at that time, as was George Guest. It's very interesting that they should be working so differently and so closely [Guest at St. John's, Cambridge, Willcocks at King's, Cambridge].

JS: What did you find inspirational?

PS: The whole experience, really. The raw emotional response to great choral music, sung very well in a great building. At John's they were doing all those wonderful Haydn Masses with orchestra, and the performances were just so vibrant. At King's they were doing all the great cathedral music and so much besides in that building which I have always thought of as the eighth wonder of the world!

Also, I think that I was rationalizing at that stage that they had approached problems to which they had found solutions, and that for one's self, the lesson was that there must always be ways to grow and develop. Having no formal conducting tuition as a choral specialist in those days, it was encouraging to feel that there was a way to get through that mist you have as a youngster to the clarity beyond.

JS: Whose work do you admire, today?

PS: Eric Ericson is someone whom I've admired for a very long time. He actually started a choral tradition. Virtually everything being done in Sweden today is the result of that one man. Interestingly, he started that choral tradition by being inspired by David Willcocks and Boris Ord at King's.

JS: Ericson was in Cambridge?

PS: Yes. He spent some time here and took it all back and developed his own way. What he has created is incredible. So Ericson is someone I really, really admire.

Another person in this country whose recordings I admire is Matthew Best and the Corydon Singers. He is a quite outstanding musician; very, very special. He brought his Corydon Singers to a festival I run and conducted a *Missa Solemnis* – a super concert. Then he turns up at the Three Choirs Festival in Gloucester some weeks later singing *Parsifal*. And Richard Hickox is quite remarkable, too.

A lot of my inspiration, however, actually comes from within the music I do. The kind of sound I look for is a mirror of what I envisage that music needing to sound like.

JS: Could you give an example?

PS: A piece which I feel very strongly about which hardly anybody knows is the *Sequence for St. Michael.* If you know the background to Howells' life, you will know that that particular piece is special in more than just musical terms. Howells had a son called Michael who died at the age of nine of polio. Howells was in mourning from 1935 to the end of his life because of this. This piece, written in the 1960's for St. John's, Cambridge, starts with three choral shouts of "Michael." If you know about the tragedy behind this work, the agony implied is intensified a million-fold. The inflection you can get in these opening cries is incredible.

JS: How do you rehearse your groups, especially the amateur choir?

PS: We always warm up, starting with a physical warm-up. We make sure there is enough elbow space to stretch. We start with hand-shaking and foot-shaking to get circulation moving. The vocal exercises I do almost always are related to what we are singing or to some aspect of vocal technique. An example would be to sing, say, sequential octaves moving by half steps because it gets people to thinking about how to approach the singing of an interval. Because we do a lot of Bach, we sing a wide variety of light, fast patterns – the types of sequences we'd find in the music.

Another thing is to work through the vowel plain, making sure of placement and clarity of vowels. These things are essential to choral blend. I've already mentioned the usefulness of chromatic scales.

With the amateur singers we do this for about five or six minutes. However, with the Finzi Singers, who are professional, I don't bother warming them up. They are supposed to come warmed up.

JS: Beyond the importance of text study in your score preparation, what else do you do?

PS: Yes, text first, but it depends on the score, very often. On the whole, I look for what the possible problems are going to be in terms of pitch or other difficulties and I prepare myself aurally for those spots. Also, something a lot of people tend to ignore are the small markings which the composers put in. These can be very confusing because a composer might write lines or accents or individual markings over notes on one part and not the other. You have to try to see your way through all of that. It's really trying to get under the skin and find the inspiration.

JS: How does scholarship inform your work?

PS: I don't do a lot of pre-Baroque repertoire. With Bach and Handel, I try to be more informed about it. With the twentieth century it is a difficult thing altogether anyway, and that's partly why I like doing twentieth-century music. Although these days, music is much more clearly annotated in terms of a composer's wishes, there is a greater flexibility that is implied because you can interpret around what you pretty well know the composer's intentions to be. With early music it's so much more conjecture.

JS: How do you select music for recording?

PS: On the whole, because our recordings have been rather successful, they allow a reasonably free hand in the choice of repertoire. I go about it through wanting to make more discoveries and to encourage people to listen more broadly to the music of composers who have a much larger compositional output than people know about it. We record single- or double-composer discs. This is a pragmatic requirement of the recording industry because with more than two composers on a disc, it can be difficult to sell.

JS: As someone who enjoys illuminating little-known works, what gems might you recommend?

PS: On my pet subject of Howells, we've mentioned the *Sequence of St. Michael*, but a piece which I adore is *The House of the Mind*, which is an extended anthem. The text is a religious-based poem by Joseph Beaumont. It is a sensationally beautiful work, very emotionally intense. Another piece is Finzi's *Lo, the Full Final Sacrifice*. The "Amen" of that piece you will take with you to your grave!

David Temple

Born: 1954

Crouch End Festival Singers
Cryes of London

Education: Southlands College of Education

Interview: January 18, 1999, Royal Festival Hall, London

David Temple does not fit any standard model of the professional conductor. Trained as a teacher, he had no musical experience at all until he was drafted (as an eighteen-year-old) by a friend into the London Philharmonic Choir. To this day, he is entirely self-taught as a musician. Temple co-founded the Crouch End Festival Singers in 1984 and has built them into a choir known for innovation, high performance standards, and unusual communicative power.

An amateur chorus of about one hundred-forty, the Crouch End Festival Singers specialize in imaginative programming and maintain a strong commitment to new music through frequent commissions. The Singers' programming often juxtaposes a standard choral/orchestral work with a new commission. The CEFS's recording, *Cinema Choral Classics II*, rose to number eleven on Billboard's "Crossover" charts.

Website: cefs.org.uk

David Temple

Photo: David Voce

David Temple
Crouch End Festival Singers

JS: Please tell me about your background.

DT: Let me begin by saying that I may disappoint you with some of my answers. I have no background whatsoever in music. I never studied music in school (wasn't interested in music) – came to it very late. When I came to London at the age of eighteen, I could not read music and went to a Methodist church and started singing in the choir. Someone in the choir said, "You're a tenor," and so they said, "Come along with me to the London Philharmonic Choir and have an audition. We sing with all of these famous conductors like Haitink and Solti and Giulini." I'd never heard of any of these people. So I went along and sang a song, and the conductor gave me some sight-reading. I didn't know what I was doing. But because I was eighteen years old and a tenor, he allowed me in, so I very quickly learned how to read music. The first time I ever heard a symphony orchestra, I was actually singing with Georg Solti in the Festival Hall in London performing Berlioz's *La Damnation de Faust*. Rather like St. Paul on the road to Damascus, I had a conversion to classical music which happened virtually overnight. I have never learned to play an instrument, but after a few years of singing, I decided I wanted to be a conductor. So I taught myself how to do it (I never had any lessons), and now I make my living at it. Even though I say I've never had any lessons, I was able to sing with people like Solti and Haitink and Giulini. They are the greatest teachers you could ever have. And in my own conducting, that is the standard I've always aspired to.

I think sometimes orchestras are quite rightly insulted by choral conductors because choral conductors tend to concentrate on the choir. They beat far too big most of the time, and they also sometimes think of the orchestra as a glorified piano accompaniment.

JS: Is the Crouch End Chorus your only choir?

DT: No, I have a Chamber Choir called "Cryes of London," named after the Orlando Gibbons' piece. It has between thirty and sixty singers. We've just been working in Lyons on *Porgy and Bess*.

JS: Are there professionals in the CEFC?

DT: There are none in the group, but occasionally we bring in some extra voices if I feel that the choir needs that extra bit of quality. For example, four or five years ago we had only sixteen to seventeen tenors in the choir and they just had to shout in order to be heard over the rest, so we needed some extras. About a year ago we decided that we were not prepared to put up with that anymore, so we had a big recruitment campaign. We now we have more and better tenors. Now we have twenty-six nicely blended tenors, and we don't have to have people screaming their heads off.

JS: How did you recruit these tenors?

DT: It's a bit like, if you're shopping and you see two greengrocers, one has a queue, the other doesn't. Which one do you go to? The one with the queue because you know you're going to get good value and good produce. So, if you have a choir with twenty-five tenors, it's no problem to make it to thirty. If you have a choir with five tenors, it's very hard to make it to six.

JS: How do you get to twenty-five in the first place?

DT: I think the answer is to put on works that other choirs do not. The good amateur tenor in London can pick and choose what he wants to sing. He can go from one choir to the other each night of the week, and if he doesn't want to do a piece, he doesn't do it. So, we attract tenors because of our repertoire. Once they're attached, they usually stay; but attracting them is the difficult part.

JS: How do you retain them?

DT: Well, it's partly to do with the quality of the group, and partly to do with the camaraderie and pride within the group. If you're good, you can choose to be with any choir you like. So, you tend to choose choirs where you enjoy your evening, where you can enjoy drinking together in the pub after rehearsal. We rehearse on Friday night, which is very unusual. It sometimes works against us because it's the end of the week. Many people are exhausted. There are some rehearsals which are an absolute disaster, especially if we're doing something really difficult and they don't like it. It's quite hard to get people warmed-up and motivated. But over the years, I've worked hard to try to compensate for that. If the rehearsal works really well, instead of being the end of one week, it's the beginning of the weekend. When we do rehearse on other nights of one week, which we occasionally do if we are very busy, everyone just goes straight home afterwards. A lot of church choirs meet on Friday night, but most of the choir are non-believers, despite our religious music.

JS: What do you like to focus on in rehearsal?

DT: The thing that means most to me about music is actually getting to the core of the meaning and the architecture of the music – getting that across to the choir, and the choir getting that across to the audience. It doesn't matter if the audience doesn't understand what is coming across, but they must understand that something is coming across, that there is an interpretation there. There may be choirs in this country that are better than my choir, but I don't know of any choir that communicates as well. If you hear us do a piece like *A Child of Our Time* and Verdi's *Requiem*, both of which have a drama to them, the intensity of the singers' communication with the audience is quite unique.

JS: How have you been able to persuade amateurs to sing so much contemporary music like Paul Patterson, Panufnik and some of the works you've commissioned?

DT: When we sang *The Plague* [Gerhard], quite a few singers dropped out, and we were left with about ninety-eight to 100 singers. They gave everything they had, and for those ninety-eight singers, it was one of the highlights of their musical lives. It created an even closer bond among those singers – we thought of having t-shirts made that said, "I survived *The Plague!*" So when we go back and do the Verdi *Requiem*, the singers who had dropped out return saying, "I heard *The Plague* was really good," and they actually regretted that they dropped out. So from then on I had this incredible sense of trust. For example, this Friday I can take a piece of music to rehearsal that nobody's ever heard of before, and they might hate it but they'll all be back the next week. That's the only way you can work; you have to have that trust. The other thing is that when you commission works, you never know what you're going to get. That's the biggest risk of all.

JS: How do you audition your singers?

DT: When we started, there were no auditions at all. After five years we had what we call "the voice test" which basically meant that if you could sing "Happy Birthday" you were in; if you couldn't you weren't. Two or three years later, we made it a bit more sophisticated but still no sight-singing. One of the reasons why I don't have sight-singing in my auditions is that I would never have got into a choir, originally, if I'd had to sight-read music. So I'm always looking for potential. I think the greatest way to teach people to read music is to give them confidence and an immense variety of music. Because I think that reading music is about recognizing patterns, the more patterns you give people the more they recognize them the next time they see them. It's a non-academic approach.

JS: How do you approach blend?

DT: One way is through the choice of singers. I'm not interested in anybody who thinks they are more important than the choir itself. So, in a way you actually create 150 soloists who then create a blend rather than create 150 automatons.

The one thing I find very interesting is, if you went to another planet, how would you actually describe what a choir sounds like? Does it sound like one person singing very loud, and should that be the aim? Should one be going for SATB sections that sing so well together that they actually sound like one person on a part; is that the desired outcome? I don't think it is. I think it should have some kind of organic quality to it that actually does make it sound like a lot of people, but within that you get the discipline of singing together. So, I'm very much against this totalitarian way of choral conducting used by a lot of my choral colleagues. I'm more in favor of appealing to the individual who wants to blend with the group – working as a team, not as regimented foot soldiers.

JS: These ideas seem opposite from the stereotypical view of English approaches to blend. Where does this aesthetic come from?

DT: I got it all from John Alldis, whom I believe is one of the founders of

contemporary choral singing as we know it today. I have a recording of the London Philharmonic Choir in 1967, just before John Alldis took over, and it sounds like something out of the 1920's and 30's. You listen to the LPC two or three years later and it sounds just like the choir does today: fresh, light, pliable, versatile – more colors. He used to talk about the two colors of choral singing: silver and velvet. Before John Alldis came along there was silver in the cathedrals and velvet in the rest of the choral tradition. What he managed to do was to employ both. It's much easier to get a silver choir to sing velvet than a velvet choir to sing silver, because the velvet choir's technique and mental approach is too rich to be able to lighten.

JS: Is intonation something on which you focus?

DT: I don't want to work with a choir where the intonation is not almost perfect because I would not know where to start correcting really bad intonation. I have had choirs where that has been the case, and I haven't been able to do anything about it. It's almost like it's a different language. The choirs I work with now have all of the tuning pegged, and it's just a matter of fine-tuning, like the e-string of a violin.

JS: How have you gotten them to the stage where they have good such intonation?

DT: Partly through the selection process. The first thing I do in the audition is to ask people to sing scales. Before they've got to the end of the first scale, I know if they can sing in tune, because you cannot sing a scale without thinking harmonically. So, immediately I've got people who are singing in tune.

JS: What is your approach to tone quality?

DT: I am not a guru in all things, and I'm not at all an expert on that, so I get others to work on things like tone production. There are some things I do well and other things I don't do well at all, and what I don't do well, I bring people in to help with. What I tend to do is demonstrate myself. Though I have had no formal vocal training, I have a reasonable voice. People manage to copy my example of what I want.

In a way, the main thing for the choir is to make sure they are confident with the notes. Once they are confident, you can then work on tone production and interpretation. Until you get to that stage, tone is a luxury you can't afford to spend time on. It's almost like worrying about the color of your car when there is no engine inside.

JS: You mention your weaknesses. What are some of your strengths?

DT: I think that I've got a good sense of rhythm and a good ear for intonation. Also, I'm able to make ordinary people do extraordinary things. If I had anything written on my tombstone, that's what I'd like. I also think that my rehearsals are pretty well organized; I don't waste people's time. I can't bear people being late for rehearsals, but I always finish on time. If you fed into a computer what I can't actually do, it would say, "This man shouldn't be a choral director." But I have always ridden over that; I've felt that what I can give choirs is greater than what I cannot give.

JS: What personal aesthetics are audible in your choir?

DT: Freshness in sound, enthusiasm, rhythmic vitality, and especially the communication of the inner music to the audience. You might not actually hear that but you might notice it being different compared to another choir.

JS: What do you mean by "freshness?"

DT: If you've done a piece ten times, it must sound like you've only just discovered it. A choir must feel that the audience has never heard the piece; that we, as the choir and the conductor, must sell this piece. We must give them an experience of the piece which gives it a good chance to survive in those people's heads.

The one thing I say to my choir is that there may be other choirs that have sung a given work better, but it might be that in a performance, that one bar, bar 104, may have never, ever, been done better than in our performance. That's worth doing. That's the wonderful thing about live music-making; you never know when that one bar may happen.

JS: How do you develop such large audiences?

DT: What we do with our audience in London is unique. The other choirs that are of similar quality work with the big London orchestras, and they don't have to do anything to get an audience. We actually work very hard to get our audience. If any of the other big London choirs actually put on their own concerts, they might get 300 to 500 people but we regularly get 1,500 people and more. And when we do our American concert on the fourth of July in the Barbican, we'll get 2,500 paying up to twenty-four pounds a seat. There is no paid administrator – everything is done voluntarily. We have about sixty to seventy in the choir who put in several hours per week on behalf of the choir, fulfilling various functions – librarian, staging, passing out leaflets and the like.

JS: If I were to hire you to build an audience for our next concert, what would you do?

DT: When you ask that, it's almost as if you expect that there is some secret formula. I don't think there is. That said, it's something we're always working on.

One thing we do is say to the choir, "There are 150 of you here and we've got to fill the concert hall. Some of you have lots of contacts, others fewer." We put a pyramid-shaped board up. Somebody sells forty, two sell twenty, ten sell fifteen, twenty sell ten, and everyone else sells five. At the end of the rehearsal we say, "Why don't you come up and check one of these boxes. Nobody is going to hold you to it – it's a commitment in your own head. If we get all of these boxes checked, we will have filled the Royal Festival Hall." I go first and tick forty.

I'm incredibly amateurish in my approach to my work. It really matters to me that there is an audience there, and I personally will phone around and mail out to all of my friends. I know of no other choir directors who will do this. I often refuse complementary tickets for myself because I just cannot bear not to pay for tickets which then go into my choir. It's an amateurish approach, and I feel very embarrassed about it, particularly if I speak to my esteemed colleagues who probably laugh up their sleeves at this.

JS: Amateurish in the truest sense of the word, it seems.

DT: Yes, but probably amateurish in its most demeaning sense to my colleagues. You see, if the singers see me putting my name for forty tickets, they may say, "If he can do forty I can do ten." So, in a way, if choral directors can get involved at the grass roots of their choirs, it makes a difference. For example, I put out the music stands and, after the end of the concert, the stands go back into my car and I take them home and keep them in my cupboard. Not because there are not plenty of people who would do this but because this is something I want to do. In some ways it drives me nuts, but in other ways it makes me realize that the nuts and bolts of the concerts are as much an issue to me as the music.

Another technique I use is to employ certain strategies to sell a particular work. I'll suggest we target our audience. I'll suggest to the person who designs the poster the ideas that I have about the piece which can then be worked into the imagery of the poster.

We try to get schools and colleges involved. I cannot bear walking out to conduct a concert and not see the place full. The other thing is to convince people that it doesn't matter how expensive their hi-fi system is, how sophisticated their CDs are, there is nothing in the world like live music-making! To hear the sound of a timpani being struck, live, in a concert hall, or the sound of a double bass being plucked, live, is something you can never, ever get with a hi-fi system. The hi-fi system, no matter how sophisticated, is the equivalent of showing someone a postcard of the Grand Canyon. What you really want to do is take them there. We try to promote live music. Another thing is to make sure that everyone in the town knows that the concert is happening.

JS: How do you do that?

DT: Sometimes we stand outside supermarkets or tube stations and give out leaflets for the concert. We get each singer to send a friendly letter to his and her friends. We give people discounts if they buy in bulk. I'll send a stamped, self-addressed envelope to my friends, and I encourage my singers to do the same.

What we don't do what we used to is to say, "If we don't sell out this concert, the choir will go under. If you don't sell tickets, we won't be able to do any interesting works next year." It doesn't work. It never works to do these sorts of things by coercion or fear or threats or sarcasm. It must always be positive, not in a sycophantic way, not in an insulting way, but appealing to the general side of people's humanity.

JS: How do you get the attendant expenses for such ambitious concerts?

DT: Members pay a subscription of just over 100 pounds per year.

JS: Really?

DT: Does that sound like a lot?

JS: For us, yes.

DT: Well, you ask, "How much do you spend each week on newspapers – six pounds each week?" You say, "Well, you get your choir for less than that. You get these wonderful concerts, rehearsals, you employ a chorus master and an accompanist. You get life-enhancing experiences. What do you do with your newspaper after you've read it? You throw it away. So, the chorus is a true investment. If you belong to the local golf club, if you belong to a health club, anything you belong to, you pay a subscription." No one ever questions it. So a lot of it has to do with getting past old attitudes. It's part of the re-education of singers and audiences.

Sometimes we put on fund-raising activities, the most popular of which is an auction-supper. People pay five to seven pounds to come along for the evening, and they have supper, which probably costs us around three pounds a head, and then we auction things we've got from local merchants. For example, we'll go to the local delicatessen and they'll give us cheeses and biscuits. We'll go to the local travel agent and it'll give us a weekend break somewhere; someone in the choir will have a cottage in the country and they'll say, "You can have our cottage for a week." You'll wind up with 100 to 200 lots. The bidding becomes silly and fun, and by the end of the evening we've made 6,000 to 7,000 pounds. You can't do it too often – every two to three years – but it's quite a good fund-raiser.

When you do commissions, you can apply to charitable trusts which will then pay for the music copying; everybody else will pay for the commissions, and in the end the commission hasn't cost you anything and you've got your own piece of music. Huge amounts of money come in on ticket sales. That's the biggest portion of revenue.

JS: What percentage of the operating costs for a concert comes from ticket sales?

DT: At the moment, about sixty-five percent. If you went to, say, the London Symphony Orchestra, they'd probably say they get about twenty-five percent or even less. In this concert we did this past weekend, we ended up with 3,500 pounds more than we budgeted for because of the great audience. That becomes a huge motivation to do even better on the next concert. It hasn't always been like this, but it has for the last two years. It's sort of like the thing with the tenors; the more successful you are, the more successful you become. When you are on the crest of the wave on your surfboard, you have to learn how to ride the wave. You don't take too many risks, but you don't stop taking risks.

JS: You mentioned John Alldis as an important influence. Who are some others?

DT: Haitink, Karl Richter, Tennstedt: these are people whom I perceive as having incredible charisma and character, with no ego. There are other conductors I sang with whom I admired, but they had no sense of warmth. They are fine musicians, very clear with their ideas, but they would not get the same results Haitink got. Haitink was so gentle. The greatest thing I remember about him was just seeing the love of music on his face. It was something he never talked about or communicated verbally; he just had it on his face. That's what makes you love the person and want to give everything you've got. The conductors who pound it into you, you'll give it because you respect them, but it doesn't come out of you naturally.

There's also a question of taste. I think, ultimately, you have to respect somebody's sense of taste. As you know, a conductor has to make decisions all of the time – dynamics, tempi, color, interpretation – and conductors very rarely admire other conductors because others are doing it differently. They make different decisions. So, I suppose the ones you admire are the ones whom you feel have similar tastes.

I also admire Colin Davis. He's more concerned with the architecture of a piece than the minutiae. That's what I admire about older conductors; they seem to be able to take several paces back and see a piece as a whole. I think that younger conductors are so determined, especially in the CD age, that everything has to be absolutely right. Of course things do have to be right, but not at the expense of the span.

JS: You've mentioned many orchestral conductors. Any choral directors whose work you admire?

DT: Not really. I think part of my problem is that John Alldis was so fundamental in the formation of my aesthetic that I always find something missing in the work of other choral directors. I know they have the technique and the musicianship and the knowledge, but...I just sort of latched on to one guy.

JS: Your story reminds me of someone like Charles Ives, in that you come at music from a completely different direction than most.

DT: I suppose. Funny you should mention Ives because if any piece of music encapsulates what I love about music, it's *The Unanswered Question*. It's this wonderful juxtaposition of nature and rebellion. That's why I love the *Glagolitic Mass* and the *Missa Solemnis*; most of the pieces I like are slightly crazy. I think the Mozart *Mass in C Minor* is slightly crazy while his *Requiem* is slightly more cozy.

JS: Given the scope of the repertory you have done, you seem to have an unusually ambitious group, especially for amateurs.

DT: One of the things I haven't explained is that at some point I actually left the London Philharmonic Choir and started the Crouch End Festival Chorus. One of the reasons I stopped singing with the London Philharmonic Choir is because the repertoire was beginning to go round in circles. It was all great music. I still adore the *Choral Symphony*, I still adore the Mahler *Second Symphony*, and I still adore *Messiah*, but I like to revisit them, having gone off to exotic places.

I think that when we do strange, unusual and ambitious works it's like we've gone off around the world with our backpack and we don't know whether we're going to get there or not, whether we're going to get mugged, and we love it. But when we've done it, we desperately want to come home, sit in front of the log fire and sing Verdi's *Requiem*. So, it's the journeys and the coming home. We don't want to stay at home all of the time, but we don't want to be on the hoof all of the time.

I think the repertoire we do is quite unique. If you're going to have a choir, you want it to be different from everybody else; otherwise, why bother?

JS: So much of your repertory is quite difficult. Describe the rehearsals from the distribution of scores to dress rehearsal of, say, a new commission.

DT: The first thing is that I have a wonderful accompanist. That's really important; you cannot function as a choral conductor without a fantastic accompanist. The accompanist has to be note-perfect at the first rehearsal because that is the basis on which everything else is built. So, tomorrow, I will spend the whole morning with the accompanist on the *Missa Solemnis*, a piece we are starting this weekend. Then at the first rehearsal, the accompanist and conductor are one. There's none of this business of, "I thought you were in two there..." or "You're not quite with me." The next thing is that my singers are incredibly proud of their sight-singing. They love it and view it as a personal challenge, so there is no fear whatsoever. With a new commission, we just start and have a go through it. If it falls apart, we all fall apart, laughing. The important thing in a rehearsal is to make everyone feel involved all the time so that, if you are rehearsing one section alone, what you are saying to that section has to be interesting enough that the other sections want to listen. I try not to do too much of individual lines but would rather slug through the whole thing, say, two voices forte and two voices pianissimo, and then swap it over. Then do the polishing later.

If the piece we are working on lasts forty minutes, and it's hard, I will want to have rehearsed the whole piece within the first three rehearsals. If we have not got to the end of the piece by the end of the third rehearsal, then we are going to be in trouble. I pace it all so that we rehearse it all in three rehearsals, and then I rehearse it all again in three rehearsals and then all again in two rehearsals and then all in one rehearsal, and by then we are getting close to the concert. Sometimes you have to leave alone something that is not quite right in order to make sure you are covering everything.

JS: How long are your rehearsals and how many do you need for a typical ninety-minute concert?

DT: Rehearsals are from 7:30 to 10:00 with a fifteen-minute break. For this last concert (Janacek *Glagolitic* and Poulenc *Gloria*) we had quite a generous amount of rehearsal time, for us. For *Missa Solemnis* we will have six. It's always hard to gauge how many rehearsals you will need for a piece. What I tend to do now is figure the number of rehearsals I will need and add two because you never get everyone at every rehearsal.

In this country, if you don't have kids, then you are encouraged by the system to take your holiday in the non-school holiday time. So from May to the end of October, I've always got people away on holiday. It's a real pain.

JS: Do you rehearse year-round?

DT: We have a six-week break in the summer, from about mid-July to the first of September. We hope to avoid that break in the future by getting involved in the BBC Proms. What will happen is that after about three weeks, some people will start to panic and say, "Oh, I don't think I will be ready." So somebody in the tenors will pull all of the tenors together and say, "Right; we'll meet at so and so's house on Tuesday night and we'll spend the whole night working on the tenor part." The altos will do the same, etc. Sometimes it happens naturally, and other times I will say to a section in the rehearsal, "It's not very good. I hope you will cover this section in your private rehearsal. Hint!" We also use voice tapes, which are quite common now. They're very useful, but of course, they don't exist for a commission.

JS: Describe your typical rehearsal. For example, do you employ warm-ups?

DT: As a singer I was brought up by John Alldis, whose warm-up might be simply to sing through a five to ten-minute section of the work. The purposes for this would be to warm up the voice, to warm up the head, and finally you would have already sung through a section of the work. If I were totally auto-cratic, which I am not, that would be my method. But my singers say, "We want to be warmed up." So, I reluctantly agree to it, not because I think we shouldn't but because I would rather get straight into the music. We do have a few vocal warm-ups, then. Generally, I pick a really beautiful tune like "Londonderry Air" because a lot of the music we do, we tend not to sing a melody. So it's nice to sing through a folk song or a Christmas carol. The accompanist then does a few vocal exercises and tongue twisters, but I have to say that I loathe these exercises. It's one of my failings, but I do it because the singers want it.

Geoffrey Webber

Born: 1959

Choir of Gonville and Caius College, Cambridge

Education: New College, Oxford
            Magdalen College, Oxford

Interview: January 21, 1999, Gonville and Caius College, Cambridge

Webber came to Gonville and Caius in 1982, after receiving the Doctorate of Philosophy in at Oxford University. Under his direction, the profile of the choir has steadily risen through international tours and well-received recordings of neglected repertory, including works by Janácek, Puccini, and William Child. Webber also remains active as a scholar and editor, and is the author of *North German Church Music in the Age of Buxtehude.*

The College of Gonville and Caius (pronounced "keys"), founded in 1348, is one of Cambridge University's oldest. The Choir consists of undergraduate men and women and sings regular Chapel services during the university term, and is heard regularly singing Choral Evensong on BBC Radio 3. The Choir is widely-traveled with appearances at the European Symposium on Choral Music in Ljubljana, and performing as an opera chorus in Mozart's *Idomeneo* with Opera Northern Ireland. It has also sung Handel's *Solomon* under the direction of Nicholas McGegan in San Francisco.

Website: www.cai.cam.ac.uk/music/choir.html

Geoffrey Webber

Photo: Gerald Place

Geoffrey Webber
The Choir of Gonville and Caius College
Cambridge University

JS: How large is the choir at Gonville and Caius?

GW: Twenty-one.

JS: How does that break down per part?

GW: Seven sopranos, five altos, four tenors, and five basses.

JS: Do you audition your singers the usual way, or do you have any things peculiar to your own process?

GW: There's a centrally organized competition for choral awards because when someone applies to Cambridge, they can apply to the various colleges that offer choral awards. There's a formal audition that takes place in the Music School where everyone does the same thing: that's the prepared piece, sight-reading, and ear tests. I also hear the applicants to Caius separately, when I give them more time and some different sight-reading. In the formal competition the sight-reading is normally a sixteenth-century motet, but I will give them something modern, which I would not expect them to get right, necessarily, just to see how they get on it.

JS: Like what?

GW: Oh, any piece they are not likely to get right on the first go – just to see how they cope.

JS: When students apply to Cambridge, is it up to the University or to the college to accept them? Could King's, Trinity, Gonville and Caius all accept the same student?

GW: No, because the candidates place the colleges in a particular order of preference. The Colleges admit the students, not the University. That's the strange way in which Cambridge works, but it allows each College to develop its own identity and is fundamental to the choral scene.

JS: How is it then that they audition at the University level?

GW: We hold the Choral Awards competition in September, and candidates apply by putting their list of preferences of colleges down on their application form. Then they can be accepted or rejected by any college on that list, in order. If they are accepted by their first-choice college, then they come back in December and have an academic interview (although applicants for King's and St John's are also interviewed academically in September). If they get an academic place then their choral award is confirmed with that. If the first-choice college does not want to offer a choral award to someone, but another college does, further down their list, then when the person comes back in December they have two interviews. They have an interview with the first-choice college, but they also have an academic interview with the other college that wants to make them an offer of a choral award, and if they get an academic offer from that college then they will go there. If they don't get an academic offer from that college, then they are still treated as an academic candidate for their first-choice college. So, they could end up coming to their first-choice college without a choral award, but with an academic place.

JS: Are the various colleges in competition with each other?

GW: Oh, certainly. But the system does work reasonably well and is there to insure that good people should get a choral award somewhere.

JS: So, it's not really like a bidding war?

GW: No, it's the candidates who express their preferences. We have to follow whatever they say. Sometimes there are well-informed candidates who select a sensible order of Colleges. Sometimes they are not terribly well informed and we just have to deal with that.

JS: Might they change their mind?

GW: Not once they commit themselves on paper; that is, once they put in an application form, that's it. But we have an Open Day every year in May, which attracts a large number of people and that's an opportunity for prospective candidates to find out about colleges and make a sensible decision about which colleges to apply to.

JS: If I were to hear, blindly, five different English university choirs, how would I know I was hearing your choir? That is, what values do you bring to choral sound and performance that are uniquely yours?

GW: Well, I suppose I would make musical expression and communication of the emotion and intent of the music the number-one priority. In other words, my approach is not quite so much that it be necessarily perfectly together or perfectly in tune if that means sacrificing getting across the music. I see the music as the priority and expression as being very important. English choirs are sometimes criticized as sounding rather cold, and I try to get something that is expressive and communicative, rather than simply technically excellent. Now, obviously, one tries to achieve as high a technical result as possible.

JS: And how do you accomplish that? I know it varies from piece to piece, composer to composer, style, etc. If I were to come sing in your choir, what things might I experience toward that end?

GW: I put a lot of stock by the individual vocal training of singers. All the members of the choir here have regular singing lessons which are free of charge to them, and I try not to do too much in choir that would contradict that. I don't want a situation where their singing teachers tell them to sing one way and then when they come to choir they have to sing in another way to suit the choir. It's always a difficult balance to get right. Sometimes there are things that are irreconcilable, but I would not want them to feel cramped, vocally, singing in the choir.

JS: Have you picked the voice teachers?

GW: Yes, certainly, we have an established system here where the College selects three singing teachers who teach everyone in the choir.

JS: As far as possible, you let the individuality of the singer and their training speak. What are some other ways that you encourage this expression, or teach it?

GW: Well, I think it is very important for everyone to understand as far as possible how the music fits together – what makes a piece tick. They've got to understand what the composer is trying to get at and respond to that. So, I do spend quite a lot of time trying to explain why I think a piece is as it is. And what matters, for example, in the performance of different repertoires – the different emphases you get in different traditions.

JS: Can you give an example of how you might do that?

GW: In performing early music it is important to treat with extreme caution the work of nineteenth- and twentieth-century editors, and to try to seek out the expression inherent in the music itself. To be specific, the way in which dynamic markings are added in many widely-used editions of renaissance masterpieces seems to me to be almost entirely misguided.

JS: How do you approach blend, or do you?

GW: Here we sing in a small chapel with a dry acoustic, and so we stand in alternating parts so that the back row is TBTB and the front is SASAS. And that, I think, helps the blend a lot, but I don't have any particular approach to blend. I think balance is as important as blend, but it depends on the singers. I think that with young voices, as long as you don't have any one voice protruding with a very different quality, you shouldn't have much of a problem.

JS: Do you have any particular methods towards improving, sustaining or developing intonation?

GW: Well, in difficult music we do quite a lot of rehearsing in different ways to aid with that. Sometimes it's good to rehearse if one has the time, individually, to have vertical sectionals, as I call them; to have one of each voice, so they are really on the spot, and to discover exactly what each individual is doing. Also, I try to get them to concentrate on just intonation by taking away the dynamic, taking away the words, just focusing on that. But it all depends on the particular demands of the piece.

JS: What about tone quality? Is it too much to say that you are willing to accept the tone quality that they are developing in the voice studio, or do you have a particular aesthetic that you are going for in the sound?

GW: No, as I say, I am more keen for the individuals to be developing their voices with their singing teacher as seems right to them. There's some talk about whether the top line, when you have female sopranos, should sound boyish or sound like women. My preference would be for the latter. On the other hand, the women are aged eighteen when they come here and have hugely different backgrounds in their musical training. Some of them have very straight, boy-like voices, and some have more mature voices with some vibrato. I like to take both. I quite like the mix in the choir, partly because different sounds fit different repertoires, and there is a greater variety of solo voices available.

222

Providing the difference between the two isn't that great; they can actually mix together quite well and get a good sound.

JS: Who or what have been your most important musical influences?

GW: Well, I have always been a great admirer of the technical excellence of English choirs as epitomized by King's under Willcocks, certainly, though I was always rather more emotionally touched by the sound of St. John's under George Guest, and I preferred the richer sound of this choir's style in which expression seemed to me to be paramount. So in Cambridge, certainly St. John's College. In Oxford, where I was an organ scholar at New College and then Assisting Organist at Magdalen College, Edward Higginbottom's approach at New College was highly influential, particularly in the area of understanding early music. But as in Cambridge there was also very evident in Oxford at that time the contrast between priorities of expression and technical perfection. Obtaining a balance between the two is the difficult task any choir faces.

JS: And that is what you strive for?

GW: Yes.

JS: Is there an English choral style?

GW: Well, yes. If you listen to an English choir, a German choir, and a French choir, you'll be able to identify them instantly. That's always been the case. As for what sound is currently dominant in English choirs at the moment, it's very hard to tell. The thing that has changed is the arrival of many professional choirs. Twenty to thirty years ago the top Oxbridge choirs very much led the field. The people leading the professional choirs today come from that tradition. But the main change has come in the recording market which is now largely dominated by these professional choirs – the Sixteen, the Tallis Scholars, the Cardinall's Musick, and others. Of course, they have the advantage of having more mature and experienced voices. The directors picked the best from all over Oxbridge and elsewhere and the standard is extremely high. This has led to a greater diversity of sound amongst English choirs. But despite the rise of the professional choirs, the Oxbridge choirs, with their very different *raison d'être*, continue to flourish, at times reflecting the educational aims of the university. Certainly that's what I try to do here. All the recordings I have made here have been of slightly out-of-the-way repertoires, including a lot of unpublished music that I or others have edited specially for the recording, thus making use of the resources you have at a university to discover interesting music.

JS: How do you discover repertoire, or explore it? I think you've got some Rheinberger recorded, right?

GW: I stumbled across an edition of the *E-flat Mass* in the university library quite by chance, and it grew from there. There was a lot of choral music which didn't seem to be much in circulation today and so, using the British Library, I got a hold of the original nineteenth-century editions of this music and looked through it. And I found some interesting things. But generally I do my own research into possible projects and plan a long way in advance.

JS: Do you make your own editions?

GW: Yes, if I have got time, or I work with someone else.

JS: Did you do this with Rheinberger, for example?

GW: No, because they were all nineteenth-century editions and out of copyright. But for another recent project, the music of the seventeenth-century English composer William Child, nearly all the music was edited from the original manuscript sources especially for the recording.

JS: Did you do the transcriptions yourself, or did you turn that over to someone else?

GW: Mostly myself. One member of the choir who was studying music helped.

JS: What is your approach to vibrato?

GW: At the age that they apply here to be undergraduates, the vast majority of applicants don't have a great deal of vibrato, only a slight amount. Perhaps in America the average young singer has more vibrato than here. I don't know if that is the case or not. But here it tends to be so mild that it's not a problem. It's something that they often develop quite a lot while they're here with their singing teachers, as the voice is just beginning to mature.

JS: Do you encourage it?

GW: I allow it to develop. In some voices it won't. Some are naturally straight voices, some naturally develop vibrato. I want each singer to develop their voice as is right for them.

JS: Please describe the way you prepare a score. You've got a lot of music to prepare every week, obviously.

GW: I tend to begin each term with three days of intense note-bashing rehearsals to get ahead with anything that is particularly difficult. We thus try to get underway before the term starts, so that as things come along, week by week, we get on to the performance of the music and not have to spend too much time just going over the notes. The ability of sight-reading is quite variable in the choir and so you have to be sensitive to that and not bore people who can do it. For those who find the reading difficult, additional help is given by the organ scholars.

JS: What's your impression of why people learn to sight-read so well in the UK?

GW: Well, they have to; it's because of the system of regular services. Obviously I want singers who can sight-read well, but an apparent inability is often due simply to lack of experience. I think if they're motivated and want to sing in the choir and they realize what they are taking on, if they have a natural ear – their intervals are sound – and if they're intelligent (as they obviously are if they are offered a place in Cambridge), then I have confidence that they would learn to sight-read whilst they are here. And I've seen numerous cases of this – people whose sight-reading has gone from awful to perfectly adequate in the course of a year. I mean, given the choice, I would always tend to go to someone who was vocally more interesting and maybe not such a good reader, over someone who could sight-read, but whose voice doesn't seem so good. But that's a hard judgement call to make.

JS: Do you employ any methods in which they learn to read?

GW: No. We throw them into the deep end – that's what it is like here. If they can't sight-read and they're in the choir, and all of a sudden they've got all this music to learn this week, then they will normally find their feet. There are more experienced people who can help them. But I think that they just learn by experience.

JS: How frequently do you rehearse?

GW: We sing every day, Sunday through Thursday. So, we have a rehearsal and service on Sunday, a rehearsal only on Monday, a rehearsal and service on Tuesday, rehearsal only on Wednesday, and a rehearsal and service on Thursday, then nothing Friday and Saturday. Sometimes we sing on Sunday mornings as well as at the regular Evensong.

JS: How long is a rehearsal before a service? And how long is a rehearsal?

GW: We have three-quarters of an hour before a service, and fifty-five minutes on the other days.

JS: What are you doing on those other days?

GW: On Monday evening of the regular week we would try to sing through as much of the week's music as possible.

JS: How do you select repertory for recording?

GW: I like to pursue interesting repertoire, as I was saying earlier, but I try to balance it so that it doesn't all come from one period. The next recording we're doing includes a lot of modern Swiss music. The last one we did was a reconstruction of Bach's *St. Mark Passion*, incorporating music by Reinhard Keiser. The one before that was of music by William Child, and other composers covered include Josef Rheinberger, Samuel Wesley – the father of S. S. Wesley – Janácek and Puccini, and two former directors of music here at Caius, Charles Wood and Patrick Hadley.

JS: What groups do you admire today?

GW: Many, across the various different categories of choirs, amateur and professional.

JS: Where do you stand on the question of girls in the cathedral?

GW: I think the increased opportunities given to young girls to sing at a high standard in cathedrals at the same age that young boys hitherto have been able to do is to be welcomed. Although the matter is very controversial, the advent of female clergy makes the continued use of male-only choirs in cathedrals seems increasingly odd. But it is difficult to assess at present whether in the long run it will be better to allow the girls to sing separately from the boys or together with them.

Edward Wickham

Born: 1969

The Clerks' Group

Education: Christ Church, Oxford
King's College, London, (Ph.D. in progress)

Interview: January 16, 1999, Private Residence, London

Edward Wickham founded the Clerks' Group in 1988 while a student at Christ Church, Oxford. While completing doctoral studies in fifteenth-century vocal music at King's College, London, Wickham stays active as a singer (Clerks, Tallis Scholars, et al), author, broadcaster, and publisher. As co-founder of Cantiones Press, he promotes the use of authentic notation for the performance of Renaissance music. Since 1995, he has also directed the amateur Renaissance Singers of London.

The Clerks' Group established its reputation with its recordings of the music of Johannes Ockeghem. Today, this professional consort is a mixed ensemble of six to eight voices that specializes in music of the Renaissance. In increasing demand among those who love early music, the Clerks sing from authentic notation in their performances. In 1997, they won the Gramophone "Early Music Award." The consort has toured extensively in the UK, Europe, and USA.

Website: www.users.dircon.co.uk/~clerks

Edward Wickham

Edward Wickham
The Clerks' Group

JS: How do you select the few singers that are the Clerks' and then for the Renaissance Singers?

EW: I don't audition for the Clerks' Group at all because the constituency from which I would draw is so small that I would know the people I wanted to get. For the Renaissance Singers my audition technique is similar to most people's, I would think. One of the things which is very important is sight-reading of this type of music. I would expect someone to be able to pick up something after a second reading. If they can't get it right the second time, then that's the crunch.

JS: What is your approach to blend?

EW: In terms of blend I'd answer that in the negative in that I think a lot of English choirs tend to be too hung up about blend. The Clerks' Group in particular is very keen to have a sound which is quite individual. I pick the singers because I like the sound of their voices. I don't want to sublimate that, individually, for the benefit of the group. So I like to hear individual voices. In the Clerks' Group, I try to encourage people to sing out certain things. When there's a particular feature I want to hear, I want to hear it from that particular person. In the Renaissance Singers, that's partly still the case. The previous conductor, whom I respect enormously, simply had a different approach to this kind of thing. His product was very good, but his approach was to create a blended, quite introverted sound. I wanted something that was much more brassy, to get the basses to sing out much more, for example. So, a lot of the work I've done in the last three years with the Renaissance Singers is actually just to get them to fulfill their potential as singers. To that end, I've engaged voice coaches to have one-to-one sessions with the singers. What the voice coaches have told me is that the singers have been told to sing in this particular way because that's the way to sing in an English Renaissance way, even though some of these singers have potentially huge, operatic voices.

JS: Is this non-traditional English sound aesthetic a result of your own taste or something that has been informed by your scholarship?

EW: It's a mixture of both. Initially, of course, it's my own taste. Though having been brought up in the cathedral tradition where the important thing is something ethereal, I actually feel that the music we do, Renaissance music, can suffer most of all from this tag of being ethereal. I feel Renaissance music has a very rhetorical, strong, in-your-face message about it. That's my initial impression about it. Backing that up is scholarship which is not really so much my own but a combination of all sorts of people's work, scholarship about the conditions under which this music was performed. It wasn't all terribly incense-suaved music in vast acoustics with priests. Sometimes it was very intimate, domestic. For instance, you had a Josquin motet performed whilst the Pope was dining. Sometimes, there was a sort of politico-religious aspect to the music. There are other environments for this music, more intimate but also more impactive. Considering the personal dimension makes for a different interpretation of this music. Also, I think that in the Renaissance the singers themselves were busy singing and praying on their own behalf. Audience and congregation don't come into it. They are themselves performing an act of devotion. So many people in this country and choral environment have grown up with the sense that singing in a choir is very much a holding-in kind of thing. So to get them to sing out and to use the full force of their voices is much more than just saying, "Go for it!" It's a question of building them up, and breathing is essential. I do lots of breathing exercises.

JS: How do you maintain proper intonation?

EW: I prefer not to get terribly hung up about intonation, particularly with amateur choirs. With professional choirs generally, you would expect it to ping. There is one member of the Clerks' Group who has perfect pitch, and he takes care of that. It's not really an issue in the Clerks' Group. But with an amateur choir, I don't want them to get so hung up about it that it makes it uncomfortable. My feeling about pitch is that sometimes, when things go flat, the audience feels anxious, but sometimes flatness occurs in a performance and it just doesn't matter; if they hear it at all, people just don't care. I also feel that it has to do with the way vowel sounds are produced; I'm very keen on bright vowel sounds. We sometimes have a problem in the Renaissance Singers with the tenors' pitch, but if they sing vowel sounds brightly, they tend to sing much more in tune. In the end it's to do with our own personal singing technique. I know some very good professional singers who sing flat just because there is something about their technique which isn't quite right. My view is perhaps not quite so precisionist as some in the English tradition. In terms of tuning, one of the things I'll do is to stop the singers on an out-of-tune chord and have them deliberately slide around until they find the exact intonation.

JS: How would you describe your particular sound aesthetic that can be heard by your listeners?

EW: Definitely the individuality of the voice and the "upfrontness" of the sound. The Clerks' Group recordings are more forceful than those of the Tallis Scholars. That's not saying that one's better than the other; it's simply saying that there's a qualitative difference. That's something I'm very pleased that critics have noticed. We want people to feel that the mike is very close, just there, and say, "Oh, that's James Gilchrist and that's Matthew Vine," and so on. There's a kind of personal rapport there with the group. So, I've always been very keen that the music should come across as very rhetorical.

JS: What do you mean by rhetorical, exactly?

EW: I mean that the text should be declaimed if and when the music demands. It would seem a bit of a paradox to say that about a group that has been specializing in Ockeghem, who has always been considered the composer of the most otherworldly kind of cadenceless, ethereal, heavenly music. One could quite well get away with a recording of Ockeghem which is very distantly miked in a huge acoustic. I'm not interested in that at all. I want the force, the rhetoric, the excitement and the singability of that music to be projected absolutely to the audience. He set texts, after all, and sometimes he set them in a very declamatory fashion. He was a singer himself. He's the guy who was remembered on his death more as a singer than as a composer, and there is this infectious singability about Ockeghem's lines. It's not just an issue about Ockeghem; this is Renaissance composers in general, particularly our period – the late fifteenth and early sixteenth centuries. These composers were all professional singers, and they all composed for their particular colleagues. This is also how one should interpret these canons, these puzzles that Ockeghem, Josquin and others set. They were not fodder for musicologists or scholars, though they have become that. They were puzzles for colleagues who were incredibly learned about how to read this music.

JS: Is the Clerks' Group entirely professional?

EW: Yes.

JS: What are your sources of funding for the groups?

EW: The Renaissance Singers is a much better example of how one might market these things. Whereas the Clerks' Group is promoted by festivals, and we've got agents and all that, the amateur group has a committee that does all sorts of publicity. We have a huge mailing list and "friends" system which is actually quite good.

You know, the Renaissance Singers has been going for over fifty years. In fact, it was one of the early leaders in the English choral renaissance. There's a great story about the singers. The group started in 1944, and the first concert they gave was in Marlyebone Church during a V-2 bombing raid. The story is that they were doing some Palestrina Mass and, during the intonation "Et in terra pax," a V-2 bomb went off nearby! This marked one of the starting points of the English revival, though there have been several of them. A number of singers have come up through the Renaissance Singers.

Anyway, we've got a "friends" system and we had a big "friends" reunion last year. Everyone came back, and we got the first conductor of the choir, Michael Howard, to conduct this group of singers. It was just incredibly different. Michael Howard, who is about eighty years old, was inspired most by recordings from the Sistine Chapel, and so we sang *Super flumina Babylonis* by Palestrina with a very, very slow tempo! And he would say something like, "Basses! More! More!" It was so amazing – like being transported into another world. Bruno Turner was there with tears in his eyes and said, "This takes me back to when I started getting into this music." Of course today it's changed beyond all recognition.

JS: Who or what have been important influences on your career?

EW: Well, I've been singing since I was six. My elder brother is a singer, and my father is a musician. I went through the cathedral tradition as a boy at St. George's, Windsor. When I was eighteen, I went to Christ Church, Oxford, and sang with Stephen Darlington. So the constant singing has been the most important influence. In terms of the way my career has panned out and what I aspire to, no one can be working in this area and deny the influence of the Tallis Scholars and Peter Phillips in Renaissance music. The influence is both positive and negative. The Tallis Scholars' recordings were really what introduced me to so much of the repertory, but I'd like the Clerks' Group actually to cut a different figure. The other choir which is very important to me is the Taverner Choir with Andrew Parrott. Their approach is always slightly a bit more offbeat and always a little bit more punchy.

JS: Please describe a typical approach to rehearsal with one of your groups.

EW: With the Clerks' Group, one expects them to be ready to go, but with the amateur group, I would warm them up with breathing exercises. Recently, I've been starting to get them to breathe shorter and shorter over periods of time. One thing that I find with choirs is either that they breathe and then stop breathing just before they are supposed to sing or that they are not quite at the top of their breath when they are supposed to sing. So, I'm trying to time their breathing over a beat of three. It's like the tennis player serving: the optimum place to hit the ball is when it's not going up or down.

That's one breathing exercise. Then, as I was saying before, I try to get at the best of the voice. I come into contact with Americans who dislike the Clerks' Group's way of doing things because they think we are too English. I get involved in these internet early-music discussions once in a while where I hear this. There are some people over in the States who think our Ockeghem recordings are far too English. In fact, they have liked our recent recordings because they're less so. What's so interesting to me are the things which they often like about our discs are the things which I think the English don't like at all; for example, too abrasive a sound in the upper voice. My own feeling is that actually each disc has its own character. It's not like the Clerks' Group is developing in a particular way; it's more like a certain set of circumstances produce a certain product at the end. I'm equally pleased when it sounds a bit English or when it sounds more abrasive – whatever. The thing about judging people simply on recordings is that recordings are set in stone, as if that represents what you do all the time, and it's not. It's just a snapshot.

JS: Is there an English sound or style?

EW: Only one which is imposed on it by others. The thing is that if you look at the personnel of choirs that record all sorts of different repertoire – in the Renaissance field, anyhow – The Sixteen, the Tallis Scholars, the Oxford Camerata, the Clerks' Group, you'll see similar names. But if you did a blind hearing, you'd know exactly what the differences are. There are different recording procedures; there are different styles which each choir produces. The singers actually have to adopt different styles all the time. When people talk about English choral tradition, they equate the King's College sound with everything. But women produce different sounds from boys; I think better sounds than boys. So the cathedral sound is a stereotype that people impose. Now, compared to some of the very wacky continental Renaissance groups, we are

233

quite conventional. But I think that's only partly to do with our style of singing. I think it's partly to do with something much deeper and much more to do with relationship to text and scholarship.

JS: Whose choral work do you most admire today?

EW: Well, I admire Westminster Cathedral Choir enormously. The fact that they've won this Gramophone Award is fantastic. It's a great "one in the eye" for choral music in general and a great recognition of the Catholic tradition. Catholic music in this country is slightly undervalued, I think. I love the way they approach Renaissance music as well, which is very gutsy. That's the kind of rhetorical approach to this music I really like. I have great admiration for Chris Page and Gothic Voices. They sing medieval repertoire. And Harry Christophers is very charismatic and very vital as a conductor.

JS: How do you select repertoire for recording?

EW: For the Clerks' Group, it's been selected for us, recently. A few years ago we embarked on a series of nine discs of Ockeghem's sacred music. We won the "Early Music" Gramophone Award for one last year, and we're just finishing off that project.

JS: Do you make your own editions?

EW: It's a mixture of things. Ockeghem scholarship has been really active, so it's been a collaboration.

JS: How do you use scholarship, both in terms of searching for repertory and in terms of performance practice?

EW: Just being in a position where I'm doing a Ph.D. and already looking at these manuscripts, I'm always digging up music which I'd love to perform. The way that the Clerks' Group is working more and more now is to be doing performances from facsimiles of manuscripts. That's clearly a scholarly initiative, and it's something that changes the whole way one approaches this music. It makes the whole approach much more intimate but actually much freer. To see this choral music in modern score, you're depriving it of so much because the notation is a language unto itself, and you're just translating it. So when you sing from modern editions, you lose as much as you would lose if you translated Slovac.

JS: Beyond the "tyranny of the barline," what are the advantages to this approach?

EW: You're reading from your own part, and that's the crucial thing, I think. You have only the information of your own line, so you have to take in through the ear all the information you would normally take in through the eye. You can't align your part with anyone else's, except through listening. So there's got to be an inherent sense of rhythm because there's no conductor there. Everyone is keeping a beat. Also, you're interpreting your own line as if it is the only thing that is important, which goes completely against this blend thing, and that's why I love it so much. You are responding according to the logic of your own melodic line, bringing it out when it's interesting and suppressing it when it's not, rather than seeing the whole texture and making decisions about that in a conductorial sort of way. There's none of that. You interpret it on your own with your own logic, and that's really liberating. Last year the Clerks' Group did an initial project which we premiered at Wigmore Hall. We stood around one choir book and read from the manuscript of a Barbireau Mass [a contemporary of Josquin], and the buzz was incredible. The really weird thing about it was that we had all thought that having one copy and actually looking at one another would exclude the audience completely and that they'd get bored. In fact, it was the opposite. It's the paradox of the fourth-wall drama in which no one looks at the audience and yet the audience is completely drawn in. Members of the audience said, "I felt so involved." That was really strange because there was no conductor; none of us was projecting out, and yet the audience felt drawn in.

If you were going to take anything away from this interview about how the English choral tradition is so variegated, this is my big crusade and the defining feature of my work, as opposed to others'. For this country, it is groundbreaking.

JS: How does what you have just described manifest itself in sound, say, in a recording?

EW: It's interesting you would say that because I had doubts about this. At the Wigmore Hall performance, everyone thought the sound was more focused, but the real test was when we sent a recording of singing this way to the editor who had no idea of how we'd recorded it. He said, "That's such a different sound." He said it was much more focused, much more intense, somehow, and much more intimate. Of course these adjectives are clichés, but I suppose "focused" is the most important word to describe the sound that results from singing in this way.

235

JS: Focused musically or vocally?

EW: Vocally. People are much closer together.

JS: Do the Clerks' use women?

EW: Two fine women and we've just added a wonderful mezzo. The repertory we do often is done with countertenors on top, but it depends on the music. You'll find a disc with an enormous variety in the scoring. In fact that's something I tend to like anyway.

JS: Do you tie yourself to original pitch or do you move things around?

EW: I will move things around to a certain extent. In fact my whole Ph.D. deals with this issue, not so much about pitch but scoring. I think scoring in Renaissance music has been neglected as a positive creative process of the composer. I think Renaissance composers were as concerned with the way the piece was scored and the ranges of it as they were the mode it was in or what *cantus firmus* they were using, or all of those other things which are traditionally discussed by musicologists. You'd expect this attention to scoring from composers of later periods. So I'm keen to present in the discs music which contrasts scoring. Sometimes, I'll have just solo voices; sometimes I'll use sopranos on the top and sometimes not.

JS: Is this just experimentation or the use of knowledge gained from your research?

EW: It's a mixture of both. In fact, some of my things are definitely experiments, and some of them are much more clear-cut ideas. I would never want to suggest that our Ockeghem series is definitive. It's important that other choirs go and sing Ockeghem. I hope our performances are a starting point. We have thousands of interpretations of Beethoven's symphonies; only when you get a large number of interpretations can you get a clear idea of a composer and how he works.

JS: How many on a part in your Ockeghem recordings?

EW: Again, it depends. It will very rarely be more than two on a part. Generally, my preferred scoring on a four-part piece is to have two on the top voice, one on each middle voice and two on the bass. That way we have something that is quite lucid in the middle of the texture, something that is individual, which is the bit where things can plug up, I've always found. Then, something stronger and slightly more blended in the other voices to provide a framework. I dislike a feeling of density in the middle, though sometimes it is two, two, two and two.

JS: Please describe your approach to score preparation.

EW: I guess my initial approach is very much practical – who is able to sing this? How is it possible to get these particular ranges working? The second part of it, at least in Renaissance music, is to ask how one paragraphs it.

JS: What does that mean?

EW: Where are there obvious closures to phrases? Every decent piece of music has its own pace, even in Renaissance music. And even in Ockeghem, which seems so seamless and ethereal, there are points at which it closes and picks up again a new set of imitative points, or whatever. That's how I approach a new Renaissance score, to try and locate where one idea closes and another begins.

JS: When beating the tactus, do you emphasize syncopations with your gestures and therefore call attention to them in the music?

EW: If you are too empathetic about it all of the time it becomes as tedious as if you do it the other way. It depends on the rhetoric and the context.

JS: What have you discovered about mensural relationships in this early repertoire?

EW: Scholars sometimes try to say that relationship of certain mensuration signs to one another should be such and such in terms of mathematical ratios. However, I am not obsessed with this topic, because scholars change their minds all of the time. I was at the Ockeghem conference in '97 and Meg [Margaret] Bent delivered a superb paper on the way that the circle with a slash through it didn't mean anything – that it's exactly the same as a circle! And all of these editors for the last thirty years have been presenting editions where the circle with a slash through it meant that you double the speed. In the end you've got to play it by ear. Of course, the singers have their own ideas about this too! Sometimes there are things that are unsingable if you do them by formula.

JS: Do you encourage vibrato in Renaissance repertoire?

EW: Oh, yes! I would always encourage coloring the voice. Vibrato has got a bad name. If vibrato is a compromise in the pitch, it's not something which one would encourage in this music. That said, a proper coloring of the voice is simply a constant reinforcement of the tone, and some vibratos don't actually have any pitch quality to them at all. A decent singer will have vibrato as part of his or her armory of expression and would be able to use that "weapon" at important points. But a voice without any kind of vibrato coloring is dead to me and has no interest to me at all. Sometimes one encounters singers, particularly older singers, who have been brought up thinking that Emma Kirkby has no vibrato. In fact that's not true. Emma Kirkby has a gorgeous voice which has a rich coloring to it, though you wouldn't perhaps call it vibrato. It's not completely straight at all! There are certain people who think that early-music singing is all about singing very straight, and that's not the case at all. Certain conductors are more insistent upon straight tone than others and you will find some conductors who reckon that the singer who cannot turn off the vibrato is not a good singer. My own view is the flip side of that: the good singer will use vibrato as a part of the armory. A friend was just telling me over lunch that Barbara Bonney was being interviewed recently about her different roles and she felt she could sing in all sorts of different styles.

JS: Is vibrato ever a conflict for you in rehearsal?

EW: It's very rarely an issue. There are occasions when one has to put one's foot down. With the Clerks' Group, I'm trying to get them to sing out in a soloistic way. And in the Renaissance Singers, when the basses get high they sort of "wawawawa" so you have to tone that down. Sometimes it will creep into a final chord because of laziness or when singers are out of breath.

Appendix I

Conductors' Discographies

Ralph Allwood

ETON COLLEGE CHAPEL CHOIR

Music from Eton; Choral, Organ and Orchestral Music
includes choral works by Boyle, Parry and Grier;
Capriole Records, CAPCD 1005, 1990 (re-issued, 1997).

Three Pieces from the Eton Choir Book
includes Davy "St. Matthew Passion," Lambe
"Nesciens Mater," and Nesbett "Magnificat";
Chatsworth (Future Classics), FCM 1004, 1994.

I Will Lift up Mine Eyes: 20th Century Anthems
includes works by Stanford, Howells, Radcliffe,
Bainton.
Soundalive, SAMLS, CD 501, 1996.

Top Hats and Tails
includes close-harmony arrangements of Gershwin,
Shearing, Porter and Jordan;
Herald, HAVPCD 218, 1998.

RODOLFUS CHOIR

Parry: Songs of Farewell
includes partsongs;
Herald, HAVPCD217, 1998.

Francis Grier: 'A Sequence for the Ascension'
Herald, HAVPCD158.

Mater Ora Filium: Choral Music by Bax and Villette
Herald, HAVPCD176.

Sue Barber

STOKE BRUNSWICK CHOIR

No CD recordings available.

Matthew Best

CORYDON SINGERS

Bruckner: Masses and Te Deum
Hyperion, CDS 44071/3, 1993.

Britten: Saint Nicolas
includes "Hymn to Saint Cecilia";
Hyperion, CDA 66333, 1989.

Rachmaninoff Vespers
Hyperion, CDA 66460, 1991.

Finzi: Die Natalis; Intimations of Immortality
Hyperion, CDA 66876, 1996.

Duruflé: Requiem; Fauré: Requiem
Hyperion, CDA 67070, 1995.

Berlioz: L'Enfance du Christ
Hyperion, CDA 66991/2, 1986.

Michael Brewer

LAUDIBUS

All in the April Evening
includes music by Vaughan Williams, Warlock, Elgar, Byrd, et al;
Hyperion, CDA 67976, 1999.

Crucifixus: The Music of Henry Clukas
includes "Requiem," "Stabat Mater," "Shakespeare Songs," "Sinfonia Sacra";
issued by the National Youth Choir.

Twentieth-Century Choral Classics
includes works by Vaughan Williams, Britten, Tippett,
Stanford, et al;
issued by the National Youth Choir.

NATIONAL YOUTH CHOIR

World Tour, 1996
includes works by Allain, Mendelssohn, Schütz, et al,
and folk arrangements;
issued by the National Youth Choir.

World Tour, 1999
includes works by Monteverdi, Brahms, Tchaikovsky,
Rheinberger, et al;
issued by National Youth Choir.

Peter Broadbent

JOYFUL COMPANY OF SINGERS

Jonathan Harvey: I Love the Lord, Works by Harvey
includes "I Love the Lord," "Carol," "Lauds," "The
Angels," "Forms of Emptiness," et al;
ASV, CD DCA 917, 1995.

*Barber and Schuman: Choral Music; Works by Samuel
Barber*
includes "Twelfth Night," "Reincarnations," "Agnus
Dei," et al, and William Schuman, including
"Perceptions" and "Mail Order Madrigals";
ASV, CD DCA 939, 1996.

Deutsche Motette
includes works by Richard Strauss, Mendelssohn,
Brahms, Parry, and Schoenberg;
Abbas Records, 1999.

*Music from St. Petersburg: Berezovsky Sacred
Concerto, Rachmaninoff
Sacred Concerto*
includes works by Smirnov and Bortiansky;
Meridian Records, CDE 84257, 1993.

Camilleri Choral Works
includes "Requiem," "Missa Brevis," "Celestial Voices," et al;
Unicorn Kanchana, DKP(CD) 9157, 1994.

A Garland for Linda
includes works by Tavener, Bingham, Rutter, Matthews, McCartney, R. Panufnik, M. Berkeley, Swayne, Bennett;
EMI 72435 56961 20, 2000.

Ken Burton

LONDON ADVENTIST CHORALE

Deep River

Steal Away; Spirituals

CROYDON SDA GOSPEL CHOIR

Until We Reach
songs in a variety of styles, including Latin American, soul, rap, gospel, jazz, et al;1994.

The Very Best of Gospel; Croydon SDA Gospel
includes "Oh Happy Day," "Said He Would," "I'll Take You There," et al;
Music Collection International, MCCD 310, 1997.

Andrew Carwood

THE CARDINALL'S MUSICK

William Byrd in Four Volumes
Vol. I, "Propers for Lady Mass in Advent";
ASV Gaudeamus, CD 170
Vol. II, "Propers for Christmas Day";
ASV Gaudeamus, CD 178
Vol. III, "Propers for Epiphany";
ASV Gaudeamus, CD 179,
Vol. IV, "Cantiones Sacrae";
ASV Gaudeamus.

Nicholas Ludford; Four Volumes

Robert Fayrfax; Five Volumes

William Cornysh
includes "Magnificat," "Salve Regina," and works by
Turges, Prentes;
ASV Gaudeamus, CD GAV 164, 1997.

Harry Christophers

THE SIXTEEN

Messiah, (two discs)
Hyperion, CDA 66251, 1987.

Robert Carver: Mass
includes "Dum Sacrum Mysterium," "Magnificat," "O
Bone Jesu";
Collins Classics, 14782, 1997.

The Rose and the Ostrich Feather
includes music from the Eton Choir Book, Vol. 1;
Collins Classics, 1314-2, 1992.

Britten Choral Works, Vol. III
includes "A Ceremony of Carols," "Missa Brevis," "A
Hymn to St. Columba," "Hymn to St. Peter," et al;
Collins, 13702, 1993.

La Jeune France
includes Jolivet "Epithalame," Messiaen "Cinq
Rechants," Daniel-Lesur
"La Cantique des Cantiques";
Collins, 14802, 1996.

Stephen Cleobury

KING'S COLLEGE CHOIR

Choral Evensong Live from King's College, Cambridge
includes music by Howells.

English Anthems
includes works by Wood, Bainton, Ireland, Harris,
Naylor, Howells, Britten, Harvey, Maw, et al;
EMI, CD 170, 1993.

Credo
includes works by Rachmaninoff, Penderecki,
Stravinsky, Panufnik;
EMI, CD 130, 1997.

Stanford Evening Services in C and G
includes "Three Motets," "Latin Magnificat," "Two
Bible Songs", Anthems;
EMI, CD 118, 1996.

BBC SINGERS, CHORISTERS OF KING'S COLLEGE

Richard Strauss Choral Works
includes "Deutsche Motette," op. 62, "An den Baum,"
"Daphne," "Der Abend," "Three Choruses for Men's
Voices";
Collins Classics, COL 14952, 1999.

Pamela Cook

CANTAMUS

*Magic in the Air: Collection of Folksongs, Spirituals,
and Sacred Music*
including Gounod "Sanctus," Fauré *Cantique de Jean
Racine*;
issued by Cantamus, 1993.

Michael Neaum's Arrangements Sung by Cantamus
includes arrangements of British, American, Polish and
Spanish folksongs, and popular melodies;
issued by Cantamus, 1997.

Christmas with Cantamus
includes works by Rutter, Mathias, and a variety of
arrangements of familiar Christmas melodies by
Michael Neaum;
issued by Cantamus, 1996.

Sir John Eliot Gardiner

MONTEVERDI CHOIR

Haydn: Die Schöpfung
Deutsche Grammophon Archiv, 449 217-2 AH2, 1997.

Beethoven: Mass in D Major ('Missa Solemnis')
DG Archiv, 429 779-2AH, 1991.

Handel: Jephtha
Philips, 422 351-2PH3, 1989.

Monteverdi: Vespers of the Blessed Virgin and Magnificat II (two discs)
DG Archiv, 457 660-2, 1999.

Simon Halsey

CITY OF BIRMINGHAM SYMPHONY ORCHESTRA AND CHORUS, prepared by Simon Halsey

Szymanowski: Stabat Mater
includes other works; conducted by Sir Simon Rattle;
EMI, CDC5 55121-2, 1994.

Mahler, Symphony No. 2, 'Resurrection'
conducted by Rattle;
EMI, CDS7 47962-8, 1987.

Bruckner: Mass in E minor
includes motets, conducted by Halsey;
Conifer, CDCF 192.

Delius and Grainger Partsongs
Conifer, CDCF 162.

Britten War Requiem (two discs)
prepared by Halsey, Simon Rattle conducting;
CDS 747 0348.

Stephen Layton

HOLST SINGERS

Ikon
includes works by Sviridov, Gretchaninov,
Tchaikovsky, Pärt, Gorecki, et al;
Hyperion, CDA66928, 1997.

POLYPHONY

Arvo Pärt: 'Berliner Messe'
includes "The Beatitudes," "Annum per Annum,"
"Magnificat," "Sieben Magnificat-Antiphonen," "De
Profundis";
Hyperion, CDA66960, 1998.

At Twilight
works by Grainger and Grieg;
Hyperion, CDA66793, 1995.

'Jungle Book' by Percy Grainger
Hyperion, CDA66863, 1996.

O Magnum Misterium: Twentieth-Century Carols
works by Bennett, Byrt, Howells, Leighton, Walton,
Warlock, Wishart;
Hyperion, CDA66925, 1996.

Requiem and other works by John Rutter
including "Hymn to the Creator of Light," "Cantate
Domino," "A Choral Fanfare," et al;
Hyperion, CDA66947.

Richard Marlow

CHOIR OF TRINITY COLLEGE, CAMBRIDGE

Sweelinck: Cantiones Sacrae
Volumes, 1 and 2;
Hyperion, CDA67103 and CDA 67104, 1998.

Bach Family Motets
fourteen motets by Johann, Johann Christoph, Johann

Michael, Johann Ludwig, J. S., and Johann Christoph
Friedrich;
Conifer, 75605 51306 2, 1997.

Michael Praetorius: In Dulci Jubilo
choral motets for Advent, Christmas and Epiphany;
Conifer, 75605 512562, 1995.

Brahms: The Motets
Conifer, CDCF 178 74321.

Poulenc: The Sacred Music for Unaccompanied Choir
Conifer, CDCF 151 74321.

Paul McCreesh

GABRIELI CONSORT AND PLAYERS

A Venetian Coronation, 1595
choral and instrumental music of Andrea and Giovanni
Gabrieli, et al;
Gramophone Award Winner;
Virgin Classics, VC7 91110-2, 1990.

Music for Philip II
featuring Morales "Requiem," Lobo "Versa est in
Luctum";
DG Archiv, CD457 597-2, 1998.

Bach: Epiphany Mass (two discs)
Includes J. S. Bach's "Missa Brevis in F" (BWV 233),
"Sanctus in D Major" (BWV 238), "Cantata, Sie
Werden aus Saba alle Kommen" (BWV 65), "Cantata,
Schmücke dich, o liebe Seele" (BWV 180);
DG Archiv, CD 457 631-2.

Messiah (two discs)
Foundling Hospital Version, 1754;
DG Archiv, CD453-464-2.

*Praetorius Mass: Lutheran Mass for Christmas
Morning*
as it might have been celebrated around 1620;
DG Archiv, CD 439 250-2, 1993.

James O'Donnell

WESTMINSTER CATHEDRAL CHOIR

Frank Martin: Mass for Double Choir and Pizzetti Requiem
Hyperion, CDA 67017, 1997.

The Music of the Westminster Cathedral Choir
including works by Elgar, Britten, Poulenc, Panufnik, Mawby, Holst, Stanford, Palestrina, et al;
Hyperion, WCC100, 1998.

Palestrina Missa aeterna Christi Munera
also includes "Magnificat Primi Toni," "Sicut Cervus," "Super Flumina Babylonis," "Aeterna Christi Munera," et al;
Hyperion, CDA 66490, 1991.

Panis Angelicus: Favourite Motets from Westminster Cathedral
includes works by Byrd, Philips, Tallis, Allegri, Palestrina, Parsons, Monteverdi, et al;
Hyperion, CDA 66850, 1993.

Maurice Duruflé
includes "Requiem," "Mass cum Jubilo," "Quatre Motets sur des Thèmes Gregoriens";
Hyperion, CDA 66757, 1994.

Andrew Parrott

TAVERNER CONSORT, CHOIR AND PLAYERS

J. S. Bach: Magnificat and Easter Oratorio (two discs)
Virgin Veritas, CDVB 5 61647 2, 1999.

The Promise of Ages: A Christmas Collection
includes traditional and non-traditional music by Holst, Davies, Niles, Weir, Madan, et al;
Sony, SK 60713, 1998.

Stabat Mater
Stabat Mater settings by Palestrina, Pärt and Browne;
Virgin Classics, VC 5452722, 1996.

J. S. Bach: Heart's Solace
includes "Komm, Jesu, Komm," "Jesu meine Freude,"
"Trauer-Ode: Lass, fürstin, Lass noch einen Strahl";
Sony, SK 60155, 1998.

Purcell: Te Deum and Jubilate
includes "When on my Sick Bed I Languish," "Beati
Omnes qui Timent," "Te Deum," "Jubilate," et al;
Virgin Veritas, VC 545061 2, 1995.

Peter Phillips

THE TALLIS SCHOLARS

The Tallis Christmas Mass
includes "Missa Puer Natus est Nobis," "Magnificat"
(four vols.), "Ave Dei Patris," et al;
Gimell, 389454 934-2, 1998.

The Best of the Renaissance (two discs)
includes Allegri "Miserere," Tallis "Spem in Allium,"
Josquin "Missa Pange Lingua," Palestrina "Missa
Papae Marcelli";
Philips, 289 462 862-2, 1999.

Live in Oxford
includes Obrecht "Salve Regina," Josquin "Gaude
Virgo," Taverner "Gaude Plurimum," Mundy "Vox
Patris Caelestis," et al;
Gimell, 289 454 998-2, 1998.

Lamenta: The Lamentations of the Prophet Jeremiah
Lamentation settings by Ferrabosco the Elder, Tallis,
Palestrina, Robert White, and Brumel;
Gimell, 454 996-2, 1998.

Johannes Ockeghem
includes "Missa De plus en plus," "Missa Au Travail
suis," et al;
Gimell, 454 935-2, 1997.

Rore: Missa Prater rerum seriem, Motets
Gimell, CDG1M029, 1994.

Palestrina: Masses and Motets
Gimell, CDG1M020, 1990.

Josquin: Desprez Masses
includes "Missa Pange Lingua," "Missa Sol fa re mi";
Gimell CDG1M009, 1987.

Vivien Pike

CANTORES NOVAE

An Hour in the Company of Cantores Novae
includes works by Palestrina, Mellnäs, Hovland, Carter,
Poulenc, folksongs and arrangements of popular
melodies.
Recorded items span seven years (1990's).

Paul Spicer

FINZI SINGERS

Howells: Choral Works
includes "Three Carol-Anthems," "God is gone up,"
"Te Deum," et al;
Chandos, CHAN 9458, 1996.

English Romantic Choral Music: Howells and Vaughan Williams
includes Howells' "Sequence for St. Michael," "The
House of the Mind," "Requiem"; Vaughan Williams'
"Lord, Thou hast been our Refuge," "Prayer to the
Father of Heaven," et al;
Chandos, CHAN 9019, 1992.

Britten Choral Edition, in Three Volumes
Vol. I includes "A.M.D.G.," "Gloriana, Choral
Dances," "Rejoice in the Lamb," "Hymn to the Virgin,"
et al;
Chandos, CHAN 9511.

Vol. II includes "Jubilate Deo in E-flat major," "A Wedding Anthem," "Te Deum in C major," et al; Chandos, CHAN 9598.

Vol. III includes "Five Flower Songs," "Advance Democracy," "Sacred and Profane"; Chandos, CHAN 9701.

David Temple

CROUCH END FESTIVAL CHORUS

Cinema Choral Classics
Silva Classics, SILK 6015, 1997.

Cinema Choral Classics II
Silva Classics, SILKD 6017, 1998.

Britten: The Company of Heaven; Will Todd: The Burning Road
Silva Classics, SILKD 6021, 1999.

Geoffrey Webber

THE CHOIR OF GONVILLE AND CAIUS COLLEGE, CAMBRIDGE

Joseph Rheinberger
includes "Mass in E flat, op. 109," "Requiem," et al; ASV, CD DCA 989, 1997.

Patrick Hadley and Edmund Rubbra
includes Hadley's "Lenten Cantata," et al, Rubbra's "Missa in Honorem Sancti Dominici," "Three Motets, op. 76";
ASV, CD DCA 881, 1993.

Puccini and Janacek
includes Puccini "Requiem" and Janacek "Mass in E-flat";
ASV, CD DCA 914, 1995.

William Child: Sacred Choral Music
ASV, CD GAV 182, 1998.

Charles Wood
includes "The Passion of Our Lord According to St. Mark";
ASV, CD DCA 854, 1993.

Edward Wickham

THE CLERKS' GROUP

Ockeghem: Requiem and Missa Fors Seulement
works by de la Rue and Brumel;
ASV Gaudeamus, CDGAU 168, 1997.

Ockeghem: Missa Prolationum
includes Josquin "Illibata Dei Virgo Nutrix," and motets by others;
ASV Gaudeamus, CD GAU 143, 1995.

Obrecht: *Missa Malheur me bat*
also "Magnificat" and motets by Martini;
ASV Gaudeamus, CD GAU 171, 1997.

Barbireau: Missa Virgo parens Christi
includes other works by Barbireau, Obrecht, Pullois, and Pipelare;
ASV Gaudeamus, CD GAU 188, 1998.

Tintoris: Missa L'homme armé
also includes "Missa Sine Nomine";
Musique en Wallonie, CIP 3608, 1997.

About the Author

Jeffrey Sandborg, D.M.A. is Professor of Music and Director of Choral Activities at Roanoke College (Salem, VA) where he has taught since 1985. He is Director of the Chancel Choir at Second Presbyterian Church, Roanoke, and he is the founder and Director of the Canticum Novum Chamber Singers and Orchestra. For fourteen years he was Artistic Director of the Roanoke Valley Choral Society. Among his conducting credits with the RVCS are Bach's *Mass in B minor*, Verdi's *Requiem*, Mozart's *Great Mass in C Minor*, Handel's *Messiah*, and Fanshawe's *African Sanctus*, which was selected for national broadcast on the "First Art" choral series. He has prepared many other major choral works for performance with the Roanoke Symphony Orchestra with which he has appeared regularly as a guest conductor.

For his contributions to the arts Sandborg has been a recipient of the Kendig Prize for Excellence in the Arts, awarded by the Arts Council of the Blue Ridge. His instructional video, *Make a Joyful and Beautiful Noise!*, is a widely used resource by teachers and church musicians for learning and teaching the fundamentals of singing. In addition, Sandborg is in demand as a clinician and adjudicator, having worked in Texas, Georgia, Illinois, Kentucky, West Virginia, Virginia, Maryland, North Carolina, and Canada.

Index

ABCD (Association of British Choral Directors): 107

Aesthetic: xx, 19, 35, 101, 106, 114, 159, 208, 210, 214, 222, 229, 231

Alldis, John: 139, 200, 208, 213, 214, 216

Allwood, Ralph: ii, vii, xvii, 2, 3, 31, 239

Amateur (singers), amateurs: xi, xvi, xvii, xix, 16, 17, 19, 21, 36, 42, 43, 45, 47, 48, 49, 87, 99, 103, 110, 112, 113, 142, 143, 160, 183, 197, 202, 204, 206, 207, 211, 214, 226, 228, 230, 232, 233

Arnoudov, Vasily 50

Audience, audiences: xi, 8, 14, 23, 35, 37, 45, 47, 48, 59, 65, 75, 143, 150, 172, 174, 178, 207, 210, 211, 212, 213, 230, 231, 235

Audition, auditions, audition process: xii, 3, 11, 12, 19, 26, 30, 31, 44, 46, 57, 63, 75, 85, 86, 87, 94, 103, 105, 113, 121, 139, 147, 167, 182, 183, 193, 196, 205, 207, 209, 219, 220, 229

Barber, Sue: ii, vii, xvii, 10, 11, 48, 107, 240

Barbirolli, John: 50

BBC Singers: xvi, xviii, 48, 74, 79, 82, 83, 112, 144, 174, 175, 195, 244

Bedford, Steuart: 79

Bertalot, John: 86

Best, Matthew: ii, vii, xvii, 16, 17, 202, 240

Blend, choral blend: 4, 5, 6, 13, 20, 31, 32, 33, 37, 43, 45, 46, 57, 58, 63, 64, 81, 84, 85, 86, 91, 95, 104, 105, 113, 121, 123, 139, 149, 160, 161, 167, 168, 169, 170, 171, 178, 188, 196, 197, 200, 202, 208, 222, 229, 235, 237

Boulanger, Nadia: 100

Boulez, Pierre: 80

Breathing: 33, 78, 93, 126, 182, 189, 195, 230, 233

Brewer, Michael: ii, vii, ix, xvii, 26, 27, 240

Broadbent, Peter: ii, vii, xiv, xvii, 42, 43, 241

Burton, Ken: ii, vii, ix, xvii, 54, 55, 242

Cantamus: xvii, 92, 93, 94, 95, 96, 244

Cantoris: 167

Cardinall's Musick, The: xvi, 62, 63, 64, 65, 72, 73, 176, 223, 242

Carwood, Andrew: ii, vii, xvi, 62, 63, 176, 242

Children's chorus: (choruses) 110

Christophers, Harry: ii, vii, ix, xv, 74, 75, 173, 234, 243

City of Birmingham Symphony Chorus, The: xvii, 102, 103, 110, 245

City of Sheffield Girls' Choir: xvii, 180, 181
Cleobury, Stephen: ii, vii, ix, xiv, xvi, xvii, 82, 83, 115, 118, 146, 152, 243
Clerkes, The: xvi, 170, 175
Commission: 29, 34, 82, 114, 183, 204, 207, 213, 215, 216
Cook, Pamela: ii, vii, xvii, 92, 93, 184, 185, 244
Corydon Singers: 16, 17, 18, 19, 20, 24, 202, 240
Costs: 24, 45, 51, 94, 138, 175, 186, 199, 213
Crouch End Festival Singers: xvii, 204, 205
Croydon Adventist Choir: xvii
Darlington, Stephen: 70, 232
Davis, Colin: 110, 214
Decani: 167
Diction: 14, 106, 140
Dorati, Antal: 80
English approach: 43, 208
English choral style, English choral tradition: 6, 7, 67, 79, 135, 141, 223, 233, 235
English culture: 7, 24, 48, 106, 136, 141, 155, 200
English Ways: i, iii, xv, 1
Ensemble, (development of): xv, xvi, xviii, xix, 4, 33, 49, 62, 64, 73, 74, 81, 85, 86, 100, 105, 112, 120, 123, 124, 134, 138, 142, 159, 160, 161, 167, 171, 176, 181, 189, 228
Ericson, Eric: 36, 37, 43, 48, 50, 107, 201
Eriksson, Gunnar: 37
Eton College: 2, 3, 239
Expenses: 59, 94, 155, 175, 186, 212
Falsettist: 99, 136, 137
Financial support: 113, 118, 189
Finzi Singers: xvi, 192, 193, 194, 195, 196, 202, 250
Franklin, Kirk: 56
Fund, funding, underwriting, subsidize: xi, 24, 28, , 50, 51, 69, 80, 103, 113, 122, 131, 132, 153, 165, 175, 183, 193, 199, 213, 231
Gabrieli Consort and Players: xvi, 134, 247
Gardiner, John Eliot: ii, vii, ix, xiii, xvi, 8, 36, 81, 90, 98, 99, 106, 107, 116, 140, 176, 245
Girls: xvi, xvii, xviii, xix, 3, 11, 12, 14, 38, 39, 68, 69, 70, 71, 88, 89, 90, 92, 93, 94, 95, 96, 97, 110, 112, 122, 123, 127, 180, 181, 182, 183, 184, 185, 186, 187, 188, 189, 190, 198, 199, 226
Global Music Network: 131

Gonville and Caius College: xvii, xviii, 218, 219, 251
Goodwin, Frederic: 70
Gospel choir: xvi, xvii, xix, 54, 55, 56, 57, 58, 59, 60, 107, 183, 242
Graham, Colin: 79
Guest, Douglas: 90
Guest, George: xvi, 6, 67, 69, 70, 84, 90, 151, 152, 201, 223
Haitink, Bernard: 205, 213
Halsey, Louis: xv, 107
Halsey, Simon: ii, vii, ix, xvii, 15, 102, 103, 245
Herreweghe, Phillipe: 81, 175
Hickox, Richard: 43, 107, 108, 202
Hill, David: xvii, 6, 38, 68, 69, 84, 146, 152
Hilliard Ensemble, Hilliards: 4, 49, 81, 176
Holst Singers, the: xvii, 112, 113, 115, 118, 246
Holst, Imogen: 100
Hoot, hooty: 151, 171, 196
Intonation: 4, 6, 12, 13, 20, 33, 44, 46, 57, 58, 64, 84, 85, 86, 88,
    96, 103, 104, 113, 148, 161, 162, 168, 187, 197, 198, 209, 222,
    230, 232
Joyful Company of Singers, the: xvii, 42, 43, 48, 52, 241
King's College, Cambridge: xii, xvi, xviii, 2, 16, 82, 98, 102, 103,
    112, 115, 118, 154, 174, 243
Kurtag, Gyorgy: 100
Layton, Stephen: ii, vii, ix, xvi, xvii, 112, 113, 246
Lessons, (singing,voice): 3, 5, 7, 11, 12, 28, 30, 33, 68, 83, 93, 94,
    96, 97, 105, 108, 122, 131, 182, 184, 185, 187, 188, 205, 221
London Adventist Choir:
Lowe, David: 108
Lumsden, David: 200
Malcolm, George: 43, 44, 68, 84, 100, 146, 151
Marlow, Richard: ii, vii, xvii, 120, 121, 246
Masur, Kirt: 105, 106, 107
Maximum number of singers for choir:
McCreesh, Paul: ii, vii, xvi, 134, 135, 247
Meantone, meantone temperament: 88, 162
Monteverdi Choir, the: xiii, xvi, 6, 24, 80, 98, 99, 101, 143, 144,
    245
Musical scholarship:
Music education: 14, 142
National Youth Choir, the: xvii, xix, 26, 27, 28, 29, 30, 31, 38, 39,

240, 241
Neary, Martin: 114, 115
Nield, David: 8
O'Donnell, James: ii, xvii, 6, 64, 68, 70, 81, 146, 147, 176, 248
Ord, Boris: 8, 68, 84, 152, 201
Oxbridge: xi, xii, xiii, 223
Ozawa: 80
Parrott, Andrew: ii, vii, ix, xvi, 36, 70, 137, 158, 159, 164, 169, 176, 232, 248
Pärt, Arvo: 69, 100, 113, 246, 249
Phillips, Peter: ii, vii, xvi, 44, 166, 167, 232, 249
Phrasing: 4, 5, 35, 63, 64, 72, 75, 78, 85, 96, 116, 128, 140, 141, 189
Pike, Vivien: ii, vii, xvii, 180, 181, 189, 190, 250
Pitch standards: 162
Pitch: 3, 4, 31, 33, 34, 37, 57, 87, 113, 114, 121, 124, 125, 135, 136, 140, 161, 162, 193, 196, 197, 203, 230, 236, 238
Polyphony: xvi, 64, 73, 112, 113, 114, 115, 117, 124, 135, 136, 137, 149, 161, 162, 164, 174, 175, 176, 178, 179, 246
Preparation: ix, xix, 37, 78, 109, 126, 141, 153, 159, 165, 186, 203, 237
Professional (singers), professionals: ix, xi, xii, xv, xvi, xviii, xix, 14, 17, 19, 20, 43, 45, 47, 48, 49, 62, 65, 70, 71, 74, 76, 79, 82, 83, 87, 89, 98, 99, 101, 103, 104, 107, 112, 113, 114, 115, 117, 136, 141, 142, 143, 144, 147, 153, 155, 156, 160, 166, 167, 169, 176, 193, 196, 198, 200, 202, 204, 206, 223, 226, 228, 230, 231
Program, programming: 22, 23, 34, 37, 42, 44, 47, 48, 49, 50, 51, 59, 65, 66, 75, 81, 83, 87, 89, 108, 138, 149, 150, 165, 174, 177, 178, 183, 185, 186, 204
Rattle, Simon: 102, 105, 106, 107, 110, 245
Rehearse, rehearsal, rehearsals: xv, xviii, 5, 12, 13, 15, 20, 21, 22, 26, 27, 28, 29, 32, 33, 34, 35, 36, 37, 38, 40, 44, 45, 46, 50, 57, 64, 78, 79, 80, 83, 87, 94, 95, 100, 106, 107, 108, 113, 114, 116, 125, 126, 127, 138, 140, 141, 147, 149, 152, 153, 159, 160, 165, 168, 169, 170, 173, 185, 186, 187, 193, 194, 196, 197, 202, 206, 207, 209, 211, 212, 215, 216, 222, 225, 226, 233, 238
Richter, Karl: 213
Rifkin, Joshua: 165
Robinson, Christopher: 90
Rodolfus Choir: xvii, 2, 3, 8, 239

Role of choral music: 7, 24, 48, 106, 141, 155, 200
Rose, Barry: 8, 68, 97
Rose, Bernard: 79
Rozhdestvensky, Gennady: 80
Sainsbury Competition: 96, 97, 185
Scholars (choral): xii, 6, 31, 78, 82, 83, 89, 108, 109, 126, 131, 132, 136, 153, 171, 231, 237
Scholarships (choral): xii, 3, 31, 82, 154, 199
Seal, Richard: xvii, xviii, 38, 71, 89, 123
Select, selection (of singers): xii, xvi, 3, 23, 26, 31, 34, 44, 50, 65, 72, 75, 99, 101, 118, 130, 138, 149, 152, 163, 184, 193, 203, 209, 220, 221, 226, 229, 234, 253
Shanahan, Mark: 60
Shaw, Robert: 104, 105, 106, 107, 109, 114, 118
Sight-reading: xv, 3, 19, 26, 30, 31, 43, 44, 63, 75, 85, 86, 87, 94, 103, 113, 121, 122, 138, 147, 182, 183, 187, 193, 205, 207, 219, 225, 229
Sixteen, the: xiii, xv, xvi, 16, 26, 27, 44, 49, 74, 75, 76, 77, 78, 80, 173, 223, 233, 243
Size: xii, xvi, 17, 27, 35, 42, 52, 72, 73, 90, 101, 117, 122, 131, 138, 162, 163, 192, 237
Skinner, David: 62, 72
Sound: xii, xiii, xiv, xv, 3, 4, 5, 6, 12, 13, 14, 17, 19, 20, 21, 22, 24, 30, 31, 32, 33, 34, 35, 36, 37, 39, 43, 44, 45, 46, 57, 58, 59, 63, 64, 67, 68, 69, 71, 73, 76, 84, 85, 86, 90, 95, 96, 97, 101, 104, 105, 106, 109, 110, 111, 114, 115, 117, 118, 123, 124, 126, 127, 135, 136, 137, 138, 139, 140, 144, 147, 148, 149, 151, 159, 161, 164, 167, 169, 170, 171, 172, 173, 174, 175, 176, 177, 178, 179, 182, 188, 189, 195, 196, 200, 202, 208, 210, 211, 212, 221, 222, 223, 225, 229, 230, 231, 233, 235
Spicer, Paul: ii, vii, xvi, 192, 193, 250
St. John's College, Cambridge: xvi, 67, 82, 111, 151
Stanley Jones, Jean: 184
Stoke Brunswick Choir: xvii, 10, 11, 240
Swingle Singers: 200, 201
Tallis Scholars, The: xvi, 6, 44, 49, 80, 111, 135, 144, 166, 167, 170, 171, 173, 174, 176, 195, 223, 228, 231, 232, 233, 249
Tavener, John: 69, 100, 114, 158, 179, 242
Temple, David: ii, vii, xvii, 204, 205, 251
Tennstedt, Klaus: 213

Thomson, Bryden (Jack): 51
Tone quality: 4, 5, 14, 20, 33, 46, 64, 85, 99, 104, 105, 114, 139, 140, 148, 161, 170, 182, 209, 222
Trinity College, Cambridge: xvii, 120, 246
Tuning: 4, 5, 58, 64, 88, 100, 121, 123, 124, 140, 148, 162, 168, 169, 170, 173, 177, 178, 197, 198, 200, 209, 230
Vibrato: 4, 14, 20, 21, 39, 44, 46, 51, 58, 73, 91, 97, 105, 110, 111, 116, 117, 123, 124, 127, 139, 140, 151, 161, 162, 168, 170, 176, 177, 188, 189, 195, 196, 222, 224, 238
Voice lessons, training: 11, 83, 96
Walker, John: 8
Warm-ups: 5, 12, 13, 21, 30, 33, 50, 107, 152, 187, 216, 217
Webber, Geoffrey: ii, vii, xvii, 218, 219, 251
Westminster Cathedral: xvii, xviii, 7, 43, 67, 70, 71, 81, 82, 84, 100, 111, 146, 147, 151, 154, 155, 156, 176, 234, 248
Wickham, Edward: ii, vii, xvi, 72, 176, 228, 229, 252

No te comas este libro

Obra editada en colaboración con Editorial Planeta - España

© 2023, Mikecrak

Edición y fijación del texto: 2023, Rodrigo Palacios

© 2023, Editorial Planeta, S. A. - Barcelona, España

Derechos reservados

© 2023, Editorial Planeta Mexicana, S.A. de C.V.
Bajo el sello editorial MARTÍNEZ ROCA M.R.
Avenida Presidente Masarik núm. 111,
Piso 2, Polanco V Sección, Miguel Hidalgo
C.P. 11560, Ciudad de México
www.planetadelibros.com.mx

Diseño de portada: Planeta Arte & Diseño
Ilustraciones de portada: © 2023, Javier Jerez
Diseño de interiores: María Pitironte
Ilustraciones de interior: © 2023, Javier Jerez y Catalina Castillo
Plantilla de Papercraft: © 2023, MiriCraft

Primera edición impresa en España: abril de 2023
ISBN: 978-84-270-5084-6

Primera edición impresa en México: marzo de 2023
ISBN: 978-607-07-9883-2

Impreso en los talleres de Impresora Tauro, S.A. de C.V.
Av. Año de Juárez 343, colonia Granjas San Antonio, Ciudad de México
Impreso en México -*Printed in Mexico*

MIKECRACK

No te Comas Este Libro

mr

MIKE Y SUS AMIGOS
QUIEREN CELEBRAR
EL ÉXITO EN SU
ÚLTIMA AVENTURA.

¿Y QUÉ MEJOR MANERA
DE HACERLO QUE CON
UNA BUENA BARBACOA?

HAMBURGUESAS DE LAS BUENAS, COMPLETAS, CON BEICON,
LECHUGA, TOMATE, MOSTAZA... MIKE ESTÁ TAN EMOCIONADO
QUE HA VENIDO CORRIENDO A PONER LA MESA. ¡INCREÍBLE!
AKELA VA A ENCARGARSE DE COCINAR, MIENTRAS ROBIN SE
ASEGURA DE TRAER TODO LO NECESARIO.

**PERO HAY ALGUIEN QUE NO PARECE
MUY INTERESADO EN ECHAR UNA MANO...**

—¿CÓMO QUE ESTÁS OCUPADO? —PREGUNTA MIKE—. ¡TE PASAS EL DÍA SENTADO Y SIN HACER NADA!

—¡ES VERDAD! —DICE ROBIN—. ¡AYÚDANOS A PONER LA MESA!

—NO TENGO TIEMPO PARA ESO —RESPONDE EXE.

—AH, ¿NO? ¡PUES YO ESTOY HARTA DE COCINAR PARA TI! —DICE AKELA.

—DEBERÍAIS AGRADECER QUE ME PREPARE PARA LA BATALLA QUE SE AVECINA
—AÑADE EXE—. VOSOTROS NO ESTÁIS LISTOS EN ABSOLUTO.

—¡¿CÓMO DICES?! —PREGUNTA ROBIN, SIN PODER CREER LO QUE OYE.

—NO SERÍAIS CAPACES DE SOBREVIVIR NI UN MINUTO SIN MÍ —SIGUE
DICIENDO EXE—. OS LO PUEDO DEMOSTRAR.

—¡CUANDO QUIERAS! —LE RETA MIKE.

DE REPENTE, EXE ABRE UN PORTAL
DEBAJO DE MIKE Y LOS DEMÁS.

NADA MÁS VER EL LIBRO, MIKE SE RELAME.

—TENGO UN POCO DE HAMBRE... —DICE.

PERO AKELA SE LO QUITA ENSEGUIDA DE LAS MANOS.

— ¡NO TE COMAS ESTE LIBRO! —LE RIÑE—.
¡LO NECESITAMOS PARA VOLVER A CASA!

—SEGURO QUE NO HACEN FALTA TODAS LAS PÁGINAS... —PLANTEA
MIKE—, ¿UN MORDISCO, NADA MÁS?

—¡QUE NO! —RECHAZA LA GATA.

BIENVENIDOS A LA AVENTURA, NOVATOS...

EL PLAN ES MUY SENCILLO: en vuestro camino de regreso a casa recorreréis varias zonas. En cada una de ellas tendréis que pasar diferentes pruebas. Y las instrucciones para superarlas están en este libro, así que ¡CUIDADLO BIEN!

AQUÍ TENÉIS UN MAPA VACÍO. Si queréis encontrar el camino de vuelta, tendréis que completarlo como si fuera un PUZLE. Conseguiréis las PIEZAS solo si superáis las pruebas durante el recorrido.

Cada vez que logréis una pieza, tendréis que RECORTARLA, volver a esta página y pegarla en el LUGAR EN EL QUE ENCAJE.

Pero ¡cuidado! Si falláis, no lograréis completar el mapa y no regresaréis a casa jamás.

¿ACEPTÁIS EL RETO?

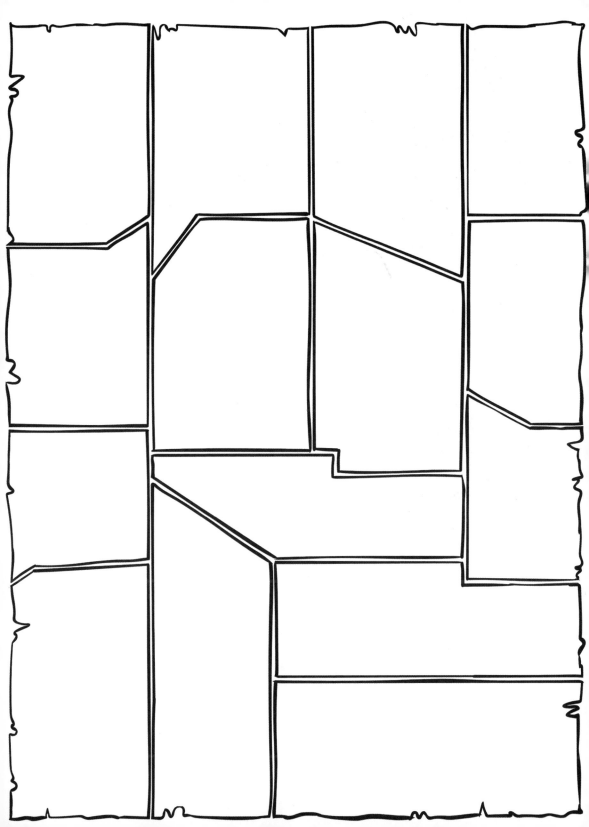

Por si no os ha quedado claro... En las pruebas más difíciles os entregaré las PIEZAS para COMPLETAR EL MAPA.

SI SUPERÁIS EL RETO, DESCUBRIRÉIS CUÁL DE LAS 3 PIEZAS QUE HAY EN EL LATERAL DE LA PÁGINA ES LA CORRECTA.

TENDRÉIS QUE RECORTARLA Y...

... PEGARLA EN EL LUGAR EN EL QUE ENCAJE DEL MAPA DE LA PÁGINA ANTERIOR.

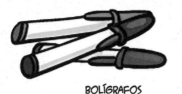

BOLÍGRAFOS

LÁPICES O ROTULADORES

TIJERAS

PARA PASAR LAS PRUEBAS TENDRÉIS QUE PINTAR, ROMPER, RAYAR, PEGAR, COLOREAR, CREAR... DEBÉIS APRENDER A IMPROVISAR CON LO QUE TENGÁIS A MANO. AQUÍ VAN UNAS CUANTAS SUGERENCIAS, PERO PODÉIS USAR LOS MATERIALES QUE QUERÁIS... *¡ECHADLE IMAGINACIÓN!*

PEGAMENTO

SI NO TIENES, PUEDES HACERLO MEZCLANDO HARINA Y AGUA.

HOJAS

GUAU!

REVISTAS

¿PODRÉ COMERME ALGO DE ESTO?

¡NO!

NECESITÁIS UN **EXE** PARA SOBREVIVIR EN MI MUNDO.

DIBUJA CÓMO SERÍA **TU VERSIÓN EXE**. PONLE UNA **BONITA** SONRISA Y UNOS **PRECIOSOS** OJOS.

¡Dibuja un **OBSTÁCULO** para que Mike no llegue a comerse el libro! Puede ser un muro, un foso con agua... ¡lo que se te ocurra!

Mike ha caído en una vieja trampa del Mundo Oscuro.
¿Crees que está asustado? ¿O solo enfadado?

¡DALE LA VUELTA AL LIBRO Y DESCUBRE LA VERDAD!

MIKE ECHA DE MENOS SU DIAMANTITO.

CREA UNO NUEVO pegando recortes de papel, cinta adhesiva de colores, cartulina, papel de regalo, pegatinas, cromos...

Para seguir adelante, tendréis que poner
a prueba VUESTRA INTELIGENCIA...

¡EMPIEZA
EL JUEGO DEL EXE!

Necesitarás enfrentarte a un amigo.
En los recuadros del tablero
SOLO PUEDES ESCRIBIR LETRAS E O X.
¡Cada palabra EXE es
un punto! ¡A ver quién gana!

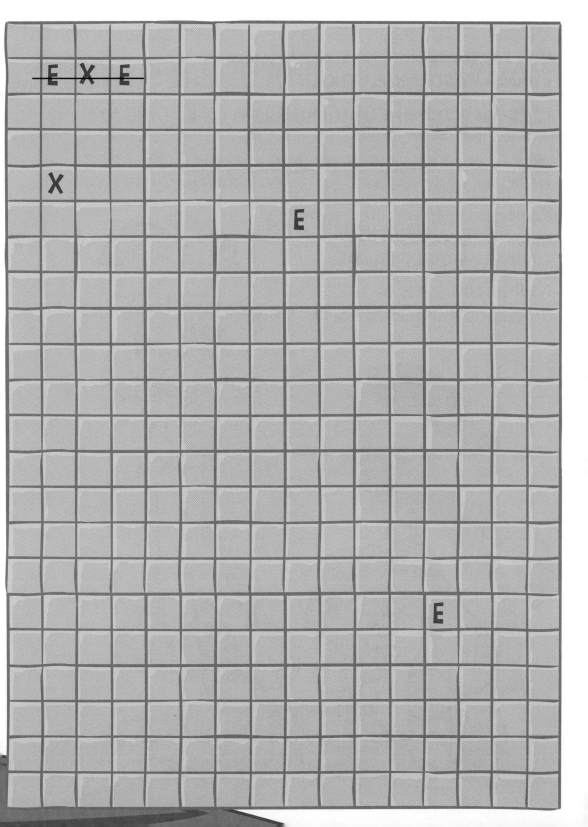

COLOREA CADA ZONA SEGÚN SU NÚMERO.
¿Puedes ver el CÓDIGO OCULTO EN EL DIBUJO?

Busca en el lateral de la página
LA PIEZA CORRESPONDIENTE A
ESE CÓDIGO. Luego pégala en el
mapa vacío al principio
del libro.

Guía de colores

357

753

375

¡CUIDADO, MIKE SIGUE TENIENDO HAMBRE!
¡ESCONDE EL LIBRO EN TU CASA PARA QUE NO SE LO COMA!

Ahora reta a tus amigos.
¿Quién tarda menos en encontrarlo?
Rellena la tabla de clasificación.

POSICIÓN	BUSCADOR	TIEMPO
1 💎		
2		
3		
4		
5		
1		
2		
3		
4		
5		

¿Cuánto tiempo creéis que aguantaréis en este mundo?
Yo pasé años a solas dentro de él.

¿QUERÉIS SABER CÓMO ME SENTÍA?

Hagamos un experimento...
Escribid la misma palabra MUCHAS VECES,
cada vez más pequeña.

Mira a un amigo a la cara
y pídele que diga lo que tienes que dibujar.
AHORA DIBÚJALO SIN DEJAR DE MIRARLE.
¿SE PARECE A LO QUE TE HA PEDIDO?

Repite el mismo juego en una hoja de papel, pero dibujando los dos a la vez, sin dejar de miraros. Hazlo una tercera vez, pero ahora, además, ¡el que se ría pierde!

¡SÍ! USA UN CEPILLO DE DIENTES Y PASTA DENTAL o pintura blanca para salpicar el cielo.

No creo que vayan a conseguirlo
ellos solos... Será mejor que
les ayudes:

CREA UNA FUSIÓN DE TI MISMO CON EL PERSONAJE QUE PREFIERAS: MIKE, EXE, AKELA, WILLY...

HABÉIS LLEGADO AL FINAL DEL MUNDO DE LOS EXE, PERO QUEDA UNA ÚLTIMA PRUEBA... DEBÉIS DEMOSTRAR QUE CONOCÉIS A LOS QUE VIVÍAN AQUÍ.

¡UN TEST SOBRE MÍ!

1. ¿DE DÓNDE SACÓ EXE LA ESTRELLA MALDITA?

a) La robó

b) La fabricó

c) Se la encontró

2. ¿CÓMO SE CONVIRTIÓ LA DIMENSIÓN DE EXE EN EL MUNDO OSCURO?

a) Pintándolo todo de negro

b) Por culpa de un fenómeno natural

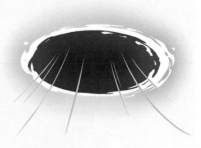

c) Por accidente, cuando Exe abrió un portal con la Estrella Maldita

3. ¿CUÁNTAS MASCOTAS TENÍA EXE CUANDO VIVÍA EN SU DIMENSIÓN?

a) Dos

b) Catorce

c) Una

4. ¿POR QUÉ RAPTÓ EXE A LOS AMIGOS DE MIKE?

    a) Para hacer una fiesta

    b) Para gastarle una broma a Mike

    c) Para protegerlos de Mike

5. ¿CUÁNTOS AÑOS PASÓ EXE A SOLAS EN EL MUNDO OSCURO?

    a) 2

    b) 5

    c) Más de 200

¿CUÁL ES LA SOLUCIÓN CORRECTA?

Mayoría de respuestas a)   ⟶   Pieza 1

Mayoría de respuestas b)   ⟶   Pieza 2

Mayoría de respuestas c)   ⟶   Pieza 3

Recorta la pieza correspondiente a tu respuesta y pégala en el mapa vacío del principio del libro.

1

2

3

MARCA LAS ACTIVIDADES QUE HAS COMPLETADO:

☐ Dibujar personaje Exe.

☐ Hacer un refugio con palillos.

☐ Dibujar obstáculo para que Mike
no se coma el libro.

☐ Darle la vuelta al libro y descubrir
si Mike está asustado.

☐ Hacer un diamantito pegando recortes.

☐ Juego del EXE.

☐ Colorear por números.

☐ Esconder el libro.

☐ Escribir la misma palabra cada vez más pequeña.

☐ Poner cola blanca y pegote de pintura.

☐ Dibujar mirando a la cara.

☐ Pintar estrellas en el cielo del Mundo Oscuro.

☐ Dibujar tu personaje fusión.

☐ Test sobre Exe.

RECORTA ESTA
PIEZA EXTRA
Y PÉGALA EN
SU LUGAR EN EL
MAPA VACÍO
DEL PRINCIPIO
DEL LIBRO.

AHORA VIENE ALGO MUCHO MÁS FÁCIL...

AQUÍ NADA ES LO QUE PARECE...

Fijaos en esos huesos que están tirados en la vía del tren. Si adivináis CUÁL ES EL MÁS GRANDE, se lo daré a Mike para que aguante un rato más sin comerse el libro.

CUANDO CREAS QUE LO SABES,
PUEDES MEDIRLOS CON UNA REGLA.
¿HAS ACERTADO?

LOS VEO MUY CONFIADOS...

Hagamos un desierto infinito para que se den cuenta de lo que tienen por delante. ¡Pega arena sobre el paisaje! Si no tienes, puedes usar pan rallado, sal, azúcar...

Todos tienen sed menos Mike, que siempre está
hambriento y está pensando en comerse el libro.
DIBUJA TU COMIDA FAVORITA
        PARA QUE MIKE SE FIJE EN ELLA.

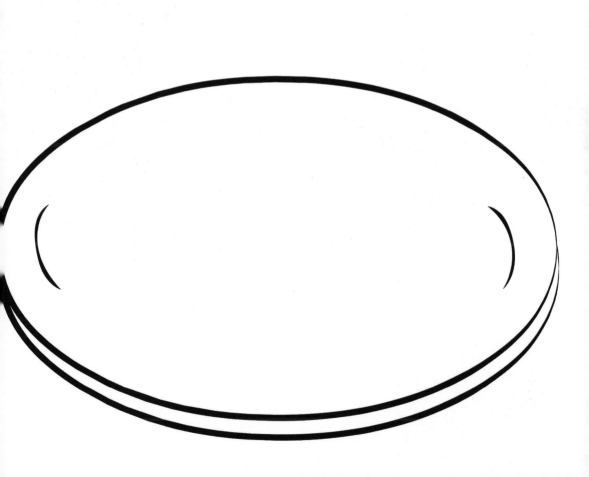

Al final de un pasillo, FORMA CON CINTA ADHESIVA TRES CUADRADOS EN EL SUELO, cada uno más pequeño que el otro, como los de abajo.

Ahora, juega con tus amigos a lanzar pelotas rodando por el pasillo, a ver quién deja las suyas más cerca del centro del cuadrado.

Repite el juego, ¡pero ya no vale que las pelotas reboten en las paredes!

VEAMOS SI TODAVÍA TE FUNCIONA BIEN LA CABEZA.

¿Puedes llegar a escribir 5?

1. _____

2. _____

3. _____

4. _____

5. _____

¡HABÉIS LLEGADO AL LABERINTO!

Al otro lado encontraréis un oasis.
Pero cuidado: si os perdéis,
podéis quedaros dentro
para siempre...

Solo un camino lleva a la
pieza correcta. Recórtala
y pégala en el lugar en el
que encaje del mapa vacío
al principio del libro.

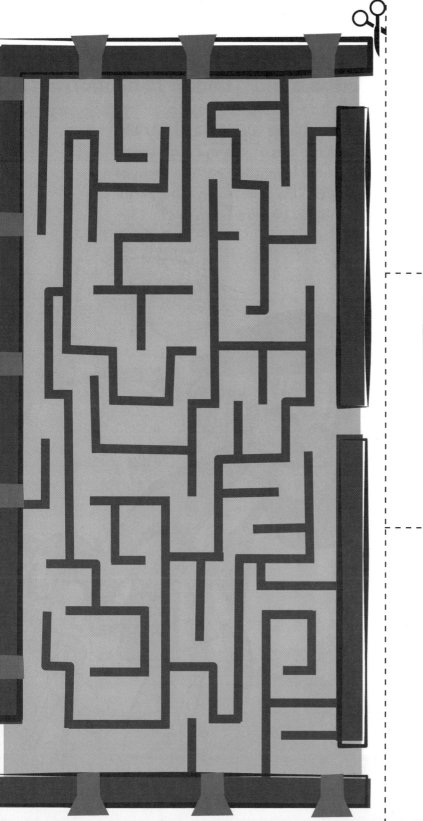

Todos han salido del laberinto MENOS MIKE. ¡¿Dónde se ha metido?!

DIBUJA A QUIEN QUIERAS QUE LE AYUDE a reunirse con el grupo. Puede ser un personaje inventado para la serie de LAS PERRERÍAS DE MIKE, un superhéroe, un amigo... ¿Qué se te ocurre?

¡MIKE SE HA QUEDADO DORMIDO!

DESPIÉRTALE PARA CONTINUAR CON LA AVENTURA: CHILLA, GRITA, ESCRIBE, GARABATEA... ¡PUEDES PEDIR AYUDA A UN AMIGO!

¡POR FIN! ¡EL OASIS!

¡CONSTRUYE UNA BALSA para Mike con los materiales que prefieras! Puedes atar o pegar lápices, palitos o cualquier cosa que se te ocurra. Luego recorta la bandera que más te guste y ponla en tu embarcación pirata. ¡Aaarrrr!

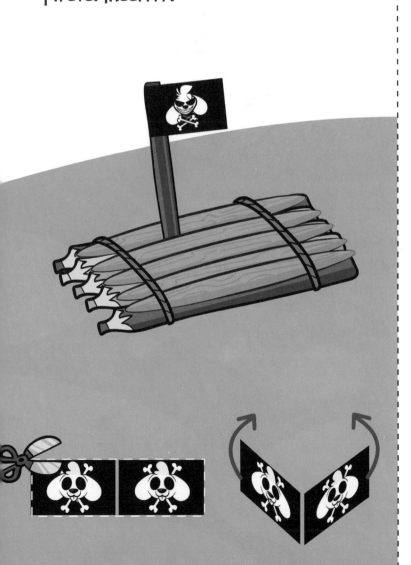

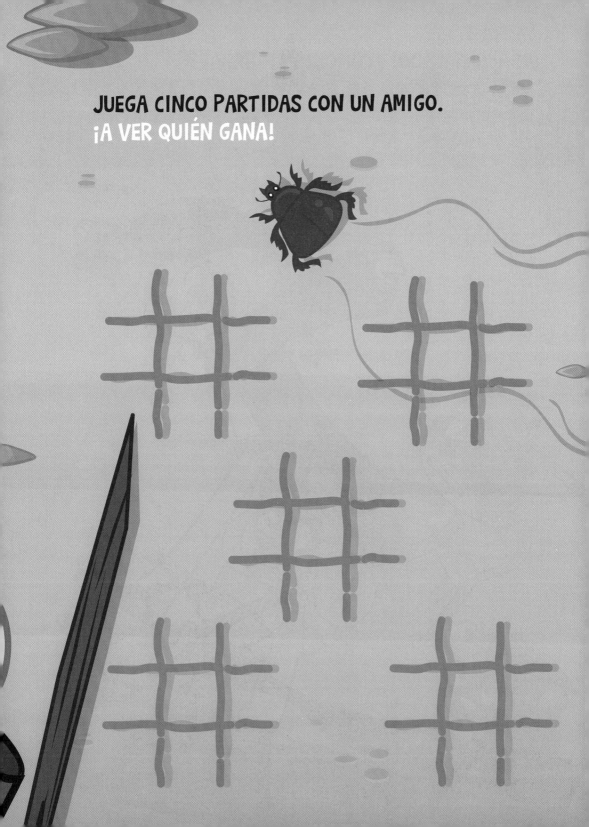

JUEGA CINCO PARTIDAS CON UN AMIGO.
¡A VER QUIÉN GANA!

¡UN ACANTILADO! ¿CÓMO VAN A BAJAR?
¿Y SI LES AYUDAS FABRICANDO UN ASCENSOR?

INSTRUCCIONES

1. Forra una CAJA DE CEREALES con papel. Si quieres, puedes pintarlo con los colores que más te gusten.

2. Haz dos agujeros en la parte superior.

3. Recorta y pega la imagen de Mike y sus amigos en uno de los laterales anchos.

4. Para hacer bajar el ascensor, pasa una cuerda por los agujeros y haz un nudo.

SE ESTÁ LEVANTANDO AIRE. ¿VIENE UN TORNADO?
DIBÚJALO CON GARABATOS.
¿HAY COSAS VOLANDO DENTRO DE ÉL?

LLEVAN DEMASIADO TIEMPO EN EL DESIERTO Y
ESTÁN VIENDO ESPEJISMOS. ¡PONGAMOS ALGUNOS MÁS! ¡JI, JI, JI, JI!

MOJA EL CORCHO de una
botella en pintura y dibuja
lo que quieras con círculos.
Cuando la pintura esté seca,
puedes pintar caras en el
interior.

PARA QUE UN EQUIPO FUNCIONE,
HAY QUE CONOCER BIEN A SUS MIEMBROS.
EMPEZAREMOS POR VER LO QUE SABÉIS

DE AKELA...

1. ¿CUÁNTOS AÑOS TIENE AKELA?

a) 143

b) Los mismos que Mike

c) 8

2. ¿CUÁL DE ESTAS COSAS SE
LLEVARÍA AKELA PRIMERO?

a) Un bocadillo

b) Un tornillo

c) Un billete

3. ¿CUÁL ES EL PODER DE AKELA?

a) Cocinar con los ojos cerrados

b) Controlar el agua

c) Hacerse invisible

4. ¿QUIÉN AYUDÓ A AKELA A ENCONTRAR A MIKE?

a) La policía

b) Robin

c) Un perro rastreador

5. ¿QUÉ LLEVA SIEMPRE AKELA EN LA MOCHILA?

a) Comida

b) Cosas que brillan

c) Lápices de colores

¿CUÁL ES LA SOLUCIÓN CORRECTA?

Mayoría de respuestas b) ⟶ Pieza 1

Mayoría de respuestas a) ⟶ Pieza 2

Mayoría de respuestas c) ⟶ Pieza 3

Recorta la pieza correspondiente a tu respuesta
y pégala en el mapa vacío del principio del libro.

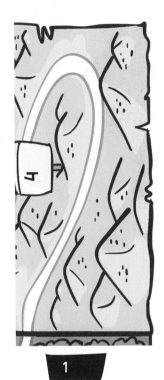

1

2

3

MARCA LAS ACTIVIDADES QUE HAS COMPLETADO:

- [ ] ¿Qué hueso es más grande?
- [ ] Llenar de arena el desierto.
- [ ] Dibujar tu comida favorita.
- [ ] Juego de los cuadrados.
- [ ] Palabras que son iguales al revés.
- [ ] Laberinto.
- [ ] Dibujar personaje para encontrar a Mike.
- [ ] Despertar a Mike.
- [ ] Construir una balsa.
- [ ] Jugar al tres en raya.
- [ ] Hacer un ascensor.
- [ ] Dibujar un tornado.
- [ ] Dibujar con un corcho.
- [ ] Test sobre Akela.

RECORTA ESTA PIEZA EXTRA Y PÉGALA EN SU LUGAR EN EL MAPA VACÍO DEL PRINCIPIO DEL LIBRO.

CREA UNA CUERDA CON HILOS DE COLORES Y PÉGALA
PARA AYUDAR A MIKE A LLEGAR A LO ALTO DEL ÁRBOL.

¡POR FIN! ¡COMIDA!

¡MANCHA LA SELVA! VIERTE EN ESTAS PÁGINAS GOTAS DE ZUMO, DE REFRESCO, DE BATIDO... CIERRA EL LIBRO Y VUELVE A ABRIRLO, A VER CÓMO HA QUEDADO.

INSTRUCCIONES:

1. Agarra un cartón de leche, saca las dos es quinas de arriba y córtalas.

2. Mete una cuerda por uno de los agujeros y sácala por el otro.

3. Ata un extremo de la cuerda en
   un punto más alto, y el otro
   en un punto más bajo, ¡para
   que la tirolina se deslice
   hacia abajo!

DIBUJA ALGO SUJETANDO EL LÁPIZ CON LA BOCA.
¿SE PARECE A LO QUE QUERÍAS PINTAR?
¿QUÉ OPINAN TUS AMIGOS?

ECHA ENCIMA DE MIKE COLONIA, PERFUME, LACA...
¿QUÉ TAL HUELE?

¡SOPA DE LETRAS! ENCUENTRA LAS 5 PALABRAS ESCONDIDAS PARA SEGUIR ADELANTE.

DIAMANTITO   CHOCOLATE   MASCOTA   AKELA   PAPEL

¿CUÁLES SON LAS LETRAS EN LAS QUE SE CRUZAN LAS PALABRAS?

MÁRCALAS CON UN CÍRCULO,
COMO EN EL SIGUIENTE EJEMPLO:

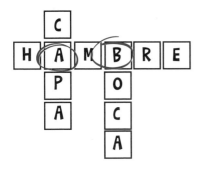

¿QUÉ PALABRA SE PUEDE FORMAR CON ELLAS?

____ ____ ____ ____ ____

APÚNTALA AQUÍ Y DESPUÉS RECORTA LA PIEZA
CORRECTA PARA PEGARLA EN EL MAPA VACÍO
AL PRINCIPIO DEL LIBRO.

CALMA

LAPAS

SACAS

CREA UN PUENTE CON PALILLOS O ESPAGUETIS
PARA LLEGAR AL OTRO LADO DEL RÍO.

¡EL PUENTE SE HA ROTO!

¡SOLO AKELA PUEDE SACARLOS DEL RÍO!

DIBUJA LO QUE HA CREADO AKELA CON SUS PODERES
PARA MANEJAR EL AGUA Y SALVARLOS. ¿BURBUJAS?
¿UN BARCO DE AGUA?

MIKE VUELVE A TENER HAMBRE: DALE DE COMER BOLITAS DE PAPEL HIGIÉNICO PEGÁNDOLAS EN SU BOCA ANTES DE QUE VENGA A POR EL LIBRO.

ESCRIBE TÚ
LA PALABRA MÁGICA.

Si quieres que sea secreta, hazlo con zumo de limón y un palillo. Para hacerla visible, solo tendrás que pedir ayuda a tus padres y aplicar calor sobre la página con una linterna.

ESTÁ BIEN...
AHORA HAREMOS
UN TEST SOBRE MIKE.

1. MIKE NUNCA SE QUITA LA CAPA PORQUE...

   a) Cree que algún día podrá volar
   como un superhéroe

   b) Le gusta el color verde

   c) Se siente desnudo sin ella

2. LA COMIDA FAVORITA DE MIKE ES...

   a) La pasta

   b) El chocolate

   c) El chocolate con almendras

3. EL PRIMER LUGAR EN EL QUE MIKE VIO A EXE FUE...

   a) Un sueño

   b) La taza del váter

   c) Un espejo

4. LA MUJER DE TROLLINO, QUE ENCONTRÓ A MIKE EN LA CALLE, SE LLAMABA...

a) Ambrozzia

b) Mari Carmen

c) Roberta

5. LA IDEA DE ADOPTAR A WILLY PERRO FUE DE...

a) Trollino, para que Mike tuviera un hermano

b) No lo adoptaron, sino que lo encontraron en la calle

c) Mike, porque quería tener una mascota

¿CUÁL ES LA SOLUCIÓN CORRECTA?

Mayoría de respuestas a) ⟶ Pieza 1

Mayoría de respuestas b) ⟶ Pieza 2

Mayoría de respuestas c) ⟶ Pieza 3

Recorta la pieza correspondiente a tu respuesta y pégala en el mapa vacío del principio del libro.

1

2

3

- ☐ Pelea de bolígrafos.
- ☐ Crear cuerda para subir al árbol.
- ☐ Manchar la página.
- ☐ Hacer una tirolina.
- ☐ Dibujar con la boca.
- ☐ Disfrazar a Exe.
- ☐ Perfumar a Mike.
- ☐ Sopa de letras.
- ☐ Puente sobre el río.
- ☐ Dibujar lo que crea Akela con sus poderes.
- ☐ Dar de comer bolitas de papel a Mike.
- ☐ Llenar la selva de cosas verdes.
- ☐ Palabra mágica con tinta invisible.
- ☐ Test sobre Mike.

RECORTA ESTA PIEZA EXTRA Y PÉGALA EN SU LUGAR EN EL MAPA VACÍO DEL PRINCIPIO DEL LIBRO.

SE HA HECHO DE NOCHE

PEGA COSAS AMARILLAS O PINTA CON TONOS BLANCOS Y AMARILLOS
PARA CREAR LUZ PARA MIKE.

Y TIENEN MIEDO

ESCRIBE UN MENSAJE A MIKE PARA QUE NO SE COMA EL LIBRO Y COMPÁRTELO EN INSTAGRAM CON EL HASHTAG #notecomasestelibro. No te olvides de etiquetar a @mikecrackyt para asegurarte de que la recibe.

Querido Mike

¿Y A TI? ¿QUÉ ES LO QUE TE DA MÁS MIEDO?

_____

_____

_____

_____

ENCUENTRA A PERSONAS QUE TENGAN ESTOS MIEDOS Y APUNTA AQUÍ SUS NOMBRES:

NADAR EN EL MAR			
LAS ARAÑAS			
LA OSCURIDAD			
LAS ALTURAS			
ESTAR EN LUGARES PEQUEÑOS (COMO UN ASCENSOR)			
LAS SERPIENTES			
VOLAR EN AVIÓN			

ARRANCA LA PÁGINA SIGUIENTE
Y PREPARA EN UN CUENCO UNA APETITOSA ENSALADA CON ELLA: AÑADE INGREDIENTES QUE LE GUSTEN A MIKE (BOLITAS DE PAPEL HIGIÉNICO, CHOCOLATE, ALMENDRAS, CHUCHES...).

PIDE A ALGUIEN QUE PIENSE UNA PALABRA Y TRATA DE ADIVINAR LAS LETRAS QUE LA COMPONEN.

CADA VEZ QUE FALLES, PINTA UNA ZONA DE AGUA, EMPEZANDO POR ABAJO.
SI LLEGAS ARRIBA DEL TODO, ¡HAS PERDIDO Y MIKE TENDRÁ QUE BAÑARSE!

BUENO, HABÉIS LLEGADO HASTA AQUÍ, PERO A VER SI PODÉIS CONSEGUIR UNA PIEZA MÁS...

RELLENA EL CRUCIGRAMA Y APUNTA LAS LETRAS QUE APAREZCAN EN LAS CASILLAS DE COLORES. DESPUÉS, ELIGE LA PIEZA CORRESPONDIENTE A ESAS LETRAS.

1: LA MASCOTA DE MIKE.

2: SUPERPODER QUE PERMITE A MIKE COMER TODO LO QUE LE DÉ LA GANA.

3: EL LUGAR DEL QUE PROVIENEN AKELA Y MIKE, Y QUE EXPLOTÓ DESPUÉS DE QUE ELLOS SE ESCAPARAN.

4: EL HOMBRE AL QUE MIKE NO PERMITE QUE SE ACERQUE AL BUZÓN.

5: LA CHICA QUE AYUDÓ A AKELA A ENCONTRAR A MIKE.

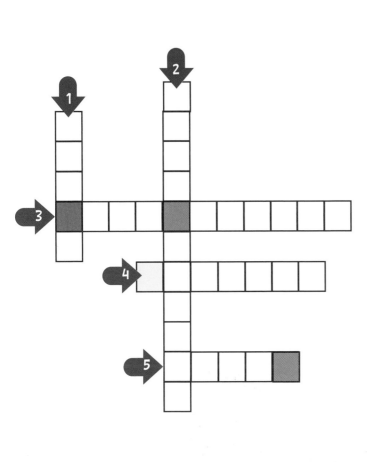

P V A R

L R C N

¿QUÉ LETRA HAS DESCUBIERTO EN CADA COLOR?
¡RECORTA LA PIEZA CORRECTA Y PÉGALA EN EL
LUGAR QUE ENCAJE DEL MAPA DEL PRINCIPIO
DEL LIBRO!

L R J T

VEAMOS SI OS QUEDA CABEZA PARA PENSAR UN POCO...

¡JUGUEMOS A LOS CUADRADOS TENEBROSOS!

Juega con un amigo. Elegid un color cada uno. En cada turno debes pintar una raya entre dos piedras. Si consigues cerrar un cuadrado, coloréalo de tu color y será un punto para ti.

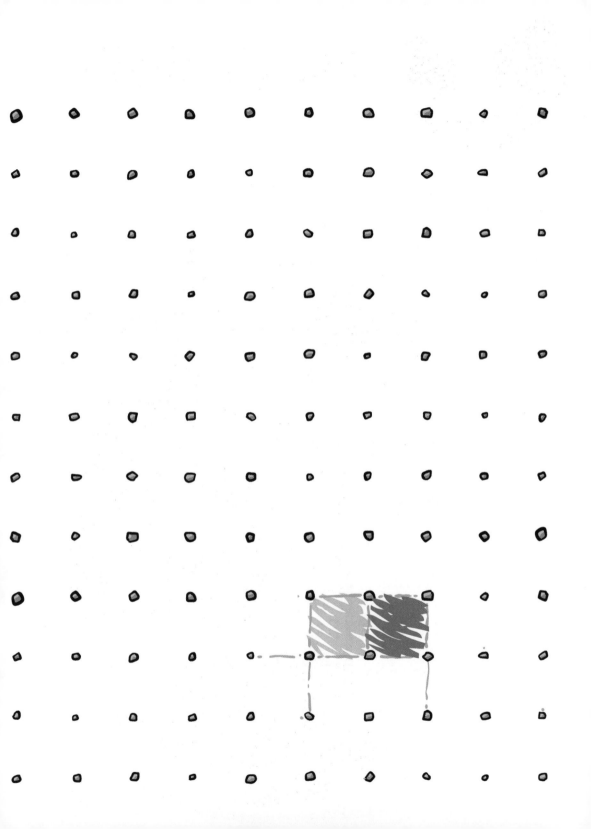

ESTOS DOS PORTALES LLEVAN AL MISMO SITIO...

¿O NO? ENCUENTRA LAS 7 DIFERENCIAS ENTRE ESTAS DOS IMÁGENES PARA CONTINUAR.

¡EXE NOS HA ENCERRADO EN EL LABORATORIO! ¿CÓMO SALIMOS?

TAL VEZ PODAMOS ENCONTRAR ALGO QUE DERRITA LA PARED.

FABRICA SLIME Y PÉGALO ENCIMA DE LA GRIETA DE LA PARED.

¿CÓMO HACER SLIME?

1. Mezcla cola blanca con un poco de pasta de dientes y dale vueltas.

2. Si todavía no ha quedado bien, echa más pasta.

3. Si tienes colorante o purpurina, ¡añádelo también!

¡VAMOS A JUGAR AL ENREDADEDOS!

Necesitas un DADO y ALGUIEN con quien jugar.

Primero, elegid cada uno con qué MANO vais a participar.
Antes de cada tirada, tu oponente debe decidir qué dedo vas a
mover. Luego TIRA EL DADO y COLOCA EL DEDO sobre cualquiera de
los SÍMBOLOS ASIGNADOS A ESE NÚMERO que esté libre.

En los siguientes turnos no podrás mover los dedos que ya tengas sobre el tablero, excepto si lo elige tu contrincante.

SI SALE UN 6, ¡PASAS TURNO!

¡El primero que se rinda pierde!

 1   2   3   4   5

ÚLTIMA OPORTUNIDAD PARA ASUSTARLOS.

PON TU MANO SOBRE LA PÁGINA DE AL LADO Y DIBUJA SU PERFIL CON UN BOLI. DESPUÉS, COMPLETA EL DIBUJO PARA QUE PAREZCA UN PERSONAJE TENEBROSO, PONIÉNDOLE OJOS, BOCA Y LO QUE CREAS QUE LE FALTA. ¡PREGUNTA A TUS AMIGOS QUÉ VEN! ¿LES DA MIEDO?

AHORA VAMOS A HACER UNAS CUANTAS PREGUNTAS SOBRE **WILLY.**
¿ESTÁS PREPARADO...?

1. ¿CUÁNTOS PERROS HABÍA EN LA PERRERA EN LA QUE ESTABA WILLY CUANDO LO FUERON A ADOPTAR?

a) 3

b) 12

c) Solo estaba él

2. ¿CÓMO CONSIGUIÓ WILLY QUE LO ADOPTARAN?

a) Poniendo ojitos tiernos

b) Demostrando que sabía hacer volteretas

c) Mordiendo a Mike

3. ¿A QUÉ JUEGAN WILLY Y MIKE EN LA BAÑERA?

a) A tirarse patitos de goma

b) A los barquitos

c) Al balón prisionero

4. ¿QUÉ SUPERPODER TIENE WILLY?

a) Ninguno

b) Superfuerza

c) Mover objetos con la mente

5. ¿QUÉ CAJA COMPARTE WILLY CON MIKE?

a) La caja de las cosas de morder

b) La caja de herramientas

c) Una caja de zapatos

¿CUÁL ES LA SOLUCIÓN CORRECTA?

Mayoría de respuestas a) ⟶ Pieza 1

Mayoría de respuestas b) ⟶ Pieza 2

Mayoría de respuestas c) ⟶ Pieza 3

Recorta la pieza correspondiente a tu respuesta y pégala en el mapa vacío del principio del libro.

1

2

3

MARCA LAS ACTIVIDADES QUE HAS COMPLETADO:

- ☐ Crear huellas terroríficas.

- ☐ Añadir cosas amarillas o blancas.

- ☐ Escribir un mensaje a Mike.

- ☐ Escribir tus miedos.

- ☐ Colorear con acuarelas.

- ☐ Preparar una ensalada para Mike.

- ☐ Adivinar la palabra.

- ☐ Crucigrama.

- ☐ Cuadrados tenebrosos.

- ☐ Encontrar las 7 diferencias.

- ☐ Fabricar slime.

- ☐ Enredadedos.

- ☐ Crear un personaje con la forma de tu mano.

- ☐ Test sobre Willy.

RECORTA ESTA PIEZA EXTRA Y PÉGALA EN SU LUGAR EN EL MAPA VACÍO DEL PRINCIPIO DEL LIBRO.

SOIS MIS PEQUEÑAS MARIONETAS, JI, JI, JI, JI.

¡HAZ LAS TUYAS USANDO ROLLOS DE PAPEL HIGIÉNICO!

Haz unos cortes en la parte superior para conseguir las orejas gatunas de Akela y pliega lo sobrante hacia dentro.

Con cartulina verde puedes hacer la capa de Mike.

El pelo de Robin puedes hacerlo con hilos de color amarillo, y después poner un círculo de cartón negro encima para que sea su boina.

Para Willy, pinta su collar negro todo alrededor.

¿HAS VISTO LA LISTA DE DESEOS DE MIKE?
¡Escribe tu propia lista! ¡Puedes incluir dibujos si quieres!

MIKE QUIERE COMER... OTRA VEZ.

¡Y AHORA VA A SER DIFÍCIL IMPEDIR QUE SE COMA EL LIBRO!
UNTA O FROTA CHOCOLATE POR TODA LA PÁGINA PARA CALMAR
SU SUPERHAMBRE.

TENÉIS CINCO MINUTOS

PARA RECOGER EQUIPAMIENTO EN EL MERCADO.
PENSAD EN LO QUE PODÉIS NECESITAR PARA COMPLETAR EL CAMINO.

¡DAOS PRISA!

MIKE ESTÁ LLENANDO SU MOCHILA. ¡LLENA LA TUYA!
¿QUÉ NECESITAS PARA LO QUE QUEDA DE AVENTURA?

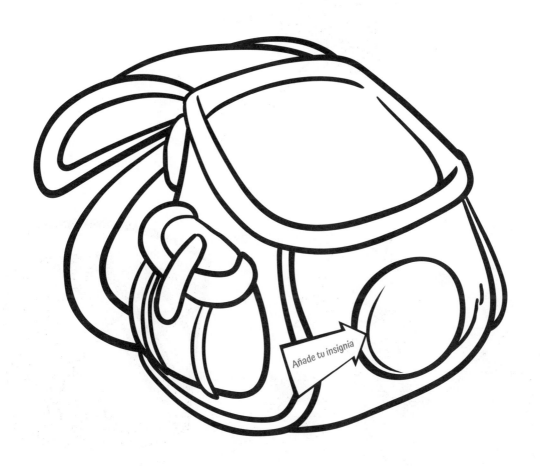

A VER CÓMO VAIS DE PUNTERÍA.

Usa un vaso para encestar bolas de papel y juega con tus amigos a ver quién es el primero en hacer 10 canastas.

Escribe los nombres de los jugadores y añade una X cada vez que hagan canasta. ¡El primero que llegue a 10, gana!

NOMBRE	1	2	3	4	5	6	7	8	9	10

¡PIENSA RÁPIDO!

Pide a tus padres que elija una letra y rellena la tabla de la página siguiente con palabras que empiecen por ella. ¡Solo tienes 5 minutos!

COSAS QUE MIKE ODIA	
FRUTA	
COSAS QUE SE COMERÍA MIKE	
NOMBRES DE ANIMALES	
COSAS QUE LE GUSTAN A MIKE	
COLORES	

PUEDES COPIAR LA TABLA EN UN PAPEL Y VOLVER A JUGAR CON TUS AMIGOS TODAS LAS VECES QUE QUIERAS.

WILLY Y ROBIN ESTÁN IMAGINANDO LO QUE DICEN MIKE Y AKELA.
¿QUIERES JUGAR TÚ TAMBIÉN?
PON UN CAPÍTULO DE LAS PERRERÍAS DE MIKE Y JUEGA CON UN AMIGO
A PONER LAS VOCES DE LOS PERSONAJES.

¿SABES CÓMO SE JUEGA AL SUDOKU?

HAY QUE RELLENAR LAS CASILLAS VACÍAS CON 4 SÍMBOLOS POSIBLES: ESPIRAL, CHOCOLATE, DIAMANTITO Y LUNA.

EN CADA FILA HORIZONTAL O VERTICAL SOLO PUEDE HABER UN SÍMBOLO DE CADA, Y EN CADA CUADRADO TAMPOCO SE PUEDEN REPETIR. ¿TE ATREVES A INTENTARLO?

A MÍ ESTO ME SUENA DE ALGO...

DESCUBRE QUÉ SÍMBOLOS ESTÁN EN LAS CASILLAS GRIS Y VIOLETA Y ELIGE LA PIEZA CORRESPONDIENTE, RECÓRTALA Y PÉGALA EN EL MAPA AL PRINCIPIO DEL LIBRO.

RECORTA LOS OJOS Y LA BOCA DE MIKE,
Y PÉGALOS EN UNA CAJA DE CEREALES.
¡ASÍ DESAYUNARÉIS JUNTOS
TODOS LOS DÍAS!

DIBUJA UNA MASCOTA COMO MIKE
CON LA MANO QUE UTILICES PEOR

(SI ERES DIESTRO, CON LA IZQUIERDA; SI ERES ZURDO, CON LA DERECHA).
¡ENSEÑA TU DIBUJO! ¿CUÁNTOS HAN ADIVINADO LO QUE ERA?

¡ATRÉVETE A DEJARLE UN MENSAJE AL CARTERO!

PÉGALO DELANTE DEL BUZÓN.

¡ESTÁN A PUNTO DE LLEGAR!

DIBUJA UN PERSONAJE NOOB QUE LOS ENTRETENGA MIENTRAS
SE ME OCURRE OTRA PRUEBA...

¡NO PUEDO CREERLO!
¡LO HAN CONSEGUIDO!

¡QUIERO ROMPER ALGO! ¡AYÚDAME! HAZLE PERRERÍAS
A LA PÁGINA DE AL LADO: RAYA, ROMPE, RASGA, PINTA,
GARABATEA...

PEGA TU FOTO EN EL ESPACIO EN BLANCO QUE HAY ENTRE NOSOTROS

Y HAZ UNA FOTO.
¡LO HEMOS CONSEGUIDO!

¡UN MOMENTO...!

AÚN QUEDA EL ÚLTIMO TEST. LE TOCA A

ROBIN.

1. ¿CUÁL FUE EL PRIMER CAPÍTULO DE LA SERIE DE LAS PERRERÍAS DE MIKE EN EL QUE APARECIÓ ROBIN?

a) El oscuro secreto de Mike.exe

b) Sonríe más 2

c) El reencuentro de Mike y Akela

2. ¿QUÉ PASÓ LA PRIMERA VEZ QUE ROBIN VIO A EXE?

a) Se marchó por donde había venido

b) Tuvo miedo

c) Lo confundió con Mike y fue corriendo a saludarlo

3. ¿QUÉ OPINA ROBIN DE QUE A AKELA LE GUSTE ROBAR?

a) Le da igual

b) Está orgullosa

c) No le parece bien

4. ¿QUÉ ARMA USÓ ROBIN PARA LUCHAR CONTRA KARMA?

a) Una pistola de agua

b) Un tirachinas

c) Nunca ha luchado contra él

5. ¿CON QUIÉN SE FUSIONÓ ROBIN?

a) Con Akela

b) Con Mike

c) Nunca se ha fusionado con nadie

¿CUÁL ES LA SOLUCIÓN CORRECTA?

Mayoría de respuestas a) ⟶ Pieza 1

Mayoría de respuestas b) ⟶ Pieza 2

Mayoría de respuestas c) ⟶ Pieza 3

Recorta la pieza correspondiente a tu respuesta y pégala en el mapa vacío del principio del libro.

MARCA LAS ACTIVIDADES QUE HAS COMPLETADO:

- ☐ Marionetas con rollos vacíos de papel higiénico.
- ☐ Escribir lista de deseos.
- ☐ Frotar chocolate en la página.
- ☐ Dibujar lo que llevas en la mochila.
- ☐ Jugar a la canasta con bolas de papel.
- ☐ Escribir palabras que empiecen por una letra.
- ☐ Poner voz a personajes de Las Perrerías de Mike.
- ☐ Sudoku.
- ☐ Poner ojos y boca a una caja de cereales.
- ☐ Dibujar con la mano que usas peor.
- ☐ Escribir un mensaje para el cartero.
- ☐ Dibujar un personaje noob.
- ☐ Hacerle perrerías a la página.
- ☐ Pegar tu foto.
- ☐ Test sobre Robin.

RECORTA ESTA PIEZA EXTRA Y PÉGALA EN SU LUGAR EN EL MAPA VACÍO DEL PRINCIPIO DEL LIBRO.

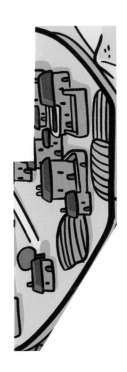

Esto aún no ha terminado...

¿HAS COMPLETADO EL MAPA QUE HAY AL PRINCIPIO DEL LIBRO?

¿Te has fijado en los números que tiene?
Para averiguar el código secreto, copia en cada círculo
el número correspondiente a su color.

CÓDIGO SECRETO

¿Ya lo tienes? ¡Ahora pasa a la página siguiente!

¡RECOGE TU REGALO!

Busca la caja que tiene el código secreto correcto y apunta con la cámara de un móvil hacia él. ¿Alguien ha dejado un mensaje para ti?

¿LO HAS LOGRADO?

¡Cuéntaselo a tus amigos!
Si no ha sido así, tal vez encuentres un poco
de ayuda en la siguiente página...

SOLUCIONES

COLOREA CADA ZONA SEGÚN SU NÚMERO
El código correcto es 357.
¡Recorta la pieza superior!

TEST SOBRE EXE
1c, 2c, 3c, 4c, 5c.
Hay cinco respuestas C, así que recorta la pieza número 3.

EL LABERINTO
La salida correcta lleva a la pieza 2.

TEST SOBRE AKELA
1b, 2b, 3b, 4b, 5b.
Hay cinco respuestas B, así que recorta la pieza número 1.

SOPA DE LETRAS
La palabra que se puede formar es CALMA.
Recorta la pieza número 1.

TEST SOBRE MIKE
1c, 2c, 3c, 4c, 5c.
Hay cinco respuestas C, así que recorta la pieza número 3.

CRUCIGRAMA

1 Willj; 2 superhambre; 3 laboratorio; 4 cartero; 5 Robin.
La solución es LRCN.
¡Recorta la pieza central!

TEST SOBRE WILLY
1a, 2a, 3a, 4a, 5a.
Hay cinco respuestas A, así que recorta la pieza número 1.

SUDOKU

¡Recorta la pieza número 1!

TEST SOBRE ROBIN
1c, 2c, 3c, 4c, 5c.
Hay cinco respuestas C, así que recorta la pieza número 3.

SI HAS LLEGADO HASTA AQUÍ ES QUE ME *JAMAS* MUCHO.

¡RECÓRTAME Y LLÉVAME SIEMPRE CONTIGO!

INSTRUCCIONES:

1. Recorta todas las piezas por las líneas del exterior, respetando las pestañas de color gris.

2. Dobla las piezas por las líneas de color negro.

3. Pon pegamento en las pestañas de color gris y pega las piezas por separado.

4. Primero, pega las orejas y la boca a la cabeza.

5. Luego pega la capa en la parte de arriba del cuerpo.

6. Ahora el cuerpo a la cabeza.

7. Pega las dos piernas en la parte de abajo del cuerpo.

8. Después los brazos a cada lado del cuerpo.

9. Pega la placa a la base.

10. Finalmente pega la figura a la base.

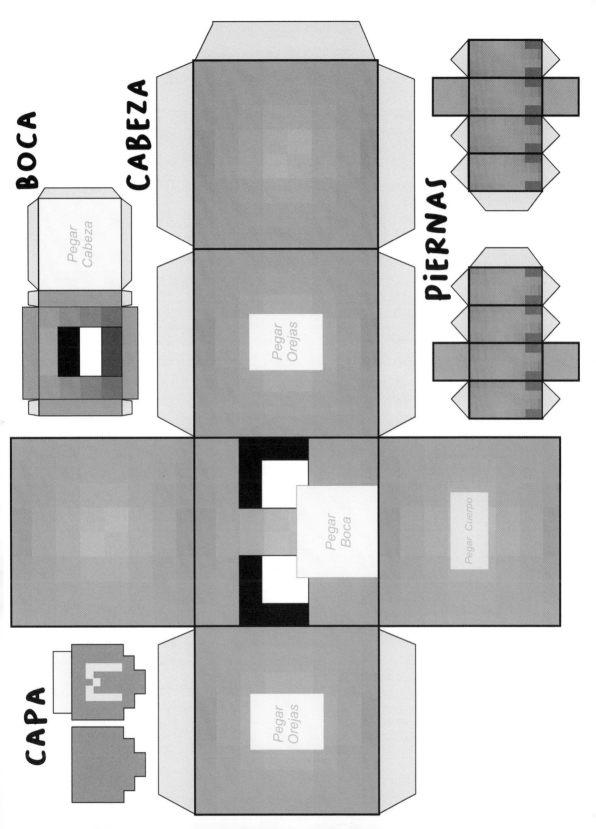

BOCA

CABEZA

CAPA

PIERNAS

Pegar Cabeza

Pegar Orejas

Pegar Boca

Pegar Cuerpo

Pegar Orejas

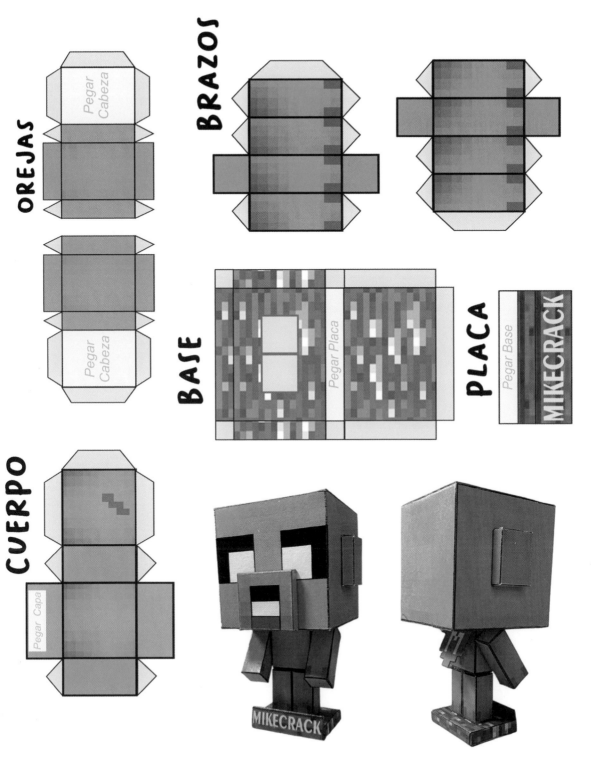

OREJAS

BRAZOS

CUERPO

BASE

PLACA

Pegar Cabeza

Pegar Cabeza

Pegar Placa

Pegar Base

MIKECRACK

Pegar Capa

MIKECRACK